# METHODOLOGY, MICROECONOMICS AND KEYNES

This volume, along with its companion volume *Money, Macroeconomics and Keynes*, is published in honour of Victoria Chick, inspired by her own contributions to knowledge in all of these areas and their interconnections. This volume represents both consolidation and the breaking of new ground in Keynesian methodology and microeconomics by leading figures in these fields.

The chapters have been contributed by some of the many who admire Chick's work: Claudio Sardoni, Meghnad Desai, Maria Cristina Marcuzzo, Alexander C. Dow and Sheila Dow, Geoffrey M. Hodgson, Roy J. Rotheim, Tony Lawson, Jan Toporowski, Giuseppe Fontana and Bill Gerrard, Athol Fitzgibbons, Suzanne W. Helburn, Brian J. Loasby, Donald Gillies and Grazia Ietto-Gillies, Fabiana Santos and Marco Crocco, Ian Steedman, David Pearce, Carmen Aparecida Feijó, Adriana M. Amado, Jochen Runde, and Peter A. Riach and Judy Rich.

The chapters cover a wide range of permutations and combinations of aspects of the three areas: methodology, microeconomics and Keynes. The volume opens with an account of Victoria Chick's academic career and ends with a list of her publications.

**Philip Arestis** is Professor and Research Director at the South Bank Business School at South Bank University. **Meghnad Desai** is Professor of Economics and Director of the Centre for the Study of Global Governance at the London School of Economics. **Sheila Dow** is Professor, Department of Economics, University of Stirling.

# ROUTLEDGE FRONTIERS OF POLITICAL ECONOMY

THE ECONOMICS OF SCIENCE
Methodology and epistemology as if economics really mattered
*James R. Wible*

COMPETITIVENESS, LOCALISED LEARNING AND
REGIONAL DEVELOPMENT
Specialisation and prosperity in smalll open economies
*Peter Maskell, Heikki Eskelinen, Ingjaldur Hannibalsson,
Anders Malmberg and Eirik Vatne*

LABOUR MARKET THEORY
A constructive reassessment
*Ben J. Fine*

WOMEN AND EUROPEAN EMPLOYMENT
*Jill Rubery, Mark Smith, Colette Fagan, Damian Grimshaw*

EXPLORATIONS IN ECONOMIC METHODOLOGY
From Lakatos to empirical philosophy of science
*Roger Backhouse*

SUBJECTIVITY IN POLITICAL ECONOMY
Essays on wanting and choosing
*David P. Levine*

THE POLITICAL ECONOMY OF
MIDDLE EAST PEACE
The impact of competing trade agendas
*Edited by J. W. Wright, Jnr*

THE ACTIVE CONSUMER
Novelty and surprise in consumer choice
*Edited by Marina Bianchi*

SUBJECTIVISM AND ECONOMIC ANALYSIS
Essays in memory of Ludwig Lachmann
*Edited by Roger Koppl and Gary Mongiovi*

THEMES IN POST-KEYNESIAN ECONOMICS
Essays in honour of G. C. Harcourt, volume three
*Edited by Peter Kriesler and Claudio Sardoni*

THE DYNAMICS OF TECHNOLOGICAL KNOWLEDGE
*Cristiano Antonelli*

THE POLITICAL ECONOMY OF DIET,
HEALTH AND FOOD POLICY
*Ben J. Fine*

THE END OF FINANCE
Capital market inflation, financial derivatives and
pension fund capitalism
*Jan Toporowski*

# METHODOLOGY, MICROECONOMICS AND KEYNES

Essays in honour of
Victoria Chick, Volume Two

*Edited by*
*Philip Arestis, Meghnad Desai*
*and Sheila Dow*

London and New York

First published 2002
by Routledge
11 New Fetter Lane, London EC4P 4EE

Simultaneously published in the USA and Canada
by Routledge
29 West 35th Street, New York, NY 10001

*Routledge is an imprint of the Taylor & Francis Group*

Typeset in 10/12 Times New Roman by
Newgen Imaging Systems (P) Ltd.
Printed and bound in Great Britain by MPG Books Ltd, Bodmin

*British Library Cataloguing in Publication Data*
A catalogue record for this book is available
from the British Library

*Library of Congress Cataloguing in Publication Data*
Essays in honour of Victoria Chick / edited by Philip Arestis,
Meghnad Desai, and Sheila Dow.
p. cm. – (Routledge frontiers of political economy; 38–39)
Includes bibliographical references and indexes.
Contents: v. 1. Money, macroeconomics and Keynes – v. 2. Methodology,
microeconomics, and Keynes. 1. Chick, Victoria.
2. Chick, Victoria – Biography. 3. Chick, Victoria – Bibliograhy.
4. Keynes, John Maynard, 1883–1946. 5. Keynesian economics.
6. Monetary policy. 7. Macroeconomics. 8. Microeconomics. I. Chick,
Victoria. II. Arestis, Philip, 1941-. III. Desai, Meghnad. IV. Dow, Sheila C. V.
Title: Essays in honor of Victoria Chick. VI. Series.

HB119.C4923 E87 2001
330 – dc21                                           2001019645

ISBN 0–415–23219–8

# CONTENTS

## CONTENTS

# TABLES

# CONTRIBUTORS

**Adriana M. Amado** is Associate Professor in the Economics Department, University of Brasília, Brazil.

**Philip Arestis** is Professor and Research Director at the South Bank Business School at South Bank University, London, UK. He is also joint editor of *International Papers in Political Economy*.

**Marco Crocco** is Professor Adjunto in the Economics Department, Federal University of Minas Gerais (FUMG), Brazil.

**Meghnad Desai** is Professor of Economics and Director of the Centre for Study of Global Governance at the London School of Economics.

**Alexander C. Dow** is Professor of the Scottish Economy at Glasgow Caledonian University, Scotland.

**Sheila Dow** is Professor in the Department of Economics, University of Stirling, Scotland.

**Carmen Aparecida Feijó** is based at the Instituto Brasileiro de Geografia e Estadistica, Brazil.

**Athol Fitzgibbons** is Associate Professor in the Economics Division, Griffiths University, Australia.

**Giuseppe Fontana** is Lecturer in Economics at Leeds University, UK.

**Bill Gerrard** is Senior Lecturer in the Interface Studies Unit, University of Strathclyde, UK.

**Donald Gillies** is Professor of the Philosophy of Science and Mathematics at King's College, London, UK.

**Suzanne W. Helburn** is Professor Emerita, University of Colorado at Denver.

**Geoffrey M. Hodgson** is a Research Professor in Business Studies at the University of Hertfordshire, UK.

**Grazia Ietto-Gillies** is Professor of Applied Economics and Director, Centre for International Business Studies at South Bank University Business School, UK.

**Tony Lawson** is Lecturer in Economics at the University of Cambridge.

**Brian J. Loasby** is Professor Emeritus in the Economics Department, University of Stirling, Scotland.

**Maria Cristina Marcuzzo** is Professor of Economics at the University of Rome, 'La Sapienza', Italy.

**David Pearce** is Professor of Environmental Economics and Associate Director, Centre for Social and Economic Research on the Global Environment at University College, London, UK.

**Peter A. Riach** is Professor and Head of the Economics and Social Sciences Department, De Montfort University, UK.

**Judy Rich** is Senior Lecturer in the Department of Economics, Monash University, Australia.

**Roy J. Rotheim** is Professor in the Department of Economics, Skidmore College, USA.

**Jochen Runde** is Lecturer in Economics and Fellow of Girton College, Cambridge. He is also Director of Studies in Management Studies at Girton College and New Hall.

**Fabiana Santos** is a Ph.D. candidate at the University of Cambridge.

**Claudio Sardoni** is Professor of Economics at the University of Rome, 'La Sapienza' Italy.

**Ian Steedman** is Research Professor in Economics at Manchester Metropolitan University.

**Jan Toporowski** is Reader in Economics at South Bank University Business School, UK.

# 1

# INTRODUCTION: ON CHICK'S LIFE AS AN ACADEMIC

*Philip Arestis, Meghnad Desai and Sheila Dow*

Keynes talked of *The General Theory of Employment, Interest and Money* as part of his 'long struggle to escape from habitual modes of thought and expression'. But these modes of thought and expression continued to prevail, requiring subsequent like-minded economists to engage in their own struggle to escape. Victoria Chick is one of the leading economists to engage in such a struggle, and to assist others in the process.

We have prepared this volume and its companion volume, *Money, Macroeconomics and Keynes*, bearing in mind the many economists, dispersed all over the world, who have assiduously sought out Victoria Chick's writings over the years to provide illumination and inspiration, who have benefited from her teaching, guidance and friendship, and who accordingly owe her a great debt of gratitude. It is therefore with great pleasure that we have invited a subset of her enormous international audience to contribute to the two volumes in her honour on the occasion of her retirement from University College London (UCL).

Victoria Chick was born in 1936, in Berkeley, California. She studied at the University of California at Berkeley where she took her Bachelor's and Master's degrees. Berkeley's Department of Economics was particularly strong and eclectic at that time. Thus, very high quality and tremendous concentration of calibre were two characteristics of the environment in which Victoria Chick developed as an economist. The important ingredient of that environment was the disparity of views that were flowing in the corridors and seminar rooms of the Department. The independent character and personality of Victoria Chick were stimulated by the diversity of theoretical views there, but she did not take sides on ideology or methodology. That came later. However, a continuity in her relationship with Berkeley was maintained through her friendship with Hyman Minsky.

At Berkeley she specialised in international trade theory and wrote a thesis on Canada's 1950s experience with flexible exchange rates. Then, in 1960 she moved to the London School of Economics (LSE) to continue postgraduate studies, where the impetus of Berkeley was maintained, indeed enhanced. That was the heyday of 'Methodology, Measurement and Testing' at the LSE. Just as at

Berkeley previously, both staff and students at the LSE were of enormously high caliber; Victoria Chick took full advantage of these opportunities. The Staff and Graduate Student Seminar chaired by Lionel Robbins, Wednesday evenings in the Three Tuns, and the London–Oxford–Cambridge graduate students' seminars provided the platform for fertile ideas to be disseminated and indeed to become firmly embedded in the economics discipline. Victoria Chick was once more in the middle of different views as to how the economy worked, but still her ideas were in their gestation period.

In 1963 she took an Assistant Lectureship at UCL, and was promoted to Lecturer during the following year. She was then moving away from international economics to monetary theory and macroeconomics. Her book, *The Theory of Monetary Policy*, grew out of her teaching, a clear indication that she takes seriously the ideal of blending teaching with research; she continues an old tradition of publishing new material as 'lectures' – a commendable way to teach. The book was a conscious attempt to impose an order on monetary theory, an order which by comparison to international economics was sadly lacking at that time. That she did extremely well.

The approach of *The Theory of Monetary Policy* was in fact simultaneously sympathetic to and critical of Keynesians and monetarists alike. Ultimately, though, she rejected both schools of thought as theoretically inadequate. Inevitably, the *IS–LM* apparatus, the accepted framework of monetary debate, had to go as well. She had uncovered a logical inconsistency in the model which was connected with its static method. The suggestion was not well received either by the Anglo-American journals or by her own colleagues. Nonetheless, she persisted and the relevant paper was published, some five years after its drafting.

As these ideas were falling into place, she attended the 1971 meeting of the American Economic Association in New Orleans, where Joan Robinson gave her famous Ely Lecture, 'The Second Crisis in Economics'. At that gathering Joan Robinson and Paul Davidson called a meeting of like-minded people, which gave Victoria Chick great courage in discovering that she was not alone and thus provided her with a tremendous impetus to carry on.

Publishing *The Theory of Monetary Policy* had created a vacuum: mainstream macroeconomics had been shown to be inadequate. Perhaps as a belated response to Hyman Minsky's earlier attempt, at Berkeley, to teach her Keynes's *General Theory* (see her *Macroeconomics after Keynes*, p. viii), she returned to that book and began teaching it to her undergraduate students and developing her views in the process. When she felt that she had a coherent and systematic story to tell, she published *Macroeconomics after Keynes*. With this book Victoria Chick made a major contribution to post-Keynesian thinking. As will become clear from the rest of this introduction and the papers that follow in the two volumes, she had already made her distinctive mark on post-Keynesian thought. *Macroeconomics after Keynes* consolidated her position as one of the more important and regular contributors to the attempt to complete and elucidate the post-Keynesian paradigm. She was promoted to Reader in 1984 and to Professor in 1993.

During the time Victoria Chick has spent at UCL, she supervised a great number of Ph.D. students, many of whom are represented in the two volumes. Victoria Chick has also taught at a number of universities throughout the world. These include McGill University in Canada, University of California at Berkeley and at Santa Cruz in the USA, Aarhus University in Denmark, University of Southampton in the UK, University of Burgundy, Dijon in France, and the Catholic University of Louvain in Belgium. As well as visiting universities, she spent a summer at the Federal Reserve Bank of New York and eighteen months at the Reserve Bank of Australia in Sydney. More recently (September–March, 2000–1) she has been appointed Bundesbank Professor of International Monetary Economics tenable at the Free University, Berlin.

Victoria Chick has been an active member of two British Study Groups, funded by the ESRC: she served on the Committee of the influential *Money Study Group* for many years; and she and Philip Arestis initiated and jointly chaired for many years the active and successful post-Keynesian Economics Study Group. Victoria Chick has also served as a member on the editorial board of the *Review of Political Economy* (1987–93), *European Journal of Political Economy* (1985–94) and *Metroeconomica* (1994–present). During the period 1991–6 she was elected and served on the Council of the Royal Economic Society (RES). Over the period 1994–6 she served on the Executive Committee of the RES.

Many of the issues raised by Vicky still remain unresolved, particularly those in monetary theory. Victoria Chick has an outstanding capacity to analyse critically the logical foundations of theoretical structures and to uncover hidden assumptions. Her analysis goes beyond the level of theory to that of method, where many of the apparent differences between theories have their source. She analyses theories on their own terms, yet she does not hesitate to point out where she regards these terms as unduly limiting with respect to real-world issues and to suggest more fruitful lines of enquiry. Nor does she hesitate to criticise Keynes's framework, with which she is most strongly identified.

Although Victoria Chick's own methodological approach has much in common with that of Keynes, she has an emphasis which he left largely implicit: the historical particularity of theories, that is the fact that different types of abstraction may be better suited to some historical periods than others. This approach encourages the fair-mindedness with which Victoria Chick explores different theoretical approaches for useful theories to deal with particular problems. She is not afraid to state her views on each theory, and on how it is used: views which are founded on a high standard of scholarship. The value of this aspect of Victoria Chick's work really cannot be emphasised enough.

We are grateful to Vicky's many colleagues and friends who responded so positively to our request to contribute to this volume. We apologise to the many more that have not been approached – this was entirely due to lack of space. We are also grateful to Taylor & Francis, and especially to Alan Jarvis, who responded so promptly and enthusiastically to our request to publish the two volumes.

# 2

# ON THE MICROECONOMIC FOUNDATIONS OF MACROECONOMICS: A KEYNESIAN PERSPECTIVE[1]

*Claudio Sardoni*

## 1. Introduction

For several years now, I have been discussing the problem of microeconomic foundations with Victoria Chick. I do hope that this chapter will provoke her reaction, so that I can keep on enjoying the pleasure of an open-minded and constructive discussion with Vicky, one of the most prominent representatives of post-Keynesian economics and a friend.

All strands of contemporary mainstream macroeconomics share the strong belief that macroeconomic theory must be based on sound microfoundations, which is generally interpreted as macroeconomics being based on neoclassical microeconomic foundations. In other words, macroeconomic analysis must be consistent with the fundamental features of the neoclassical model of the economy. In this chapter, I argue that macroeconomics must indeed be based on rigorous microeconomic foundations, but this does not imply that the microfoundations of macroeconomics must be neoclassical. Following Keynes's approach to economics, the explanation of macroeconomic phenomena can be based on an analysis of individual behavior that differs from the neoclassical model in fundamental respects.

The macroeconomics of the neoclassical synthesis of the 1950s and 1960s was criticized for its lack of sound microfoundations. Since the monetarist 'counter-revolution', the neoclassical synthesis has been accused of failing to reconcile its analysis of the macroeconomy with its underlying neoclassical vision of the working of the microeconomy. The inconsistency between the so-called 'Keynesian results' and the underlying neoclassical microeconomic model led monetarism and new classical macroeconomics to reject Keynesian macroeconomics altogether. More recently, new Keynesian economics has tried to reconcile 'Keynesian results' with rigorous microeconomic foundations. The 'old Keynesians' of the synthesis tried to explain market failures at the macro-level by introducing some obstacles (or imperfections) into the working of the economic system,[2] which were simply assumed without any analytic explanation. New Keynesians argue that, instead, these rigidities must be explained on the grounds of microeconomic analysis.

Non-mainstream economists, post-Keynesians in particular, have traditionally looked at the debate on the microeconomic foundations of macroeconomics with a great deal of suspiciousness. The attempt at explaining macro-phenomena on the basis of the neoclassical vision of the world has been regarded as a betrayal of Keynes's own theory.[3] Many post-Keynesian economists have held that what is most needed is *macroeconomic foundations of microeconomics* rather than the other way around (see e.g. Crotty 1980; Kregel 1987). Individual behavior is necessarily constrained and conditioned by crucial inherent characteristics of a capitalist market economy. It is those characteristics that must be taken into consideration in order to provide a satisfactory explanation of individual behavior.

Although I agree with the view that individual behavior is socially conditioned, I also believe that acknowledging this does not imply renouncing the development of a rigorous analysis of how individuals decide and act in a decentralized capitalist economy. Section 2 below is devoted to arguing that macroeconomics needs to be based on a rigorous analysis of individual behavior, i.e. on microeconomic foundations, even though such microfoundations must not necessarily be neoclassical and based on methodological individualism. Quite to the contrary, in my view, rigorous microeconomic foundations imply a radical critique of neoclassical economics.

In this perspective, I regard Keynes's original contribution to the analysis of the working of a market economy as fundamental. Keynes tried to base his macrotheory on microeconomic foundations that were not neoclassical. His vision of the basic features of a market economy led him to stress the importance of social conditioning of individuals' behavior. In this respect, Keynes's fundamental notion of uncertainty and of decision making within an uncertain framework plays a crucial role. Moreover, from Keynes's analysis of the working of a market economy in conditions of uncertainty, it emerges that the crucial decisional units are entrepreneurs rather than generic optimizing individuals. This interpretation of Keynes, which emphasizes the importance of microeconomic analysis, is not generally accepted; therefore, Section 3 is concerned with showing that Keynes indeed based his macroeconomic theory on microeconomic foundations that were essentially non-neoclassical.

Keynes's approach to the analysis of individual behavior represents a fundamental contribution to the construction of non-neoclassical microeconomic foundations of macroeconomics but, in my view, he left some problems unsatisfactorily dealt with and in need of further developments. Here, in Section 4, I concentrate on some problems that are more directly connected to the analysis of the decisional units that are crucial in a capitalist market economy, entrepreneurs and firms. In particular, in Section 4, attention is concentrated on two aspects that are related to one another: Keynes's hypothesis of short-period decreasing returns and his choices concerning the issue of market forms. Finally, I draw some conclusions in Section 5.

## 2. The need for microeconomic foundations

Greenwald and Stiglitz have argued that discriminating among alternative macro-economic theories is possible only if a satisfactory microeconomic analysis is developed. Statistical analyses of macro-phenomena are not sufficient to allow economists to choose among differing theories (Greenwald and Stiglitz 1993: 24). This position, though acceptable, offers only a partial justification for micro-economic foundations. More general arguments in favor of microfoundations can be found at a deeper level, in considering the very nature of capitalist market economies.

In a capitalist decentralized economy, relevant economic decisions are made by individual units rather than by some sort of central decisional agent. The comprehension of how the economy works cannot disregard the comprehension of the behavior of such individual agents. In other words, the observed macro-phenomena are the outcome of individual decisions and actions; therefore a satisfactory analysis of the working of the macroeconomy requires that individual behavior be analyzed.

Even though mainstream economics derives its methodological individualism from this basic feature of market economies, this does not mean that the neoclassical approach is the only possible theoretical derivation. The neoclassical *homo economicus*, which is at the core of methodological individualism, is an individual agent who makes unconditioned decisions in total isolation and independence. But such isolated independent individuals do not exist. Individuals are *social entities*, so that their decisions and actions necessarily are historically and socially conditioned.

Acknowledging that individual behavior is historically and socially conditioned must represent, in my opinion, a distinctive feature of a non-neoclassical approach to the development of sound microeconomic foundations of macro-economics.[4] A rigorous explanation of the behavior of 'individual agents' is necessary, but this does not imply that the notion of individual agent must be reduced to the neoclassical notion of *homo economicus*. Moreover, emphasizing the need for the analysis of individual behavior does not imply that aggregate variables can be treated as if they simply were the sum of individual variables: the whole is not the simple sum of its parts.

Keynes's theory, in this respect, offers a fundamental contribution. His analysis of aggregate phenomena was indeed based on the analysis of the behavior of individual agents, but he did not regard the decisions made by individual agents as decisions socially unconditioned and pointed out the 'fallacy of composition'. This interpretation of Keynes's approach, however, is far from being generally accepted. Quite to the contrary, many of the economists who have stressed the importance of microeconomic foundations have also criticized Keynes's macro-economics for the lack of sound microeconomic foundations. The reason why Keynes is blamed for the lack of microeconomic foundations has to be found in the mistaken identification of his own original theory with the macroeconomics of the neoclassical synthesis of the 1950s and 1960s. If the neoclassical synthesis is seen as the direct derivation of Keynes's *General Theory*, then the criticism is correct. However, as all post-Keynesians have strongly argued, Keynes's theory cannot be reduced to the neoclassical synthesis.

The issue of the microeconomic foundations of macroeconomics in Keynes must be dealt with by looking at his own works and not by vicariously considering the approach developed by the neoclassical synthesis.[5] The following section is devoted to showing that Keynes actually grounded his macroeconomic theory on microeconomic analysis and that it was significantly different from the neoclassical analysis of individual behavior. Fundamental distinctive aspects of Keynes's approach are his emphasis on uncertainty and on the fact that entrepreneurs, rather than generic optimizing agents, are the crucial decisional units in a capitalist economy.

## 3. The microeconomic foundations of Keynesian macroeconomics

When, in 1936, Keynes restated and summarized his analysis in chapter 18 of *The General Theory*, among the fundamental independent variables that explain the level of income and employment he put the three *fundamental psychological factors* (the propensity to consume, the attitude to liquidity and the expectation of future returns to capital assets) (1936 [1973a]: 246–7). If the aggregate demand for consumption, money and investment can be understood by referring to psychology, Keynes's theory was obviously based on the analysis of individual behavior. Also on other occasions, Keynes explicitly pointed out that the behavior of the economy as a whole can be satisfactorily understood only starting from the analysis of individual behavior. For him, economics differs from natural sciences as it has to do with 'motives, expectations, psychological uncertainties' and, hence, a good economist has to rely significantly on introspection. Introspection is a reflection on individual experience and reasoning through analogies from the individual level to the general level (1938 [1973b]: 295–301).

To argue that Keynes's theory is grounded on microeconomic analysis is not difficult, but more complex is the problem concerning the fundamental characteristics of his microeconomics and, in particular, the relationship with neoclassical microeconomics. Keynes himself, especially in *The General Theory*, may have contributed to engendering the idea that his microeconomics was not so different from the neoclassical. He criticized classical economics for having neglected the theory of the demand for the output as a whole rather than for having an unsatisfactory theory of individual agents' behavior (1936 [1973a]: 378–9).

Thus, one could argue that Keynes's innovations concerned only the theory of aggregate demand. However, there is a crucial factor that makes the Keynesian and the neoclassical visions of individual behavior radically different. Keynes's approach is characterized by the deep conviction that the economic, and social, environment is dominated by uncertainty that cannot be reduced to risk and treated with the traditional tools of probability theory. Keynes's notion of uncertainty is incompatible with the neoclassical analysis of individual behavior.[6]

Notwithstanding uncertainty, individuals have to make decisions and act. They do so by 'pretending' that they have behind them 'a good Benthamite calculation of a series of prospective advantages and disadvantages, each multiplied by its appropriate probability, waiting to be summed' (1937 [1973b]: 114). In order to behave in such a way, some techniques are devised. They are essentially conventions like assuming that the present is a reliable guide to the future despite the past evidence to the contrary or trying to conform to the behavior of the majority. This means that individual decisions and actions cannot be regarded as independent of one another.[7]

Furthermore, Keynes's analysis of individual behavior is concentrated on a specific class of individuals whose decisions are crucial for the working of the economy. He argued that, in a capitalist environment, investment decisions are those that are mostly affected by uncertainty. They concern events expected to take place in a relatively distant future that cannot be known (1936 [1973a]: 149). For this reason investment must be regarded as the *causa causans* of output and employment.[8] If investment is the crucial variable to understand the working of the economy as a whole, it follows that, in studying the microeconomic foundations of macroeconomics, the relevant analytical units are not generic individuals but entrepreneurs, who make their decisions within the context of the firm. The levels of output and employment and their fluctuations over time are ultimately contingent on the entrepreneurs' view of the future. By putting entrepreneurs' or, more in general, firms' decisions at the center stage of his analysis, Keynes was closer to the classical tradition rather than to the neoclassical vision of a market economy.

Thus, rigorous microeconomic foundations are primarily needed for those macroeconomic variables that most directly depend on firms' behavior. Other variables, like aggregate consumption, can be dealt with even by leaving microeconomic analysis rather undeveloped. For example, the aggregate demand for consumer goods certainly derives from individuals' decisions – which are largely influenced by social, cultural, institutional and psychological factors – but economics need not investigate these factors accurately in order to deal with the determination of the aggregate level of output. After all, what is really relevant in this context is that, for whatever reason, income is not entirely consumed, so that there is a gap between aggregate supply and demand that has to be filled by investment or by other autonomous components of aggregate demand.

## 4. Beyond Keynes's microeconomic foundations

Although, in *The General Theory*, Keynes developed a radically innovative approach to the problem of firms' decision making and behavior, he did not always succeed in carrying out his analysis satisfactorily. In my view, many of the difficulties raised by Keynes's analysis derive from the persistent Marshallian influence on his work and his inability to free himself completely from the past tradition. Moreover, in some cases, Keynes's attempt to carry out the critique of the dominant paradigm in the most convincing way may give rise to difficulties when the emphasis is shifted toward the analysis of how actual economies work. Here, I consider two topics in which these aspects of Keynes's approach appear quite clearly and further analytical developments are required. I look at the hypothesis of decreasing short-period returns and the problem of market forms, two topics that are strictly related to one another.

The notion of aggregate supply function, which plays an important role in *The General Theory*, was obtained by Keynes as an extension to the economy as a whole of the Marshallian industry supply curve.[9] He obtained an upward sloping supply curve by making the hypothesis that individual supply curves are increasing because of short-period decreasing returns. Although Keynes's, and Marshall's, notion of decreasing returns is different from the canonical neoclassical hypothesis, it is nonetheless unable to provide support to the hypotheses of U-shaped marginal cost curves and of an upward sloping aggregate supply curve.[10]

In general, the safest hypothesis on short-period returns is that they are constant and, hence, short-period marginal cost curves have a reverse-L shape, i.e. they are flat to capacity and then rise vertically. This hypothesis is supported by empirical evidence.[11] In turn, the adoption of a hypothesis of constant returns leads to the conclusion that, in general, also industry supply functions and the aggregate supply function are reverse-L shaped. In principle, such a conclusion is not necessarily true, but in order to obtain upward sloping supply curves it would be necessary also to accept other unrealistic results. If all firms in an industry are identical and have reverse-L-shaped cost curves, the industry supply function takes on the same shape. But, if it is admitted that firms are of differing efficiency, it is possible to obtain a continuously increasing supply function by arguing that the number of firms is so large and the degree of efficiency is so differentiated that all the discontinuities in the supply function are 'filled' by firms of differing efficiency. Continuously increasing supply functions obtained in this way, however, imply an unrealistic consequence. Any situation in which demand is below the level corresponding to the industry's full capacity implies that there must be some firms (the least efficient or marginal firms) that do not produce at all, while all the others produce to full capacity. Thus, if more realistic situations, in which all firms in an industry produce below capacity, have to be explained, the simplest and most acceptable hypothesis is that industry supply functions are flat up to capacity. As to the shape of the aggregate supply function, the conclusions are analogous to those reached for industry supply functions. If industries' supply functions are reverse-L-shaped, the aggregate supply function retains the same shape.

If the hypothesis of a flat to capacity (full employment) aggregate supply curve is accepted, increases in effective demand do not give rise to increases in the general price level, unless the economy reaches full employment or one or more industries experience a bottleneck.[12] Once the economy has reached full employment, the aggregate supply function becomes vertical: further increases in demand give rise only to price increases since no expansion of output is possible. If one or more industries reach full capacity earlier than others, the aggregate supply function starts increasing before it becomes perfectly vertical.[13] The rejection of the hypothesis of an upward sloping aggregate supply function has significant implications for some of Keynes's analytical results in *The General Theory*. If the aggregate supply function is not upward sloping, the general price level is no longer an increasing function of the level of output. This means that, with a given money wage rate, it is no longer true that the real wage rate is a decreasing function of the level of employment.

Since the 1920s, the rejection of decreasing returns had been associated with the rejection also of the hypothesis of perfect (or free) competition (see e.g. Kahn 1989). Keynes, however, remained firmly convinced of the validity of the hypothesis of short-period decreasing returns and never showed great interest in the issue of market forms. In 1938–9, Dunlop, Tarshis and Kalecki questioned Keynes's conclusions on the behavior of the real wage rate; and they offered an alternative analysis of distributive shares that was based on a hypothesis of constant short-period returns and the introduction of some form of imperfect competition. Keynes (1939 [1973a]) replied to these criticisms by holding that he did not see any valid reason to reject the assumption of decreasing returns, even though he reluctantly conceded that perfect competition was not a realistic hypothesis.

Apart from Keynes's analytical considerations concerning returns and competition, it also appears quite clearly that he regarded those issues as not very relevant since they did not affect his general results in a significant way. As to the returns issue, Keynes, though convinced that his hypothesis was correct, argued that an assumption of constant returns would have reinforced his policy conclusions. Expansionary measures would not produce any inflation and, hence, the opposition to his policy conclusions would be weakened. In other words, Keynes regarded the hypothesis of decreasing returns as the most favorable to his adversaries. As to Keynes's hypotheses on market forms, the picture is somewhat analogous. As well known, in *The General Theory*, Keynes took the degree of competition as a given. This suggests that he believed that his general results were fundamentally independent of the assumed market form, even though it is quite evident that in the book the market form implicitly hypothesized is perfect competition (see e.g. Tarshis 1979).

The explanations of Keynes's attitude can be explained both with 'tactical' and methodological considerations. In his attempt to convey the principle of effective demand to the profession and convince his fellow economists of the validity of his alternative vision of the macroeconomy, Keynes may have decided not to open too many fronts in his critique of orthodoxy, by avoiding dealing with issues that he did not regard as crucial. In particular, in ignoring the problem of imperfect competition, Keynes may have chosen not to question the hypothesis of perfect competition, which still was largely dominant, and to avoid giving the impression that his fundamental results were contingent on the existence of some 'imperfections' in the working of markets.

Keynes's choices probably were adequate to carry out a more convincing criticism of the neoclassical dominant paradigm. However, in my opinion, they cannot be regarded as acceptable when the emphasis of the analysis is shifted toward the explanation of how actual economies work. The hypothesis of short-period decreasing returns is affected by logical inconsistencies and does not have any convincing empirical support. A hypothesis of constant (if not increasing) returns should be regarded as more adequate in studying the working of real economies. If decreasing returns are rejected, an explicit hypothesis of some form of imperfect competition becomes necessary, a hypothesis that is largely supported by empirical evidence.[14] In such a way, a more realistic analysis of firms' behavior could be carried out, and macroeconomics would be based on foundations that are not only more realistic but also more rigorous than neoclassical microeconomics; as they would not be flawed by the logical inconsistencies that mar the traditional view of the firm.

## 5. Conclusion

In dealing with the topic of the microeconomic foundations of macroeconomics, post-Keynesian economists often tend to emphasize that what is really needed is the macroeconomic foundations of microeconomics. The insistence on microeconomic foundations essentially means to distort Keynes's theory and an explicit hypothesis of imperfect competition implies a weakening of Keynes's theory. Although I share the conviction that the behavior of individuals is conditioned by macroeconomic factors, I also believe that this should not imply that the development of macroeconomic analysis can be carried out by ignoring microeconomic issues. It cannot be ignored that aggregate outcomes derive, though in a non-simplistic way, from individual decisions and actions.

For post-Keynesians, Keynes's theory represents a radical break with orthodox economics. In his attempt to explain the world in which we live, Keynes provided a new alternative theoretical framework, which post-Keynesians try to develop further.[15] I argued that the development of Keynes's theory also requires carrying out a rigorous analysis of the microeconomy. Keynes followed this line of approach, even though he left some problems unsolved.

In this chapter, I concentrated on two aspects of Keynes's analysis that cannot be regarded as fully satisfactory, the problem of short-period decreasing returns and the problem of market forms. Post-Keynesian efforts to develop Keynes's theory should also be directed to providing a more satisfactory analysis of these topics. In this respect, Kalecki's work, and more recent work done in that tradition,[16] are an important contribution. Kalecki's analysis of firms operating in an oligopolistic regime can be coherently integrated into Keynesian analyses of the macro-economy in an uncertain context.

It is likely that Keynes did not pay much attention to the analysis of costs and to the problem of market forms also because he believed that such topics were not crucial for the validity of his principle of effective demand, and that accepting the traditional hypotheses would have reinforced his critique of the dominant paradigm. Post-Keynesians, however, should now take a different perspective.

Although a hypothesis of short-period decreasing returns can be suitable for criticizing traditional microeconomics, it cannot be accepted when trying to understand the working of actual economies. Analogous considerations can be made with respect to the topic of market forms. Although it is true that the validity of Keynes's principle of effective demand is not contingent on a hypothesis of imperfect competition, this does not mean that macroeconomic analysis can ignore that the real world does not operate in a regime of perfect competition.[17]

Accepting decreasing returns and perfect competition may be an effective choice when criticizing neoclassical economics, but the critique of the dominant orthodoxy is never sufficient to promote the development of a viable alternative paradigm. Efforts to construct macroeconomic analysis on more realistic hypotheses about market forms and costs would also allow post-Keynesian economics to contrast more effectively those new Keynesian economists who, while retaining neoclassical hypotheses on costs and returns, use a notion of imperfect competition that is as unrealistic as perfect competition.[18]

# Notes

1 I would like to thank G. Harcourt, W. Harcourt, P. Kriesler and the editors of this volume for their helpful comments on an earlier version of this chapter.
2 In particular, wage rigidities were used to provide a justification for the existence of involuntary unemployment.
3 Also the new Keynesian approach to microfoundations has been, by and large, considered as an attempt to develop macroeconomics along neoclassical lines.
4 In this respect, Marx's view is still relevant: 'In this society of free competition, the individual appears detached from the natural bonds etc. which in earlier historical periods make him the accessory of a definite and limited human conglomerate ... But the epoch which produces this standpoint, that of the isolated individual, is also precisely that of the hitherto most developed social ... relations.' (Marx 1973: 83–4).
5 In this regard, Greenwald and Stiglitz have recently taken a position that certainly is more correct. They hold that Keynes had indeed based his analysis on microeconomic foundations. However, they also view Keynes's foundations as essentially traditional and incompatible with his vision of the working of the macroeconomy (Greenwald and Stiglitz 1993: 25n). Greenwald and Stiglitz take chapter 18 of *The General Theory* as an example of the traditional character of Keynes's microfoundations (Greenwald and Stiglitz 1987: 127–31); but post-Keynesians (e.g. Shackle 1967) have traditionally looked at Chapter 18 as one of the chapters where the innovative character of Keynes's economics appears most clearly.
6 Keynes's famous 1937 article in the *Quarterly Journal of Economics* (1937 [1973b]: 109–23) is perhaps the clearest exposition of his vision of uncertainty and how individuals cope with it: 'By "uncertain" knowledge, let me explain, I do not mean merely to distinguish what is known from what is only probable. The game of roulette is not subject, in this sense, to uncertainty ... The sense in which I am using the term is that in which the prospect of a European war is uncertain ... About these matters there is no scientific basis on which to form any calculable probability whatever. We simply do not know.' (1937 [1973b]: 113–4).
7 For Kregel, 'individual actions are constrained by the actions of other individuals which cannot be predicted with certainty and thus when taken together form an aggregate or global or macroeconomic constraint which is not the simple, linear, and therefore predictable summation of individual behaviour' (Kregel 1987: 528).

8 Among the factors which determine output, 'it is those which determine the rate of investment which are most unreliable, since it is they which are influenced by our views of the future about which we know so little' (1937 [1973b]: 121).

9 On Keynes's aggregate supply function, see Tarshis's (1979) excellent analysis.

10 For Keynes, like for Marshall, decreasing returns are due to the heterogeneity of factors of production rather than to the varying quantity of homogeneous factors employed. For more details on this topic, see Sardoni (1994).

11 Sylos Labini (1988: 276) refers to some empirical studies that confirm the hypothesis of reverse-L-shaped direct cost curves.

12 This, of course, is true under the hypothesis that the money wage rate is constant until full employment is reached.

13 On the other hand, it is reasonable to think that reaching a bottleneck, which causes the prices of some goods to rise vertically, might give rise to changes in the demand composition. In such a case, even if one or more industries reach full capacity earlier than others, the aggregate supply function could remain flat until full employment is reached: the increase in the prices of the goods in shortage could induce a shift of demand toward goods whose prices are still unchanged.

14 An explicit assumption of imperfect competition 'is not one for which you have to make an apology, you have to apologise when you are assuming perfect competition which manifestly does not exist' (B. Reddaway, in Harcourt 1985: 96–7).

15 Also recently, post-Keynesians have offered important contributions to the development of several aspects of Keynes's theory. See e.g. the recent essays by eminent post-Keynesians on a 'second edition' of The General Theory (Harcourt and Riach 1997).

16 For a recent work on microeconomic foundations from a Kaleckian perspective, see Kriesler (1996).

17 See e.g. Shapiro (1997), where it is argued that imperfect competition is irrelevant for Keynes's analysis, but see also Marris (1997) for an opposite viewpoint.

18 On this, see Harcourt's contribution to this volume.

# References

Crotty, J. R. (1980) 'Post-Keynesian Economic Theory: An Overview and Evaluation', American Economic Review 70(2): 20–5.

Greenwald, B. and Stiglitz, J. E. (1987) 'Keynesian, New Keynesian and New Classical Economics', Oxford Economic Papers 39: 119–32.

Greenwald, B. and Stiglitz, J. E. (1993) 'New and Old Keynesians', Journal of Economic Perspectives 7: 23–44.

Harcourt, G. C. (ed.) (1985) Keynes and His Contemporaries. London: Macmillan.

Harcourt, G. C. and Riach, P. (eds) (1997) 'A Second Edition' of The General Theory. London and New York: Routledge.

Kahn, R. F., 1989 (1929), The Economics of the Short Period. London: Macmillan.

Keynes, J. M. (1936) [1973a] The Collected Writings of John Maynard Keynes, Vol. 7, The General Theory of Employment Interest and Money. London: Macmillan.

Keynes, J. M. (1937, 1938) [1973b] The Collected Writings of John Maynard Keynes, Vol. 14, The General Theory and After – Part II. London: Macmillan.

Keynes, J. M. (1939) [1973a] 'Relative Movements of Real Wages and Output', Economic Journal, Reprinted in The Collected Writings of John Maynard Keynes, Vol. 14, pp. 394–412.

Kregel, J. (1987) 'Rational Spirits and the Post Keynesian Macrotheory of Microeconomics', De Economist 135(4): 520–32.

Kriesler, P. (1996) 'Microfoundations: A Kaleckian Perspective', in J. King (ed.), *An Alternative Macroeconomic Theory: The Kaleckian model and Post-Keynesian Economics*. Boston: Kluwer, pp. 55–72.

Marris, R. (1997) 'Yes, Mrs Robinson', in Harcourt and Riach, 1997, Vol. 1, pp. 52–82.

Marx, K. (1973) *Grundrisse*. London: Penguin.

Sardoni, C. (1994) 'The General Theory and the Critique of Decreasing Returns', *Journal of the History of Economic Thought* 16(1): 61–85.

Shackle, G. L. S. (1967) *The Years of High Theory*. Cambridge: Cambridge University Press.

Shapiro, N. (1997) 'Imperfect Competition and Keynes', in Harcourt and Riach, 1997, Vol. 1, pp. 83–92.

Sylos Labini, P. (1988) 'The Great Debates on the Laws of Returns and the Value of Capital: When Will Economists Accept their Own Logic?', *Banca Nazionale del Lavoro Quarterly Review*, No. 166, pp. 263–91.

Tarshis, L. (1979) 'The Aggregate Supply Function in Keynes's General Theory', in M. J. Boskin (ed.), *Economics and Human Welfare*. New York: Academic Press, pp. 361–92.

# 3

# THE NATURE OF EQUILIBRIUM IN KEYNES'S *GENERAL THEORY*

## Meghnad Desai

> Thus, short of final equilibrium there are some outcomes which we describe as equilibrium at one level and disequilibrium at another. Since whether or not we are entitled to call something equilibrium depends on where in these nested sets of concepts we decide to locate, any definition short of final equilibrium can be regarded as provisional.
>
> Victoria Chick and Maurizio Caserta (1997b: 228)

## 1. Introduction

The core of Victoria Chick's (VC hereafter) work has been Keynes, the *General Theory* and money. She has espoused a non-dualistic (non-Cartesian) and non-formalistic, open-systems-oriented and historically grounded approach to economic theorising, sensible of the inevitable ambiguities and aware of the institutional specificities. In this essay in her honour, I want to take up a theme in her work which relates intimately to the core of her concerns – the nature of equilibrium in Keynes's *General Theory* (*GT* hereafter). This also connects with her methodological writings on formalism in economics. Equilibrium is also a theme which she has pursued in a consistent way over the twenty-five years of her published work and even longer in her lectures and conversations. I shall pay particular attention to the most recent of her writings on the subject in which she put forward the notion of provisional equilibrium (PE) (Chick 1997b).

In Section 2 I discuss the notion of equilibrium as it is taught in economic theory. This is a somewhat pedagogic section but nonetheless useful in demonstrating the range of equilibrium concepts which are currently in use. Then in Section 3, I discuss VC's notion of PE which is her most mature characterisation of Keynes's equilibrium in the *GT*. In Section 4, I put the notion of PE on a formal footing taking advantage of the discussion in Section 2. I develop a more explicit and formal description of PE though no proofs are provided at this stage. Much remains to be done as I point out in the concluding section.

## 2. Equilibrium in economic theory

In economics, equilibrium is a concept which is constructed for a theoretical purpose. Economic theory is faced with enormous complexity, especially, but not exclusively, to do with time and openness. Complexity is made manageable by imposing constraints on what adjustments are allowed and what can reasonably be kept constant.

(ibid., p. 228)

Equilibrium is at once the most commonly used idea in economics and the most confusing to many economists and non-economists. Grown-up men and women have been unable to agree on its meaning and scope. Some like Nicholas Kaldor have traversed a path from a firm belief in the concept to total agnosticism over a lifetime in economic theorising (Kaldor 1934, 1972). A crude version of the concept – supply-equals-demand – has entered popular imagination so much that even a sophisticated financial expert like George Soros asserts that that is all there is to economics (Soros 2000). So let us go a step at a time.

*Static partial equilibrium.* The simplest notion is of course the static partial equilibrium notion of demand-equals-supply. Formally, it is the intersection of the demand schedule and the supply schedule in the price–quantity space (or equivalently the solution to the demand and supply equations). It is presumed in textbook diagrams, though it is not necessarily true, that (a) such an intersection is in the positive orthant and yields a non-negative, indeed positive, price and quantity as solutions, and/or (b) that it is unique. Textbooks discuss only the most restrictive case presuming a unique equilibrium in the positive orthant.

Of course the simple notion is the popular one. It is also the easy one to teach. Multiple equilibria are quite possible. They are mentioned sometimes when the discussion moves on to the stability of equilibrium. Textbooks contrast Marshallian and Walrasian notions of stability by highlighting that one can be stable and the other unstable, given certain configurations of demand and supply. In cases of multiple equilibria some can be stable and others unstable. Stability may of course only be local rather than global.

Thus even the simplest case of demand-equals-supply is fraught with a multiplicity of possibilities. We may have locally/globally stable/unstable unique/multiple positions of equilibrium even in the partial static case. But even this simple listing exposes gaping holes in the simple notion of equilibrium within its own terms. Thus two questions need to be asked:

1.   Where do the demand and supply curves come from?
2.   How can we speak of stability or instability in a static model since one involves movement and hence time and the other rules both out?

The answer to the first question involves aggregation. The supply curve is pretty straightforward for a competitive industry with price-taking firms. The supply

16

curve is a summation of the marginal cost curves of price-taking firms (see, however, Chick 1991). If firms are not price taking – imperfectly competitive or monopolistic – then there can be no supply curve, though many textbooks and even articles in learned journals draw supply curves for imperfectly competitive industries. But the difficulty is even more formidable with the demand curve. The aggregation of individual consumer demand curves into a market demand curve is almost insuperable without stringent assumptions about the homotheticity of preferences. All Engel curves have to be linear through the origin (or at least affine) (Gorman 1953). The more thoughtful economic theorists confine themselves to models with a single representative consumer for that reason (though how such a consumer can have competitive supply conditions which require many firms is not an issue often addressed).

The second question epitomises all the troubles VC has had with the economic theorising of the mainstream. Much of her critique concerns comparative statics with its half denial and half pretence of modelling movement in time while ignoring the process of change as it passes through time. The problem I highlight here is that if economists took their own definitions seriously, they would not discuss stability in the context of static demand and supply schedules. If $D(P)$ and $S(P)$ are demand and supply schedules, their intersections are just points in the price–quantity space. They can be neither stable nor unstable. They are just there. In order to discuss stability, one would require $D[P(t)]$ and $S[P(t)]$ at the very least with some explicit theory of the dynamics.

*General equilibrium.* When we move away from partial to general equilibrium, the scenario is still static or stationary. There are extensive results on the existence, uniqueness and stability of general competitive equilibrium (Arrow and Hahn 1971). But here again the second question raised above crops up. How can we discuss stability in a model with only price-takers? Who changes the price when faced with excess demand or supply? It was Arrow who not only pioneered discussions on stability, but posed this awkward question in his 1958 article. A large literature grew up on the 'disequilibrium' approach to stability but it did not get anywhere and is now ignored (Arrow 1958; Fisher 1983).

So all we can say rigorously is that a static partial or general equilibrium may exist and may be unique or not. Even then the economy has to be perfectly competitive. We do not have any rigorous story of general equilibrium for non-competitive economies (see, however, Hart 1985). Of stability we should not speak unless we are clear as to who has the incentive to be a price-setter in an economy of price-takers.

*Dynamic equilibrium.* Other notions of equilibrium are more helpful in describing history and time. In dynamic systems, we may have a variety of outcomes which are equilibrium in the sense that they constitute a solution to the system of equations. Thus taking a two-variable dynamic system as our model, we may have a steady state, or a saddle point, or a limit cycle, all of which are equilibrium solutions. The limit cycle is an interesting equilibrium concept because the system is not 'at rest', nor going along a predetermined steady path.

It is cycling if the variables happen to be in a particular region of the phase space. Away from it the system may explode or collapse down to a static equilibrium.

One of the most interesting equilibria is that of the predator–prey-type system of Richard Goodwin (Goodwin 1967). This two-equation system has a pair of imaginary roots. The system has an equilibrium but it is a virtual equilibrium since the system will never approach equilibrium unless it starts there. This makes a very important distinction between the existence of equilibrium and convergence towards it if you start away from it. Yet the Goodwin system is not unstable in the ordinary sense of the word since the solution traces out a cycle which is infinitely repeated. Initial conditions totally determine where the cycle will start and stay.

The Goodwin system has inspired a large literature (Desai 1973; Goodwin *et al.* 1984; Veneziani 2001). A basic result is that the Goodwin system is structurally unstable. This means that for small perturbations of the parameter values, the system's qualitative properties change drastically. Thus in the Goodwin system, if the parameter for money illusion in the wage bargain changes from zero to a small positive number, the system becomes globally stable instead of a centre with a perpetual cycle around it. While in the previous parametrisation the equilibrium is unreachable, now it is immediately reached (Desai 1973).

Goodwin's model thus shows that economic models may have non-robust properties. Parameters may change, say, due to learning. Probability distributions themselves may not be stable. Structurally unstable models also lead to chaotic dynamics. Within the two-variable phase space the system's behaviour may alter from stable to cyclical to chaotic as we move from one region of the phase space to another as parameter values change. Few economic models are such that their parameters are exact within narrow ranges. Structural instability may be more pervasive than we admit. Keynes's picture of the stock market as changing between normal times when speculation is just bubbles on the surface, to when it becomes a whirlpool of bubbles at other times, is a picture of a structurally unstable system (*GT*, chapter 12, p. 159).

*Temporary equilibrium.* The most useful model for macroeconomic reasoning is of course Hicks's temporary equilibrium (TE) model. First, unlike in the Walrasian general equilibrium model (especially its Arrow–Debreu version), time can be explicitly introduced in a way that makes a difference whether we are speaking of *ex ante* or *ex post*. (Debreu's clever device of contingent commodities and simultaneous instantaneous clearing of all markets in equilibrium annihilates both time and uncertainty.) Second, it allows for agency in discussing who does what when an equilibrium is arrived at, unlike in all the other notions of equilibrium discussed thus far. Third, it allows for modelling of the interaction of agents explicitly. Fourth, of course, we can deal with expectations and uncertainty rigorously in the TE framework although the uncertainty is not in Keynes's sense (Grandmont 1988).

Thus TE leads to a notion of equilibrium which is not demand-equals-supply, or even of market clearing necessarily, but in terms of behaviour of agents. This is best captured by Hahn's definition of equilibrium. To quote Chick and Caserta again, 'Hahn proposes to define equilibrium as the situation in which "the economy" is giving agents signals which do not cause agents to alter their theory (Hahn 1973: 59)' (ibid., p. 227). Agents act on the basis of the theory they hold of the economy. They base their expectations on their theories, and if the outcome is such as not to falsify their theory they do not change behaviour or their theory. It is possible that different agents have different theories unlike in the standard rational expectations (RE) case where everyone knows the unique 'true' model. There is also the possibility of Bayesian learning. TE does however make heroic assumptions about perfect information. The solution concept of a Nash equilibrium which is most often used does assume that each agent knows the strategies of all the other agents. (Recent game theoretic work has introduced new solution concepts such as perfect equilibrium. I leave them aside partly for want of space and largely for lack of expertise on these topics.)

Equilibrium in economic theory is thus a very rich notion, though even at the end of this inventory one is aware how much simpler models are than the world they are purporting to describe. Thus it is not surprising that many economists are impatient with the notion of equilibrium and wish to speak of disequilibrium. But if equilibrium is difficult to model, disequilibrium is impossible. This is so in the sense that in disequilibrium anything can happen, and if one wants to sketch out the behaviour of an economy in disequilibrium it is impossible to do so without saying something about systematic (i.e. consistent) predictable (i.e. derivable from some theory) behaviour. Sometimes when people speak of disequilibrium, they may merely mean a dynamic rather than a static or comparative static model, for example a limit cycle rather than a static equilibrium. At other times they may be rejecting a particular class of restrictions, for example the assumption in RE models that everyone has the same model. Or they may prefer a non-linear model to a linear one. The rich array of equilibrium concepts available allows for much flexibility and they need to be exhausted before one may plunge into the uncharted waters of disequilibrium analysis.

## 3. Provisional equilibrium

With that background how do we characterise the equilibrium in *GT*? There have been many views expressed – that it is a disequilibrium model disguised as comparative statics, that it is a comparative statics model overlaid with dynamic literary additions, that whatever it is it is inconsistent with microfoundations, that is, with Walrasian general equilibrium. VC has explored this question in a series of papers spanning twenty-five years (Chick 1973/7 1978/92, 1983, 1991, 1992, 1997a, b). There are some constant themes but there is also progression in the articulation of the *GT* model. The constant themes are:

1. *GT* is a static model of a dynamic process.
2. A Marshallian periodisation has to be imposed on what seem to be simultaneous decisions about production, financing and consumption (see figure 2.1 in 1983).

3.  The nature of the monetary economy with the pivotal importance of credit in financing production leading to a causal primacy of investment over saving.

As I said above, it is in the article written with Maurizio Caserta that the most recent and in my view most mature of these analyses occurs. I shall therefore discuss that article.

Provisional equilibrium (PE) is a variation of TE. While TE can be modelled in terms of the one-period-ahead expectations of all agents for all commodities, in PE there is an additional complication that investment decisions by entrepreneurs are conditional on long-term expectations. Thus, unlike TE, a PE is a consistent solution of short-term expectations of many agents conditional on the long-term expectations of the entrepreneurs. Long-term expectations of investors are volatile partly because the future values of the marginal efficiency of capital are unknown and unknowable and partly because of the influence of animal spirits. (Other factors mentioned in the article cited are signal extraction and analytical convenience for choosing PE as a way of describing *GT* equilibrium.)

The equilibrium is provisional in the sense that it is not final, that is, stationary or steady state. Nor is it clear that the sequence of PE will converge to a long-term or final equilibrium. This could be the case if agents' long-term expectations as well as short-term expectations could be fulfilled. But, as the authors say, Keynes never worried about the long-period equilibrium. This is because 'he considered the question of whether entrepreneurs' expectations of long-term profits would be realised (the long-period equilibrium of his short-period equilibrium) to be irrelevant. The result would not guide entrepreneurs' future action, as the circumstances surrounding the investment decisions may have changed.' (ibid., p. 230). This leads the authors to an important conclusion: 'Thus, "progress" towards the neo-Ricardian final equilibrium depends, if it is to happen at all, on continual recalculation and the repeated exercise of animal spirits, in new and always uncertain circumstances. Convergence is far from guaranteed.' (ibid., p. 230).

## 4. Understanding provisional equilibrium

The *GT* equilibrium is one where involuntary unemployment can persist. Thus it conflicts with a Walrasian equilibrium. The argument above says that this is a PE which departs from the typical TE inasmuch as it is contingent on the fragile and volatile long-term expectations of the investors. How do we model this?

The structure of TE is well understood. A pair of equations constitutes the model. The first equation says that the actual outcome is conditional upon the forecasts of the agents about the outcome. The second equation shows how agents generate those forecasts. The equilibrium is established by showing that the two are consistent. A simple outline will do here. Let $x$ be the $n$ vector of commodities and let there be $I$ agents labelled $i$ each. Then we have (* denotes short-term expectations)

$$x\,t = f\,\{x^*it + 1: \text{for all } i \text{ in } I\}, \tag{1}$$

$$x^*it + 1 = gi \, [xt, xt-1, xt-2, xt-3, \ldots]. \tag{2}$$

Substituting (2) into (1) we get the equilibrium equation:

$$xt = f\{g1(xit, xit-1 \ldots)\, g2(xit, xit-1, \ldots)\, g3(xit \ldots) \ldots\}. \tag{3}$$

Note that each agent can have a different forecasting rule (Grandmont 1988, introduction).

In the Keynesian case there are different types of agents – consumers, workers, producers, rentiers and entrepreneurs. There is an overlap between these categories. Thus producers and entrepreneurs overlap, as do consumers and workers. But the distinction is as to what they focus on in generating their short-term forecasts. Thus as VC showed in *Macroeconomics after Keynes*, one has to periodise as between the action of these different agents. Within the unit period, producers have primacy in generating their forecasts of what the demand will be and deciding on how many workers to hire and what to pay given their wage and price expectations. Consumers/workers make their plans but may revise them in light of what the producers decide by way of hiring. Entrepreneurs have long-term expectations about profitability which are fragile (high variance) but they also have animal spirits. Rentiers have expectations about the course of the money supply and interest rates.

Thus we can distinguish between agents and confine their expectations to a subset of the variables. This is not necessary since everyone can have expectations about everything but there is some convenience to using common sense to simplify the problem. So we denote $X_c$ consumers and $X_l$ workers, $X_k$ producers, $X_r$ rentiers and $X_e$ entrepreneurs. The variables are aggregate supply price $Z$, aggregate demand price $D$, $N$ is employment, wages $w$, price $p$, interest rate $r$. We assume a single commodity besides labour, bonds and money. The production function of the single commodity is a standard one and capital stock is given as usual in a $GT$ model.

Producers generate expectations about $D$ knowing the production function and decide on wages and the price level. Consumers/workers having formed initial expectations about $Z$ estimate their incomes $wN$ and decide on consumption which is part of $D$. Producers hire and pay wages and workers receive and spend wages. The difficult element in the equilibrium is investment. This depends on entrepreneurs' expectations about long-term profitability and animal spirits. Let us say that the timing and size of investment demand is erratic because of this. This makes the estimate of $D$ erratic. Therefore analogous to eqn (1) above, the $X$ vector in the present case, comprising $\{Z, D, N, w, p, r\}$, can be written as follows:

$$Xt = f\{X_k^* \, (D,w,r), X_r^*(r, p); X_{c,1}^* \, (Z,w,p); X_e^{**}(Z,p,r)\}. \tag{4}$$

Here I have indicated the expectations of the producers as $X_k$, of entrepreneurs as $X_e$, etc. In the arguments of each are the relevant variables. To emphasise who decides first, I have clubbed together producers and rentiers whose expectations determine the cost of credit and the size of output/employment. Then consumers/workers decide on their demand given expected income. Lastly all this depends on the entrepreneurs' long-term expectations. Long-term expectations are denoted by a double asterisk. The analogues of (2) and (3) can be easily written.

Equation (4) is just a formal exercise. We have to go further and put some flesh on the bare bones of the equilibrium. Let me for the present take the rentiers' expectations as given, and hence take the interest rate as given as well. In line with *GT* chapter 3, we can then trace out the aggregate demand aggregate supply equilibrium as follows. Given the expectations about $D$ and $w$ and $r$, producers decide on employment. They do this by inverting the aggregate supply curve derived from the production function (see Chick (1983) for details).

$$N = F\left[\left(\frac{D}{w}\right)^*\right]. \tag{5}$$

This says that employment is decided on the basis of expected aggregate demand and wages. The function $F$ is the inverse of ø which is the standard notation for aggregate supply. Now $D$ is the sum of consumption and investment. Consumption is decided as follows:

$$C = C\left[\left(\frac{Z}{p}\right)^*\right]. \tag{6}$$

For investment we have to compute profitability. Profits are equal to $\{Z - wN\}$. But $Z = w$ 'φ' $[N]$. So profits are $w$ 'φ' $[N] - N]$. Given capital stock $K$ the profit rate is then a function of $w$ and 'φ'. Price is equal to $w$ divided by the marginal product of labour derived from the production function. (For details again see Chick 1983, chapters 3–5.) Let profitability be denoted by $G(w)$ ($G$ is a function of $w$ and $p(w)$). Then investment is determined as follows:

$$I = I\left(G(w) - r\right)^{**}\exp u. \tag{7}$$

In (7) I have introduced animal spirits crudely by putting in $u$ which appears in an exponential way. Assume that $u$ is a random variable which takes values between 0 and 1. There are also the long-run expectations about profitability relative to the rate of interest. It is admittedly only a very sketchy investment function. Now

$$D = C + I. \tag{8}$$

In equilibrium we have $Z = D$. So we have

$$F\left\{\left(\frac{D}{w}\right)^*_k\right\} = F\left\{C\left(\frac{D}{p(w)}\right)_c + I\left(G(w) - r\right)^{**}_e \exp u\right\}. \tag{9}$$

Equation (9) is then the PE of the Keynesian *GT* model. In each case it is made clear as to whose expectations they are by putting in the subscripts k, c and e. We have also the superscripts * and ** to clarify whether these are short- or long-run expectations. The question is, will (9) be solvable, that is, do the two sides really equal each other?

In chapters 3 and 5 where Keynes discusses this output employment equilibrium, he dwells mostly on the expectations of the firm, that is, of the producers. If we had k instead of c in the first term on the right-hand side of (9), that is with the consumption function $C$, only the long-term expectations of the entrepreneurs will remain as a complication. Here again since producers overlap with entrepreneurs, we could get away by saying that these are the short- and long-run expectations of the same people.

This will not quite do. But even if that was the case, we still have animal spirits to deal with. Let me offer the following scenario.

We may have low animal spirits $u=0$ and then $D=C\{D/p(w)\}+I\{G(w)-r\}$. This is a low demand scenario. If $u$ takes on a higher value, then $D$ will be higher and so will be $N$ which then will feed back on $C$ and so on. So animal spirits will make the PE fragile in any case.

But the really important insight is that there are long-term expectations about profitability of the entrepreneurs who will be a subset of the producers and they may differ from those who are not investing but merely producing. Thus our PE departs from a TE in the vital sense that both short- and long-run expectations are involved in its determination. The situation which will be realised will thus depend on the investment decision for this double reason – fragility of long-term profitability expectations, and animal spirits. It can be anywhere in the range given by $u$ as it varies from 0 to 1, as shown in Fig. 3.1.

In any case the left-hand side of (9) less the first term on the right-hand side will equal investment at some level. So it all depends on $I$. Equilibrium will thus depend on $I$.

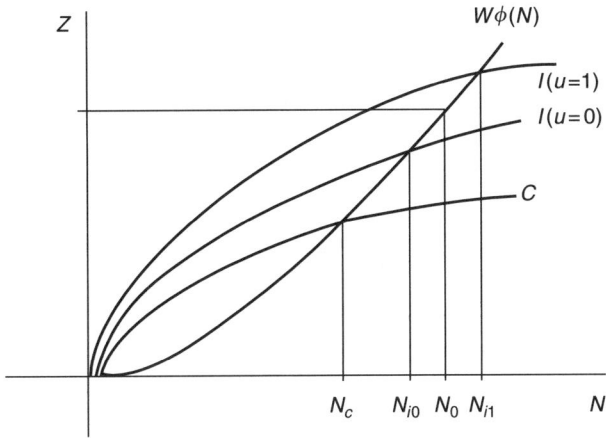

*Figure 3.1* The provisional equilibrium.

It is very difficult to say anything about long-term convergence since it is not the spirit of *GT*. But the sort of a story a Walrasian or his twin neo-Ricardian will tell is clear from eqn (9) above. Fix $u$ at its expected value (assuming moments exist of the pdf of $u$). Then, given $r$, there will be a value of $w$ at which, after repeated iterations, the model will converge. So profitability will be that in the long and the short run which satisfies (9), given a mean value of $u$. It is not a story that VC would buy.

## 5. Conclusion

I have attempted a very crude and simple demonstration of PE of the Keynesian model. Its connections with TE have been shown and an attempt was made to set up the chapter 3 model in the framework of PE. Much work remains to be done of course, but then there are plenty of years ahead for all of us to do just that.

## References

Abramovitz, M. *et al.* (eds) (1958) *The Allocation of Economic Resources*. Stanford, CA: Stanford University Press.

Arrow, K. J. (1958) 'Towards a Theory of Price Adjustments', in Abramovitz (1958).

Arrow, K. J. and Hahn, F. H. (1971) *General Competitive Analysis*. San Fransisco, CA: Holden Day.

Arrow, K. J. and Honkapojha, S. (1985) *Frontiers of Economics*. Oxford: Basil Blackwell.

Chick, V. (1973/7) *The Theory of Monetary Policy*. London: Gray Mills/Oxford; Parkgate Books, Basil Blackwell.

Chick, V. (1978/92) 'The Nature of the Keynesian Revolution: A Reassessment', Australian Economic Papers June. Reprinted in Chick (1992).

Chick, V. (1983) *Macroeconomics After Keynes: A Reconsideration of the General Theory*. London: Philip Allan.

Chick, V. (1991) 'The Small Firm Under Uncertainty: A Puzzle of the General Theory', Discussion Papers in Economics 91-10, UCL.

Chick, V. (1992) In P. Arestis and S. Dow (eds), *On Money Method and Keynes: Selected Essays*.

Chick, V. (1997a) 'The Multiplier and Finance', in G. C. Harcourt and P. A. Riach (eds), *A Second Edition of General Theory*, Vol. 1, Chapter 11. London: Routledge.

Chick, V. (1997b) 'Provisional Equilibrium and Macroeconomic Theory', with Maurizio Caserta, in P. Arestis, G. Palma and M. Sawyer (eds), *Markets, Unemployment and Economic Policy: Essays in Honour of Geoff Harcourt*, Vol. 2, London: Routledge.

Desai, M. (1973) 'Growth Cycles and Inflation in a Model of the Class Struggle', *Journal of Economic Theory*, Vol. 6, pp. 527–545, December.

Feinstein, C. E. (ed.) (1967) *Socialism, Capitalism and Economic Development*. Cambridge: Cambridge University Press.

Fisher, F. M. (1983) *Disequilibrium Foundations of Equilibrium Economics*. Cambridge: Cambridge University Press.

Goodwin, R. M. (1967) 'A Growth Cycle', in Feinstein (1967).

Goodwin, R. M., Krueger, M. and Vercelli, A. (1984) *Nonlinera Models of Fluctuating Growth*. Berlin: Springer-Verlag.

Gorman, W. M. (1953) 'Community Preference Fields', *Econometrica*, 21, June.

Grandmont, J.-M. (ed.) (1988) *Temporary Equilibrium*. New York: Academic Press.

Hahn, F. H. (1973) *On the Notion of Equilibrium in Economics: Inaugural Lecture.* Cambridge: Cambridge University Press.

Hart, O. H. (1985) 'Imperfect Competition in General Equilibrium: An Overview of Recent Work', in Arrow and Honkapojha (1985).

Kaldor, N. (1934) 'A Classificatory Note on the Determinateness of Equilibrium', *Review of Economic Studies*, Vol. 2, February.

Kaldor, N. (1972) 'The Irrelevance of Equilibrium', *Economic Journal* 82, Vol. 82, pp. 1237–55.

Veneziani, R. (2001) 'Goodwin's Growth Cycle: An Overview of the Literature', Discussion Paper, Department of Economics, University of Sienna (forthcoming).

# 4

# FROM THE FUNDAMENTAL EQUATIONS TO EFFECTIVE DEMAND: 'NATURAL EVOLUTION' OR 'CHANGE OF VIEW'?

*Maria Cristina Marcuzzo*

## 1. Premise

One of the difficult tasks, which any scholar of Keynes's writings is confronted with, is that of tracing the relationship between the *General Theory* and the *Treatise*. To this controversial matter, which has spawned a large literature, I would like to contribute with a further element which does not seem to have received as much attention as others, namely an investigation into Keynes's own assessment of the relationship between his two books.

Keynes was convinced that there was a fundamental continuity between the *Treatise* and the *General Theory*. Throughout the process which led him from the former to the latter book, he repeatedly claimed that the *Treatise* analysis was in fact compatible with that of the *General Theory* and that he had made the new argument only 'much more accurate and instructive' (Keynes 1936 [1973b]: 77).

In fact, the transition from the *Treatise* analysis, as presented in the Fundamental Equations and that of the *General Theory*, as incorporated in the principle of effective demand, required the introduction of new concepts and a change in definitions, which eventually made the latter approach quite distinct from the former. However, Keynes wanted his readers to believe that 'under the surface [...] the essential ideas are the same' (Skidelsky 1992: 442), and presented his new book as a 'natural evolution' in his line of thought. (Keynes 1936 [1973b]: xxii).

In this paper I follow this evolution step by step, comparing Keynes's own measurement of the distance from his previous framework of analysis with our present understanding of the change involved in the process of building up the new one. To spin the narrative, I divide the five years spanning from the publication of the *Treatise* to that of the *General Theory* into three time-legs, which I have marked as Stages I, II and III. The first dates from comments and criticism on the *Treatise* (autumn 1930) to the early material for the new book and lectures (spring 1932). Stage II spans from the Easter Term 1932 lectures, which were attended by members of the 'Circus', to the summer 1933, when the writing of the new book was well under way. The final stage runs from the 1933 Michaelmas Term lectures and the contemporary fragments of versions of the *General Theory*, when the principle of effective demand was clearly expounded, to the final touches to the proofs in December 1935.

## 2. Stage I: Autumn 1930–Spring 1932

It will be remembered that in the *Treatise* the equilibrium condition of the overall system is given by the equality of the value of investment ($I$) to its cost of production ($I'$) and by the equality of the value of investment to saving ($S$). This corresponds to a situation of zero extra profits in the consumption ($Q_1$) and investment sectors ($Q_2$), and to equality of investment to saving. Total profits ($Q$) are then the equilibrating mechanism not only between cost of production and the value of output, but also between saving and investment (Keynes 1930 [1971]: 124):

$$Q_1 = I' - S,$$

$$Q_2 = I - I',$$

$$Q = Q_1 + Q_2$$

$$= I - S.$$

There are different effects on the system, according to how profits are spent. In the 'widow's cruse' example (Keynes 1930 [1971]: 125), if entrepreneurs spend their extra profits on consumption goods, the positive gap between the cost of investment goods and saving widens: the price of consumption continues to increase, and so do profits. When profits are positive, entrepreneurs have an incentive to increase output and employment; if losses occur, both output and employment will be reduced. However, adjustment of output is not the object of the analysis in question, although in the 'banana plantation' example (Keynes 1930 [1971]: 158ff.) the effect of losses (due to an autonomous increase in saving) on output is taken up to show the potential instability of the system (Barens 1987). If, starting from an equilibrium condition (prices = costs of production, saving = investment), there is an increase in saving, the price of consumption goods fall, entrepreneurs incur losses and so cut back on employment. A new equilibrium position is reached only when either: (a) output is reduced to zero; (b) the reduction in saving no longer occurs; and (c) investment increases and exceeds saving (Keynes 1930 [1971]: 160). The possibility that equilibrium is reached at a positive level of output was not envisaged.

The Fundamental Equations apparatus was the object of criticism from the outset. Hawtrey, Robertson, Pigou and Kahn objected to some of Keynes's definitions and conclusions. In particular, three issues came to the forefront: (a) the 'independence' of the forces underlying determination of the two price levels; (b) the definition of saving; and (c) the price–output adjustment mechanism.

As a result of the various criticisms, a few months after publication of the *Treatise* Keynes recast his argument in a new form. The first evidence of a change in formulation is the account which he gave in the Harris Foundation lectures (June 1931) of the reason for expecting a positive equilibrium level of output to be reached:

> A given deficiency of investment causes a given decline of profit. A given decline of profit causes a given decline of output. Unless there is a constantly increasing deficiency of investment, there is eventually reached, therefore, a sufficiently low level of output which represents a kind of spurious equilibrium.
>
> (Keynes 1973a: 356)

Unlike the 'banana plantation' example, the possibility that the equilibrium level of output may be less than zero is now given, on the basis of the assumed behaviour of saving: '[...] as soon as output has declined heavily, strong forces will be brought into play in the direction of reducing the net volume of saving' (Keynes 1973a: 356). This result was anticipated in a letter to Kahn of 17 April 1931 (during the 'Circus' period): '[...] when $O$ [output] is falling, unless entrepreneurs' expenditure on consumption falls faster than $O$, there is a *reduction* of saving' (Keynes 1979: 12). What, however, remained to be determined was at which level of profit entrepreneurs are no longer inclined to continue production, or, on the other hand, have an incentive to expand production. The solution was found in a new relationship, which Keynes attributed to Kahn (Keynes 1973a: 368), the aggregate supply curve.[1]

During the summer of 1931, Keynes worked to pin down cases where 'points of equilibrium output can be reached which fall short of maximum and zero' (Keynes 1973a: 374). The mechanism he submitted to Kahn in a letter of 20 September 1931 may be outlined thus: an increase in investment ($I$) raises profits ($Q$), part of the increase in profits going into savings ($S$); at the same time, an increase in profits raises output ($O$), along the aggregate supply curve, and thus brings about a further increase in savings. However, the profit per unit of output ($Q/O$) declines as output increases since profits fall as savings rise. Keynes's conclusion was that 'If $Q/O$ reaches zero before $O$ reaches maximum, we have "long-period unemployment", i.e. an equilibrium position short of full employment.' (Keynes 1973a: 374).

Kahn was not totally convinced (Keynes 1973a: 375); it was clear that the question was far from being settled. Keynes had to work out the new formulation afresh, which is what he set out to do in the autumn of 1931. He told Lydia on 22 November: 'I have begun again quietly in my chair writing about monetary theory' (Skidelsky 1992: 432). In fact, early in 1932, in a draft,[2] he was able to present the 'vital generalisation' of the proposition that entrepreneurs tend to increase or decrease their output according as their profit is increasing or decreasing, which runs as follows:

> [...] increases and decreases in the volume of output and employment depend upon the changes in disbursement relative to earnings (which is the alternative mode of expression I now offer to the reader) or in investment relatively to savings (which is the mode of expression I employed in my *Treatise on Money*).
>
> (Keynes 1973a: 380)

The condition for equilibrium was specified accordingly:

> [...] provided $\Delta S$ [changes in saving] and $\Delta E$ [changes in earnings] have the same sign, and that investment does not change, *any* level of output is a position of stable equilibrium. For any increase of output will bring in a retarding factor, since $\Delta S$ will be positive and consequently $I$ being assumed constant, $\Delta Q$ will be negative; whilst equally any decrease of output will bring in a stimulating factor, since $\Delta S$ will be negative and consequently $\Delta Q$ positive.
>
> (Keynes 1973a: 386–7)

Summing up, in Stage I Keynes inherited a framework of analysis based on the Fundamental Equations, in which profits were the 'main spring of change', through variations in the price levels of consumption and investment goods. As a consequence of much criticism within the 'Circus' and by Robertson, Hawtrey and Pigou, with the main focus on the supposed independence in determination of the two price levels and the neglect of output as opposed to price adjustment, Keynes was led to forge new tools. In the Harris Foundation lectures we find the first 'hints' (Keynes 1973: 79) of a move towards a different approach. During the summer of 1931 and until he resumed lecturing in April–May 1932, he searched for the conditions for an equilibrium of output to occur, at less than full employment. His solution rested on what he believed to be only a 'generalisation' of the old argument, but which was instead a switch of focus: from investment-relative-to-saving to expenditure-relative-to-income.[3]

## 3. Stage II: Easter Term 1932–summer 1933

When Keynes resumed[4] lecturing in April–May 1932[5] he presented his new argument as a 'generalisation' of that of the *Treatise*:[6]

> [...] fluctuations of output and employment for a given community over the short period [...] depend almost entirely on the amount of current investment. This goes beyond the contention of my *Treatise*, where

it was meant to depend on the amount of investment *relatively* to saving [...] This less restricted generalisation is the result of taking account of the probable effect on saving of a change in the amount of investment.

(Keynes 1979: 41)

This result was reached on the 'presumption' (Keynes 1979: 41) that changes in saving, following a change in investment, rather than offset, reinforce the effects of the change in investment on profit and output. The main argument was that changes in investment and output were positively correlated: an increase in output is equal to an increase in sales receipts (=income); an increase in investment is equal to an increase in sales receipts (=income) *minus* expenditure on consumption; consumption and income are positively correlated, therefore changes in investment and changes in output have the same sign. This 'proof' was challenged by Kahn, Austin and Joan Robinson who signed a Manifesto and offered an 'alternative' (as Keynes put it) or 'complementary' (as Joan Robinson had it in her subsequent correspondence) solution (Keynes 1973a: 378). The authors of the Manifesto claimed that demonstration would be better handled 'by the method of supply and demand' (Keynes 1979: 43). The increase in investment – they argued – leads *directly* to an increase in the level of output because it raises the demand for consumption goods; assuming as given the supply conditions of these goods, the new level of output of consumption goods and thus the aggregate level of output can *immediately* be determined.[7]

Keynes was reluctant 'to scrap all my present half forged weapons' (Keynes 1973a: 378), as he wrote to Joan Robinson, but shortly afterwards he gave in. In the lectures of Michaelmas Term 1932, when he changed the title of his course to 'The Monetary Theory of Production',[8] he took up the 'method' of the Manifesto. However, once again he pledged that 'a change in demand as a whole relatively to supply as a whole due to deficient disbursement [...] is the same thing as what in my *Treatise on Money*, I have called an excess of saving over investment' (Keynes 1979: 53).

In those lectures, windfall profits are the signals which induce entrepreneurs to revise their production decisions, but whether or not entrepreneurs are making profits is now made dependent on whether disbursements (i.e. expenditure) are greater than earnings. According to his new terminology (Rymes 1989: 57), unlike the *Treatise*, total income, $E'$, includes profits, being defined as

$$E' = E + Q,$$

while $E$ retains its old meaning of earnings. Moreover, the 'new term' (Rymes 1889: 57) disbursement, $D$, is defined as the sum of investment, $I$, and expenditure on consumables, $F$, which are made equal to income. Then we have

$$D = I + F = E' = E + Q$$

and

$$Q = I - (E - F),$$

hence

$$Q = I - S.$$

Parallel to the change in the definition of income, a new concept of saving was introduced, which Keynes labelled 'surplus', retaining $S$ ($= E - F$) for saving:

$$S' = S + Q.$$

Equality is said always to exist between investment and surplus, the adjustment mechanism being provided by the price of consumables (Rymes 1989: 62); saving being here described as 'something that has to occur to make more investment possible at the existing price level' (Rymes 1989: 61).

The ambiguity of Keynes's position at the time – his formulation being halfway between the *Treatise* and the *General Theory* – is well revealed by the following passage from a fragment from which he appears to have lectured on 14 November 1932:

> [...] if, starting from a position of equilibrium with saving and invest-
> ment equal, the price level stable and the factors of production fully
> employed, there occurs a change which causes the rate of interest exist-
> ing at the moment to become such as to cause saving to be in excess of
> investment[9] prices will fall, rates of earnings will fall, and output will
> fall, in accordance with the argument in my *Treatise of Money.*
>
> (Keynes 1979: 56)

Certainly, unlike the *Treatise*, we have here a mechanism preventing output (and/or prices) to be falling to zero or infinity: 'neither prices nor output will fall forever; and they will [...] come to rest again at some position from which they will have no further tendency to depart' (Keynes 1979: 57). The mechanism is provided by the assumption that expenditure always increases less or decreases more than does income ('whenever there is a change in income, there will be a change in expenditure the same in direction but less in amount'; Keynes 1979: 38). However, saving is not yet fully integrated as dependent variable in the output-adjusting mechanism.

Early in 1933, the changed political climate prompted Keynes to write four articles for 'The Times' (published between 13 and 16 March 1933) to give his new approach an airing and to relaunch a plan for public spending. These articles were subsequently published as a pamphlet, *The Means to Prosperity*. A further contribution came with the article *The Multiplier* (where the term, later to become familiar, made its first public appearance) published in 'The New Statesman' of 1 April 1933.

Moggridge is persuaded – unlike Patinkin (1976) – that by the time of this article the 'penny had firmly dropped for the theory of effective demand' (Moggridge 1992: 564). Certainly, a visible leap forward from the *Treatise* was accomplished in Stage II, with the crucial discovery of the income–expenditure approach, which provided the framework where the multiplier could be fully accommodated.[10]

As late as 17 August 1933 writing to Macmillan Keynes appeared to think that he could revise the *Treatise* accordingly, believing that he was just putting off revising it 'until my next book has appeared' (Keynes 1973a: 420). As we know, the revision was not to be and perhaps could never have been.

## 4. Stage III: Michaelmas Term 1933–December 1935

On the basis of the evidence of the lectures of Michaelmas Term 1933, and the contemporary[11] fragments of versions of the *General Theory* that came to light in Tilton's 'laundry hamper', most commentators (Dimand 1988: 167; Moggridge 1992: 562; Patinkin 1976: 79; 1982: 33; 1993: 656) agree that by that time the conception of effective demand had been accomplished.

In 'an early typed and hand-written draft of what eventually became chapter 5 of the second 1933 draft table of contents' (Keynes 1979: 68), Keynes presented again 'our fundamental equations'; the only changes of notation (from the lectures in the previous year) are $C$ for $F$, consumption expenditure, while $Y$, income, makes its first appearance:

$$Y = E + Q = C + I = D$$

or

$$Q = D - E = I - (E - C).$$

Facing once again the task of accounting for the change in the definition of saving from the *Treatise*, Keynes presented the following:

$$S = Y - C = E + Q - C,$$

and then explained that he had decided to retain the notation, $S$, and the word *Saving* for $Y - C$ and to define $S'$, corresponding to the definition of saving in the *Treatise*, as *Economising* (Keynes 1979: 69). He then rewrote the price equations of the *Treatise*, insisting that, although the definitions were not identical with those given in the previous book, 'they deal with substantially the same concepts which I was then driving at' (Keynes 1979: 72).

We have now two definitions of savings ($S$ and $S'$) and two corresponding definitions of profits ($Q$ and $Q'$) to distinguish their meaning from that in the *Treatise*, according to the following expression:

$$S' = E + Q' - C.$$

He stressed the compatibility of his present treatment with the *Treatise*, by saying that $Q'$ was the 'flow of quasi-rent relevant to long-period expectations', while $Q$ is relevant for the short period (Rymes 1989: 107; Keynes 1979: 72).

The Fundament Equations had by now (Rymes 1989: 110) become

$$Y = E + Q = C + I = D,$$

$$S = E + Q - C = Y - C,$$

$$\Delta S = \Delta Q + \Delta(E - C) = \Delta I,$$

$$\Delta S' = \Delta(E - C),$$

hence

$$\Delta Q = \Delta S - \Delta S'$$

and

$$\Delta Q = \Delta I - \Delta S'.$$

When $\Delta Q$ is positive, because investment is increasing faster than the community is economising (Rymes 1989: 111), firms increase output. To be noted is that in this formulation the role of profits has changed, since now the level of output is dependent on a *prospective* rather than *actual* magnitude. In fact, in the fragment corresponding to the first 1933 draft table of contents, Keynes wrote that the level of output depended 'on the amount by which the sale proceeds of output as a whole are expected to exceed their variable cost' (Keynes 1979: 64); in other words the relevant magnitude had become *ex ante* or expected profits and not the *ex post* or realised profits, as in the *Treatise*.[12] Eventually, in the fragment of the version of chapter 3 corresponding to the last index of 1933 (December), he made quite clear that the introduction of the principle of effective demand represented the novelty in the *General Theory* treatment:

> In my *Treatise on Money* the equality of saving and investment, as then defined, was a condition equivalent to the equality of aggregate expenditure and aggregate costs, but I failed to point out that this by itself provided only for neutral equilibrium and not for, what one might call, optimum equilibrium.
>
> (Keynes 1979: 91–2)

In March 1934 Keynes was convinced that the book was by then 'nearing completion' (Keynes 1973a: 422). From this period we have the versions of chapters 6–12 of the index to the book, which now bore the title *The General Theory of*

*Employment, Interest and Money*, written before his journey to the United States in June 1934, and the provisional versions of chapters 8–9 written over the summer.[13] In those drafts he insisted on compatibility with the *Treatise* analysis, by referring to entrepreneur's windfall profits or losses as the difference between effective demand and income (Keynes 1973a: 425) and explaining the change in the definitions of income and saving as 'a change of terminology and not a change of view' (Keynes 1973a: 476).

The issue of explaining the relationship between the new book and the old one arose again. On 29 November 1934, he wrote to a Spanish correspondent, Luc Beltram:

> [...] in a work of mine which will probably come out in about a year's time I deal with the underlying theory on what at any rate on the surface, would appear to be lines rather different from those adopted in my *Treatise on Money*. Under the surface, however, the essential ideas are the same.
>
> (Skidelsky 1992: 442)

The *General Theory* was finished in late December 1935. In the final version Keynes carefully indicated where his new argument departed from the old. First, there was the change in the definition of income:

> [...] I should at once remind the reader that in my *Treatise on Money* I defined income in a special sense. The peculiarity in my former definition related to that part of aggregate income which accrues to the entrepreneurs, since I took neither the profit (whether gross or net) actually realised from their current operations nor the profit which they expected when they decided to undertake their current operations, but in some sense (not, as I now think, sufficiently defined if we allow for the possibility of changes in the scale of output) a normal or equilibrium profit; with the result that on this definition saving exceeded investment by the amount of the excess of normal profit over the actual profit.
>
> (Keynes 1936 [1973b]: 61)

Second, there was a new mechanism for output adjustment:

> [...] by an excess of saving over investment I meant [i.e. in *The Treatise*] that the scale of output was such that entrepreneurs were earning a less than normal profit from their ownership of the capital equipment; and by an increased excess of saving over investment I meant that a decline was taking place in the actual profits, so that they would be under a motive to contract output.
>
> As I now think, the volume of employment (and consequently of output and real income) is fixed by the entrepreneur under the motive of

seeking to maximise his present and prospective profits [...]; whilst the volume of employment which will maximise his profit depends on the aggregate demand function given by his expectations of the sum of the proceeds resulting from consumption and investment respectively on various hypotheses.

(Keynes 1936 [1973b]: 77)

Third, there was determination of the equilibrium level of output at less than full employment:

In my *Treatise on Money* the concept of *changes* in the excess of investment over saving, as there defined, was a way of handling changes in profit, though I did not in that book distinguish clearly between expected and realised results.[14] I there argued that a change in the excess of investment over saving was the motive force governing change in the volume of output. Thus the new argument, though (as I now think) much more accurate and instructive, is essentially a development of the old.

(Keynes 1936 [1973b]: 77–8)

Summing up, reinterpreting in Stage III his former approach based on the Fundamental Equations in the light of the latter, based on Effective Demand, Keynes claimed to have established compatibility between the two. The 'expected increase of investment relatively to saving' as defined in the *Treatise* had become 'a criterion of an increase in effective demand' (Keynes 1936 [1973b]: 78). So he felt confident to present the escape from his 'old ideas' as continuity in his line of thought, granting that the exposition in the *Treatise* was 'of course, very confusing and incomplete in the light of the further developments here set forth' (Keynes 1936 [1973b]: 78).

## 5. Conclusion

Throughout the writing of the *General Theory*, Keynes was at pains to make the new approach compatible with the *Treatise*. First, he presented the argument, reached probably at the end of 1931, according to which changes in the volume of output and employment 'depend upon the changes in disbursement relative to earnings' as a 'generalisation' of the old argument, where it was dependent upon changes in investment relative to saving. Second, during the second half of 1932, in adopting the new 'method' – a fall in output and employment depended on 'a change in demand as a whole relatively to supply as a whole due to deficient disbursement' – he presented it as 'the same thing' as an excess of saving over investment. Third, when in the autumn of 1933 he introduced effective demand and showed that equality of aggregate expenditure to aggregate costs may well occur at a level of output below full employment, he very cursorily mentioned that in the *Treatise* he just 'failed to point [this] out'.

Keynes managed to present his former approach as compatible with the latter by: (a) reinterpreting profits of the *Treatise* 'as determining the current expectation of profit'; and (b) presenting a change in the excess investment over saving of the *Treatise* as 'a criterion' of an increase in effective demand. However, he must have had doubts that his attempted reconciliation was entirely successful, since he wrote in the Preface to the *General Theory*:

> what in my own mind is a natural evolution in a line of thought which I have been pursuing for several years, may sometimes strike the reader as a confusing change of view.
>
> (Keynes 1936 [1973b]: xxii)

The scope for the history of economic thought is to review existing records and textual evidence in order to provide evidence for interpretations and to explain developments of ideas. Unfortunately, the evidence is rarely unambiguous and interpretations are often the by-product of the purpose for which the historical investigation is undertaken. It thus happens that those aiming to discover compatibility among theories conceived at different times tend to draw a line of continuity, whereas those who are mindful of the time at which they were presented are likely to emphasise changes and discontinuities. In the quest for further clues, it may sometimes be attempted to make use of the narrative of the development of ideas given by the author. In this context, I think I agree with what one of Keynes's biographers wrote: 'I believe that one should accept Keynes's retrospective account of how he came to his conclusions.' (Moggridge 1992: 559). However in assessing those conclusions, I cannot but interpret the approach based on effective demand as a 'dramatic' change of view.

## Notes

1 'You have over a short period something of the nature of a supply curve which tells you that for a given level of prime profit [i.e. the difference between gross receipts and prime costs] there will be a given level of output, that if you have a certain amount of prime profit, that would be sufficient to bring a certain quantity of potential output over the prime cost level [...] so if you have a supply curve which is valid over the short period only [...] you could only increase employment and output by increasing prime profit.' (Keynes 1973a: 368).

2 According to Moggridge's dating (Keynes 1973a: 380), this is the 'earliest' of the fragments of the 1931–2 period of writing. Moggridge's dating of the early *General Theory* fragments was questioned by Patinkin (see Patinkin 1993: 654–6). I do not see enough evidence supporting Patinkin's claims.

3 See also the letter to Hawtrey, 1 June 1932: 'I put less fundamental reliance on my conception of savings and substitute for it the conception of expenditure.' (Keynes 1973a: 172).

4 Keynes postponed the lectures he was to have held in the 1931 Michaelmas Term to April–May 1932 feeling that a 'theoretical clean up' was needed before he could 're-lecture stuff which is available in print'. Letter to Austin Robinson of 28 September 1931 (EAGR papers, Marshall Library, box 9).

5　We have fragments from which he appeared to have lectured on 25 April and 2 May.

6　'I believe that [Keynes] thought then [in April 1932] and I think he thought later – of the *General Theory* as supplementing rather than replacing the *Treatise*.' (E. A. G. Robinson 1986: 7).

7　In 1980 Joan Robinson reviewed Vol. XXIX of the *Collected Writings of J. M. Keynes*, where the Manifesto was first published. She argued that: '[…] Keynes, in his lectures, was still using the cumbersome *Treatise* definitions, which turn on a difference between saving and investment, but he was using them to get the same results' (Robinson 1980: 391).

8　Of these lectures there survive fragments from 10 October and 14 November.

9　In retrospect Kahn was startled by this proposition: 'It is disconcerting in these October [sic] lecture notes to read of the rate of interest "such as to cause saving to be in excess of investment".' (Kahn 1984: 113n).

10　In the retrospective evaluation of his 'multiplier' article, Kahn wrote: 'I was handicapped having to translate my thinking into the definitions of the *Treatise*.' (Kahn 1984: 100).

11　In fact, there is no evidence on whether the fragments corresponding to the first and second 1933 draft table of contents (Keynes 1979: 63–75) were written during the summer, but it is a plausible inference.

12　Dimand (1986) noticed that the *Treatise* profits are always *ex post* windfalls magnitudes, except for one passage (Keynes 1930 [1971]: 143) in which they are considered as an *ex ante* measure of profitability.

13　By the autumn of that year he was using chapters 2–14 of the first drafts of the *General Theory* for his lectures (Keynes 1973a; Rymes 1989).

14　My method there was to regard the current realised profit as determining the current expectation of profit.

# References

Barens, I. (1987) 'From the "Banana Parable" to the Principle of Effective Demand: Some Reflections on the Origin, Development and Structure of Keynes's *General Theory*', in D. A. Walker (ed.), *Twentieth-Century Economic Thought*. Aldershot: Elgar.

Dimand, R. W. (1986) 'The Macroeconomics of the *Treatise of Money*', *Easter Economic Journal* 12(4): 431–50.

Dimand, R. W. (1988) *The Origins of the Keynesian Revolution*. Aldershot: Elgar.

Kahn, R. F. (1984) *The Making of Keynes's General Theory*. Cambridge: Cambridge University Press.

Keynes, J. M. (1930) [1971] 'A Treatise on Money', in D. Moggridge (ed.), *The Collected Writings of John Maynard Keynes*, Vol. V. London: Macmillan.

Keynes, J. M. (1973a) 'The *General Theory* and After: Preparation', in D. Moggridge (ed.), *The Collected Writings of John Maynard Keynes*, Vol. XIII. London: Macmillan.

Keynes, J. M. (1936) [1973b] 'The General Theory of Employment, Interest, and Money', in D. Moggridge (ed.), *The Collected Writings of John Maynard Keynes*, Vol. VII. London: Macmillan.

Keynes, J. M. (1979) 'The General Theory and After. A Supplement', in D. Moggridge (ed.), *The Collected Writings of John Maynard Keynes*, Vol. XXIX. London: Macmillan.

Moggridge, D. (1992) *Maynard Keynes: An Economist's Biography*. London: Routledge.

Patinkin, D. (1976) *Keynes's Monetary Thought: A Study of its Development*. Durham: Duke University Press.

Patinkin, D. (1982) *Anticipations of the General Theory? And Other Essays on Keynes*. Oxford: Blackwell.

Patinkin, D. (1993) 'On the Chronology of the *General Theory*', *Economic Journal* 103: 647–63.

Robinson, E. A. G. (1986) 'Symposium to celebrate the 50th anniversary of the Publication of Keynes's *General Theory*', Cambridge, mimeo.

Robinson, J. V. (1980) 'Review of *The Collected Writings of John Maynard Keynes*, Vol. XXIX: The *General Theory* and After – A Supplement', *Economic Journal* 90: 391–3.

Rymes, T. K. (1989) *Keynes's Lectures, 1932–1935*. Ann Arbor: University of Michigan Press.

Skidelsky, R. (1992) *John Maynard Keynes. The Economist as Saviour 1920–1937*. Vol. 2. London: Macmillan.

# 5

# THE RELEVANCE OF HISTORICAL EXPERIENCE FOR ECONOMICS

*Alexander C. Dow and Sheila C. Dow*

## 1. Introduction

At the 1999 Meeting of the UK History of Economic Thought Conference in Glasgow, Victoria Chick presented a paper on Karl Niebyl's *Studies in the Classical Theories of Money*. Drawing our attention to a little-known author, Chick explains the circumstances of chancing on his work, so that we could understand the context of discovery. We are treated to an insightful and thought-provoking account. But above all, as with Keynes's *Essays in Biography*, the account of Niebyl's methodology is as significant for our reading of Chick's work as it is for our reading of Niebyl himself.

We are told that the attraction of the book was its methodology, which involves an emphasis on history, both economic history and the history of economic thought, and their interconnections. We therefore take this paper as a starting point for a discussion of the role of history in economics. There is a large and growing literature on the study of the history of economic thought (see e.g. the survey in Coats 2000), but little attention is paid to the more general issues of the role of history, such as economic history, in economics. It is the purpose of this chapter to look at some of the history of ideas on history in economics in this latter sense, focusing on British economic thought. This limited sampling of ideas reveals that, even among those who see history as important for economics, there are differences over what exactly is entailed. Just as Weintraub (1998) has argued that, because mathematics itself evolves, the question of whether or not economics should be mathematical is incomplete, so there may be a similar issue with respect to history and economics.

It is not uncommon for heterodox economists in particular to advocate the importance of a historical time approach to economics (see e.g. Robinson 1978: 126–36). The distinction between historical time and the logical-time framework of orthodox economics is fundamental to the argument for the historical approach. But there is rarely any detailed discussion of what exactly is meant – what kind of history, how it relates to theory and theory construction, and so on. Chick's work is a notable exception in that she not only provides a rationale for integrating history and economics, but also exemplars of how it should be done.[1] In the third section we focus on Chick's views of the role of history in economics (with reference to Niebyl), and the way she employs these views in monetary economics. The chapter concludes by broadening out the discussion of the role of history in economics by considering its reinvention for modern economics.

## 2. Historical analysis of history and economics

Within history, one of the subcategories of particular interest to economists is economic history. According to William Cunningham, a prominent member of the English Historical School of Economics,

> Economic History is not so much the study of a special class of facts, as a study of all the facts of a nation's history from a special point-of-view.
> (Harte 1971, introduction, p. xxi)[2]

The history of economic thought similarly could be seen as taking an economics perspective on the broad scope of intellectual history. But there are other forms of history of potential interest to economists which are specific to 'a specific class of facts': labour history, for example. But within the two categories there is still scope for different historical approaches.

We focus our attention first on the ideas current during the professionalisation of economics, around a century ago, in England.[3] The academic study of history was then only slightly older than that of economics itself within the university. The method was narrative; and if economic history was concerned with statistics, it was descriptive in their use. At the University of Cambridge, economics broke away from history in terms of the University's institutional structures. But even Alfred Marshall, who spearheaded the move to make economics a distinct discipline, still studied economic history and made use of it for copious illustrations in his published work. Likewise Keynes looked to the past, for example including a chapter on Mercantilism in *The General Theory* (Keynes 1936, chapter 23).

A century ago the academic battle was fought which has led ultimately, by its outcome, to the present situation in UK economics of inattention to history. The English Historical School of Economics argued strenuously for an economics to which history was integral. The names commonly associated with this school are Cliffe Lesley, John Kells Ingram (both Irish), Arnold Toynbee, L. L. Price, William Ashley, W. A. S. Hewins and William Cunningham. Their impact at the time was considerable. In the words of Gerard Koot, author of *English Historical Economics, 1870–1926*:

> The failure of the English Historical Economists to become a dominant School of Economics in Britain, to say nothing of the dominant one, should not lead us to conclude that they were of little or no importance

in the history the Economic Thought or to history in general. Even in the history of Economic Thought, in which Whiggish interpretations of history often still flourish, their importance has been acknowledged. Their chief historical significance lies in three areas. First, they helped destroy the over-confidence, the insularity, and even the dogmatism that often characterised English classical economics. Second, in a field of economic policy, the Historical economists generally expounded the need for a national, and even an Imperial, scheme of economic policy and social reform that has become so characteristic of the 20th century. Third, they played a major role in the development of Economic History as a recognised field of study. This became their most lasting and specific legacy.

(Koot 1987: 2)

The arguments put forward by the English historical economists for their view that history and economics were inseparable reflect the contemporary, narrative approach to history. In 1878 J. K. Ingram delivered a lecture on 'The present position and future prospects of political economy' to Section F of the British Association.[4] Here he laid out his objection to deductive economics without a historical dimension. The contents of this address are summarised by Koot:

His objections to deductive economics were fourfold. First, economic phenomena could not be studied in isolation from other aspects of society, but must be 'subsumed under and absorbed into sociology'. Second, the conceptions of economists were necessarily abstract and did not correspond to real conditions. The most dangerous of these abstractions was what he assumed to be the Ricardian premise, that 'this sole human passion or motive which has economic effects is the desire for wealth'. Third, and closely related to the second, he objected to orthodoxy's logical structure. Noting that Mill himself had conceded that deduction could be used only as verification for inductively derived conclusions, Ingram maintained that 'social phenomena are ... too complex, and depend upon too manifold conditions' to be capable of a priori treatment. Finally, the excessive abstractions of the dominant economics had made its conclusions unnecessarily insular: 'In most enunciations of economic theorems by the English school, the practice is tacitly to presuppose the state of social development, and the general history of social conditions to be similar to that of modern England.' For Ingram, neither England nor any other society of a particular time could serve as a model of universal economic conclusions.

(Koot 1987: 56)

It is this final point which distinguishes much of modern economics most fundamentally from Ingram and the English Historical School of Economics. Thoroughly instilled into the psyche of modern economists is the notion that the generalisations of the discipline are applicable in all times in all places.[5] The price mechanism is a universal wonder. Individual self-interest always plays a dominant role in economic outcomes. Opportunity costs are perceived and provide incentives. A few examples sustain this perception – cigarettes in prisoner of war camps and the effect on wages of the Black Death in medieval England are frequently cited. What is the point of having students of economics study history (at the cost of not learning more mathematical techniques) if universal principles are discernible in the current economic environment anyway? Why introduce a historical perspective to the economic analysis of a particular issue if nothing is added by so doing?

But the predominantly narrative historical approach of the English Historical School was not the only approach in British economics. In looking back to the flowering of economics more than a century earlier in Scotland, the Scottish tradition of the twentieth century had absorbed naturally the Scottish Enlightenment approach to social science which was imbued with history. Knowledge across the disciplines was built on a theory of human nature which in turn was built on detailed historical study. Among those who inspired the Scottish tradition, David Hume was known to his contemporaries as a historian rather than a philosopher, and Smith's *Wealth of Nations* is full of detailed historical passages which recognised the specificity of context while searching for common principles.

The Scottish Enlightenment approach to history itself was distinctive:

> The distinctive nature of the theory of history...may be found in its scientific temper and emphasis on economic forces as fundamental to historical and sociological investigation. The particular feature of this contribution...[may be]...that of finding principles which reduce the apparent chaos of history to order and thus enable us to understand our *present* condition.
>
> (Skinner 1965: 22, emphasis in original)

The ensuing Scottish tradition in political economy carried forward this particular, analytical, historical approach to economics (Dow *et al.* 1997). Therefore there was also in Scotland, at the turn of last century, a body of support for an integral role for history in economics, where history was more analytical than narrative. J. S. Nicholson, the second appointment as Professor of Economics at the University of Edinburgh, and William Smart, the first Professor of Economics at University of Glasgow, were both sympathetic to this historical approach to economics.

## 3. Chick on history in economics

The arguments of the English Historical School (and the Scottish tradition) are now likely, by their own standards, to require reformulation as economics has professionalised and grown, and as society has run the rapids that were the twentieth century. History, furthermore, while often still narrative in form, has developed modes of analysis influenced by literary criticism and anthropology. This contrasts with modern economic history which, subsequent to the cliometric revolution in the 1960s, became quantitative and formally analytical. (Ironically this transformation does not seem to have improved the currency of the historical dimension within the economics profession at large.)

In considering how we might incorporate history into modern economics, we therefore need to consider a range of approaches. Victoria Chick has identified in the writing of Niebyl a set of ideas which makes the case for an integral role for history. Both Niebyl and Chick are particularly apposite in that their methodological thinking is presented along with exemplars of how it may be applied.

Niebyl is concerned to understand money. In order to do this, he argues, we need to understand the history of the real economic processes which moulded the development of modern institutions. Further we need to study the historical development of monetary theory in relation to the contemporary real economic context within which it developed so that 'we shall be able to attain an invaluable insight into the necessary technique of coping with our own concrete problems' (Niebyl 1946: 2).

But the three layers (production, the institution of money and monetary theory) may get out of phase with each other. Niebyl identifies periods of stable growth (he focuses on the late eighteenth to the early nineteenth centuries), as being when monetary arrangements settle into phase with the mode of production. In contrast, periods of recession instigate institutional change. Further, Niebyl identifies classical monetary theory with that period of economic and institutional stability. But these ideas persisted in spite of subsequent instability, and change in the mode of production and in money. The resulting disjunction between theory and reality can persist either because of a view of theory as being detached from history, or because of 'the functional part that the reviewers play in the given economy' (Niebyl 1946: 164). As a corollary, as Chick makes clear, once we take account of context, we can understand some theoretical disputes as being empty, since each position was in phase with a different historical context.

History is then important at three, interconnected levels: the historical development of real economies, the historical development of the institutions of production and the historical development of ideas. Money provides an excellent case study for such a methodology because of its institutional nature, and because monetary history is so tied up with the role of the state, which in turn is the product of the history of ideas.

This concern with the history of production, the history of institutions and the history of ideas is something we can see traced through Chick's work. Nowhere is this more evident than in her own path-breaking contribution to money and banking theory: the stages of banking development framework, first set out in Chick (1986) and developed further in Chick (1988) and Chick (1993).[6] Here she shows how money and banking systems develop according to their own logic, through a series of historical stages, in response to the needs of the real economy.[7]

The significance of the framework has several dimensions. First it highlights the logic of banking development, and the importance of the institutional structure for generating confidence. The framework is based on English banking history. But the framework provides a benchmark by which to analyse any national banking system, and thus has general application.[8]

Second it shows how different economic theories make sense depending on the stage of development of the banking system. In particular, as soon as the banking system can create credit as a multiple of deposits, the economy is no longer constrained by prior saving. Chick's framework demonstrates that Say's Law, based on an effective saving constraint, ceases to be relevant with the early development of the banking system.

Third, different stages of banking development justify different monetary theories. For example, as soon as the central bank introduces the lender-of-last-resort facility, it is no longer the case that the money supply can reasonably be treated as exogenous. Monetary policy is more appropriately analysed in terms of interest rate policy than control over monetary aggregates (see Goodhart 2001). In parallel to Niebyl's argument, classical monetary theory is no longer relevant, and indeed has not been relevant for a considerable period of time.[9]

History, then, is important in helping us understand the evolution of the institution of money in relation to production. It is also important for helping us understand the evolution of ideas about money, and their translation into monetary policy and the design of public monetary institutions. It is ironic that the real economic consequences of the modern application of classical monetary ideas should support a governmental system in Europe with a deflationary bias and a lack of attention to financial stability (as a result of excessive attention to monetary stability). These are exactly the opposite of the conditions which Niebyl specifies for the kind of stable institutional environment which could feasibly justify the classical approach. Current conditions then could be said to justify reintegrating history into economics.

## 4. History and modern economics

We turn now to focus more specifically on what kind of role history could perform in modern economics. The relationship of history to economics can focus on the following roles for history widely defined and, more narrowly, for economic history:

- history is a test bed for economic theory,
- history widens, and possibly enriches, economics education, and
- history is an integral part of economic analysis, especially where such analysis is conducted with a policy focus.

Of course, it is possible that history could fill all three roles, or any two of them. In practice, our perception is that, with honourable exceptions such as Victoria

Chick, only the first role listed is credited within the profession today, and that probably only by a minority. In what follows we consider the case for history to fill all three roles.

Modern economics has become a discipline based on mathematical modelling, which may or may not be oriented towards economic data. Often economists seem to regard this method as the only legitimate one by which to pursue knowledge of an economic sort (see e.g. Krugman 1998). Other methods are regarded as 'soft' or simply ruled out. But there is still some possibility for reintroducing the historical approach. When it comes to pedagogy, for example, other methodologies may be admitted. Thus David Colander can publish an article in the *AEA Papers and Proceedings* calling for a historical approach to the teaching of the Principles class (Colander 2000). Also some methodological evolution is apparent in the practice of economics. Even an apparent formalist such as Arrow (1985) has spoken out in favour of the role of history in economics.

Were it the case that we were considering simply using history as a test bed, there might be little nominal resistance within the profession.[10] Many applied economists would express themselves happy to use data from the historical past. But the point is that the historical approach pays much more attention to the context in which data originate, including the institutional configuration and the cultural background, than is now usual in applied economics.[11] The call for historical perspective is an appeal for a particular mindset (one evident in the approach of Adam Smith and Alfred Marshall), in which the particulars of history are considered alongside statistical measures.[12]

It is in this regard that cliometrics, once the 'New Economic History', may have erred. Robert Solow put this idea more than a decade ago:

> As I inspect current work in economic history, I have the sinking feeling that a lot of it looks exactly like the kind of economic analysis I have just finished caricaturing: the same integrals, the same regressions, the same substitution of *t*-ratios for thought. Apart from anything else, it is no fun reading the stuff any more. Far from offering the economic theorist a widened range of perceptions, this sort of economic history gives back to the theorist the same routine gruel that the theorist gives to the historian.
>
> (Solow 1985: 330)

When it comes to the suggestion of history as a component part of the studies to be undertaken by economists in training, there are both pragmatic and principled considerations. Regarding pragmatic considerations, the lesson of cliometrics may have wider relevance to economics in its entirety. Many students find the conventional, formalist Principles class daunting. As suggested by Colander (2000), a historical approach to Introductory Economics could be pedagogically valuable and result in increased recruitment at this level. Such an approach would involve the teaching of economic principles within the context of current economic arrangements and conditions, something which is difficult within the formalist approach. Then a historical approach would explain how current conditions arose, and provide different examples of economic phenomena to be explained by theory.

As an academic profession economics sits atop a pyramid with a wider student base and narrower apex than most other academic disciplines. The resources which support the academic profession of economics are thus predominantly obtained in the teaching of first- and second-year undergraduates. Often the students are pursuing degree programmes other than economics. If these disciplines were to decide they did not wish their students to pursue a (formalist) Introductory Economics module, the student shortfall would be devastating for the employment of economists in the academy.

Of course, there is a high ground too on which to argue the case for a historical dimension in the learning required at an introductory and intermediate level. Developing the skill of dealing with the structural change characteristic of open systems is a major benefit of the historical approach in undergraduate education. (Unlike the orthodoxy with respect to history we do not disparage, or seek to eliminate, the teaching of mathematical and quantitative methods, though in a fixed timetable there is clearly a trade-off.) Further, the communication of (non-formalist) economic knowledge to a wider, more receptive audience must be good for the discipline; the English Historical School, to its credit, was greatly interested in promulgating economic knowledge as widely as possible.

As an intellectual training a graduate education in economic history could enhance the Ph.D. in economics. The case for this is that it encourages lateral thinking. Charles Kindleberger in his book *Historical Economics* remarks:

> Art, instinct, intuition, hunch and pattern recognition may be among the missing ingredients of the economic tyro and the unrecognised asset of the magisterial one. Exposure to Economic History, if necessary at some cost in giving up courses in advanced mathematics in the Economics curriculum, will push the student a slight distance in the development of these capacities.
>
> (Kindleberger 1990: 350)

While a study of views on US graduate economics education concluded that it was too narrowly formalistic, the emphasis for change was in fact put on more applied work in general rather than specifically historical instruction (see Hansen 1991). However, it should be noted that applied political economy, in the Scottish tradition at least, retains a strong role for history (see Dow *et al.*, 2000). As a prominent policy-oriented economist in the Scottish tradition, it is not surprising to find the following view expressed by Alec Cairncross in an address to economic historians:

> It is hard to be sure that you understand how the economy works now without looking at evidence that is largely historical; and if you want to

know how it might work it is useful to look quite a long way back. You have to examine how the different economic forces operated on one another in the past in order to judge the strength of their interactions currently. To form an accurate view of what matters and what does not matter in the performance of the economy, or parts of it, you badly need an historical perspective, a truth too little appreciated by those whose business it is to manage or control the economy.

(Caincross 1989: 175)

These arguments suggest that an alert historical perspective should be part of the expertise of every economic analyst, not only to emphasise the importance of context, but also in order to draw on other contexts to inform modern debate. But integrating history successfully into economics requires a knowledge base which has been eroded by recent trends in economics education. Can economists be persuaded again to have students exposed to historical experience as they were until the final third of the twentieth century?

When the case for including a historical dimension in economic analysis in general is considered, more philosophical issues thus arise, such as the problem of historical specificity (Hodgson 2001). Can the analyst generally understand the crucial aspects of a situation by reference to a few general economic principles, backed up (in the more thorough investigation) by econometric estimation? Or, are there unique aspects to each economic reality such that a historical clarification of the context is necessary to guide and embellish the application of economic principles involved? This provides a strong case for (narrative) history's role as integral to economic analysis.

There still remains the issue of the approach to history which is to be used for any analysis. The arguments are being rehearsed in the history of economic thought as to the balance between the different approaches (see e.g. Weintraub 1999); mirroring developments in the field of history itself (see e.g. Tully 1988). There is an important issue as to how context is to be understood and what contextual specificity implies for our understanding of context and our ability to draw conclusions from history. In the same way, we have seen a difference within the historical approach to economics over the balance between the analytical and the narrative. An analysis of the role of history in modern economics requires that these issues be brought to the fore.

## 5. Conclusion

Embedded in all of Chick's work, and made explicit in her account of Niebyl as well as her stages banking development framework, is a focus on the history of economies, institutions and ideas, and their interactions. This contrasts with the current norm in economics, which is an inattention to history. There has been in fact over the centuries a discourse on the role of history in economics. It is not simply a matter of whether or not to refer to history, but also a matter of the role of historical evidence. How far, for example, can history be treated as providing massive data sets by which to formulate or assess theory?

Chick has more recently (Chick 1998, for example) become much more explicit on methodological issues. It is therefore fitting to take her views of history in the context of monetary economics, and relate the discussion to a more general discussion of history in economics. Echoing Niebyl, we can see that the development of ideas on history and economics itself requires a study of history.

The way in which both Niebyl and Chick have used history is closer to the analytical approach than the narrative approach. A great attraction of Chick's stages of banking framework is that it allows us to attempt to identify forces at work underneath the mass of historical detail. At the same time, there is a modern trend towards emphasis on the specificity of context. There appears to be considerable scope for discussion as to how exactly to proceed with a historical approach to economics. In that sense, this chapter has simply attempted to expose some of the scope for such debate.

But a firmer conclusion can be reached with respect to economics education. There are good (resource and educational) arguments for including economic history in the standard economics curriculum. But, if the arguments that history should be integral to economics hold for the modern era, then educating economists in history is not to be regarded as an optional extra. The generation of economists for whom history was part of their economics education will soon be succeeded by a generation of whom the majority received no historical education. If the reintroduction of the historical approach is to be on the agenda at all, those who make the decisions need to be convinced soon.

## Notes

1 Another exemplar is provided in Arestis and Howells (2001).
2 The original reference is Cunningham, W. (1882: 5).
3 We therefore do not aim here to consider other traditions in which history played an integral role in economics, such as the German Historical School or the American Institutionalists.
4 Ingram was President of Section F. He also gave the lecture to the Statistical and Social Inquiry Society of Ireland.
5 It should be noted that the notion of generality is not unproblematic; see for example Dow and Chick (forthcoming).
6 Some precursors have subsequently been identified in the work of Mireaux (see Fontana 1999) and De Viti De Marco (see Realfonzo 1998).
7 In later stages, Chick argues that it is the needs of the banking system itself which come to dominate.
8 Thus, for example, we can see how the US banking system oscillated for a long time between stages one and three until a successful central banking system was set up to allow progress to later stages.
9 This argument also echoes Keynes's argument about the particularity of the classical approach. Similarly, in the early drafts of the *General Theory*, Keynes compared the characteristics of pre-capitalist economies with capitalist economies. Thus Chick, like Keynes and Niebyl, employs history in order better to understand the present. In this they seem to be closer to the analytical approach to history than the narrative approach.

10 This view of history is best exemplified in monetary economics by Friedman and Schwartz (1963).
11 The issues raised here are the same as those raised by Davidson's (1994) analysis of non-ergodic systems, and by Lawson's (1997) critique of orthodox econometrics.
12 The distinction is perhaps less marked for the historical approach of the German historical school and the American institutionalists.

# References

Arestis, P. and Howells, P. (2001) 'The "Great Inflation", 1520–1640: Early Views on Endogenous Money', in P. Arestis, M. Desai and S. Dow (eds), Money, Macroeconomics and Keynes. New York: Routledge.

Arrow, K. J. (1985) 'Maine and Texas', *AEA Papers and Proceedings* 75(2): 320–23.

Cairncross, A. K. (1989) 'In Praise of Economic History', *Economic History Review* 42(2): 173–85.

Chick, V. (1986/92) 'The Evolution of the Banking System and the Theory of Saving, Investment and Interest', *Economies et Sociétés, serie Monnaie et Production*, No. 3: 111–26; Reprinted in P. Arestis and S. C. Dow (eds), *On Money, Method and Keynes*. London: Macmillan.

Chick, V. (1988) 'Sources of Finance, Recent Changes in Bank Behaviour and the Theory of Investment and Saving', in P. Arestis (ed.), *Contemporary Issues in Money and Banking: Essays in Honour of Stephen Frowen*. London: Macmillan, pp. 30–48.

Chick, V. (1993) 'The Evolution of the Banking System and the Theory of Monetary Policy', in S. F. Frowen (ed.), *Monetary Theory and Monetary Policy: New Tracks for the 1990s*. London: Macmillan, pp. 79–92.

Chick, V. (1998) 'On Knowing One's Place: The Role of Formalism in Economics', *Economic Journal* 108(451): 1859–69.

Chick, V. (1999) 'Karl Niebyl's Methodology: Classical Monetary Theory in Historical Context', Paper presented to the History of Economic Thought Conference, Glasgow Caledonian University.

Chick, V. and Dow, S. C. (forthcoming) 'Formalism, Logic and Reality: A Keynesian Analysis', *Cambridge Journal of Economics*.

Coats, A. W. (2000) 'The Historiography and Methodology of Economics: Some Recent Contributions', Paper presented to the HES Annual Meeting, Vancouver, July.

Colander, D. (2000) 'Telling Better Stories in Introductory Macro', *AEA Papers and Proceedings* 90(2): 76–80.

Cunningham, W. (1882) *The Growth of English Industry and Commerce*. Cambridge: Cambridge University Press.

Davidson, P. (1994) *Post Keynesian Macroeconomic Theory*. Cheltenham: Elgar.

Dow, A., Dow, S. C. and Hutton, A. (1997) 'The Scottish Political Economy Tradition and Modern Economics', *Scottish Journal of Political Economy* 44(4): 368–83.

Dow, A., Dow, S. C. and Hutton, A. (2000) 'Applied Economics in a Political Economy Tradition: The Case of Scotland from the 1890s to the 1950s', *History of Political Economy*, 32 (Supplement): 177–98.

Fontana, G. (1999) *Essays on Money, Uncertainty and Time in the Post Keynesian Tradition*, Ph.D. thesis, Leeds University.

Friedman, M. and Schwartz, A. (1963) *A Monetary History of the United States: 1867–1960*. Princeton: Princeton University Press.

Goodhart, C. A. E. (2001) 'The Endogeneity of Money', in P. Arestis, M. Desai and S. Dow (eds), *Money, Macroeconomics and Keynes*. New York: Routledge.

Hansen, W. L. (1991) 'The Education and Training of Economics Doctorates', *Journal of Economic Literature* 29(3): 1054–87.

Harte, N. B. (1971) *The Study of Economic History*. London: Frank Cass.

Hodgson, G. M. (2001) 'General Theorising versus Historical Specificity: A Problem for post-Keynesians', in P. Arestis, M. Desai and S. Dow (eds), *Methodology, Microeconomics and Keynes*. New York: Routledge.

Keynes, J. M. (1936) *The General Theory of Employment, Interest and Money*. London: Macmillan.

Kindleberger, C. P. (1990) *Historical Economics: Art or Science?* Hemel Hempstead: Harvester Wheatsheaf.

Koot, G. M. (1987) *English Historical Economics, 1870–1926*. Cambridge: Cambridge University Press.

Krugman, P. (1998) 'Two Cheers for Formalism', *Economic Journal* 108(451): 1829–36.

Lawson, T. (1997) *Economics and Reality*. London: Routledge.

Maloney, J. (1976) 'Marshall, Cunningham, and the Emerging Economics Profession', *Economic History Review* 39(3): 440–51.

Niebyl, K. H. (1946) *Studies in the Classical Theories of Money*. New York: Columbia University Press.

Realfonzo, R. (1998) *Money and Banking: Theory and Debate* (1900–1940). Cheltenham: Elgar.

Robinson, J. (1978) *Contributions to Modern Economics*. Oxford: Blackwell.

Skinner, A. S. (1965) 'Economics and History: The Scottish Enlightenment', *Scottish Journal of Political Economy* 32: 1–22.

Solow, R. M. (1985) 'Economic History and Economics', *AEA Papers and Proceedings* 75(2): 328–31.

Tully, J. (ed.) (1988) *Meaning and Context: Quentin Skinner and His Critics*. Oxford: Oxford University Press.

Weintraub, E. R. (1998) 'Axiomatisches Miβverständnis', *Economic Journal* 108(451): 1837–47.

# 6

# GENERAL THEORISING VERSUS HISTORICAL SPECIFICITY: A PROBLEM FOR POST-KEYNESIANS

*Geoffrey M. Hodgson*

I was prompted to write this chapter for two reasons. First, although I am an admirer of the works of John Maynard Keynes and of many modern post-Keynesians, I have long had nagging doubts about Keynes's emphatic claim to build a *general* theory. Second, in September 1999, Victoria Chick gave an excellent talk at the University of Hertfordshire on the evolution of financial institutions and their relevance for monetary theory and policy. This presentation was based on her important but unduly neglected paper on the same theme (Chick 1986). Vicky's outstanding talk (delivered amazingly without any use of notes or prompts) helped me develop my ideas on the difficulty that I had perceived within the Keynesian tradition. The purpose of this chapter is to outline this problem.[1]

What I call 'the problem of historical specificity' starts from the supposition that different socioeconomic phenomena may require theories that are in some respects different from each other (Hodgson, 2001). An adequate theory of (say) the feudal socioeconomic system will differ from an adequate theory of (say) capitalism. Furthermore, an adequate theory of (say) nineteenth century British capitalism will differ from an adequate theory of any other capitalist system in different time or space. Any common aspects of these theories will reflect common features of the real systems involved. Nevertheless, differences between different systems could be so important that the theories and concepts used to analyse them must also be substantially different. A fundamentally different reality may require a different theory. This is the problem of historical specificity. The problem was central to the economics both of Karl Marx and of the German historical school.

In contrast, a general theory presumes that 'one theory fits all'. It is claimed that one theory can deal adequately with diverse phenomena within a wide – if not universal – historical and geographical range of socioeconomic systems. Examples of such claims to generality are common in mainstream economics, from the assumption that the subject is the universal 'science of choice' to the idea that 'general equilibrium theory' applies to many human societies. Another such claim is found in the work of Keynes.

Section 1 of this chapter discusses the generality of Keynes's *General Theory*. It is argued that the theory is not as general as its author claimed. Section 2 deals with the earlier claim, by Joseph Schumpeter, that Keynes's theory was not truly general in its scope. Section 3 focuses in detail on a specific aspect of the problem with the 'general theory' claim, by using the example of money. Section 4 situates the overall problem within the post-Keynesian tradition. Section 5 concludes the chapter.

## 1. How general is the General Theory?

Despite the gigantic secondary literature on Keynes and Keynesianism, the question of its alleged generality has rarely been discussed. Yet Keynes attributed to it some importance. Near the beginning of his *General Theory* he wrote:

> I have called this book the *General Theory of Employment, Interest and Money*, placing the emphasis on the prefix *general*. ... I shall argue that the postulates of the classical theory are applicable to a special case only and not to the general case, the situation which it assumes being a limiting point of the possible positions of equilibrium. Moreover, the characteristics of the special case assumed by the classical theory happen not to be those of the economic society in which we actually live, with the result that its teaching is misleading and disastrous if we attempt to apply it to the facts of experience.
>
> (Keynes 1936: 3)

The first chapter of the *General Theory* consists solely of the single paragraph from which the above quotation is taken. Here Keynes was playing a double rhetorical game. First, the term 'general theory' was used to create a contrast with the allegedly special theory of the neoclassical economists. Keynes made the convincing argument that the 'classical' theory misses something, especially concerning issues such as uncertainty and disequilibria. He wanted a 'general theory' that encompassed such missing elements.

Second, Keynes made the claim that his theory applies to the specific 'economic society in which we live' – again in alleged contrast to the classical theory. He suggested that a more general theory is able to embrace contemporary reality more closely. This particular claim is contestable. If the 'economic society in which we live' is different in one or more important respects from other socioeconomic systems, then a *general* theory, embracing all or several such systems, could not include any features that were unique to contemporary reality. A theory of greater generality would fail to identify the particular mechanisms that were relatively more important at a specific historical juncture. Contrary to

Keynes, by making a theory more general we may make it less able to focus on the important aspects of the 'economic society in which we live'. We cannot have it both ways.

Keynes missed the possibility that such a high degree of generality might be gained at the cost of a loss of explanatory power. A set of general statements might encompass contemporary economic reality, but be unable to explain very much. Universality is gained at the cost of an ability to discriminate between and explain concrete particulars.

In economics, a theory with sufficient explanatory power would have to focus on the key economic relations and processes that were of importance in understanding the nature and behaviour of the system in question. In contrast, a general theory that covered a wide variety of different structures, would not be able to focus on these special relations and processes. Keynes did not consider that a theory with substantial explanatory power that applied to the 'economic society in which we live' might have to be a *special* theory. Indeed, a 'general theory' might underemphasise some of the historically specific features of the economic system and the causes of the prevailing unemployment of the 1930s. Keynes overlooked the possibility that a special theory could start from historically specific assumptions concerning economic institutions, and end up with much greater explanatory power.

Keynes was concerned to criticise those 'classical' theories that claimed to show that markets would clear and the economy would reach a full employment equilibrium. But the fact that Keynes considered disequilibria, and multiple equilibria below full employment, is not enough to make his theory *general*. It still rested on historically specific assumptions. The classical theory is not general, in part because it excludes price inflexibility and radical uncertainty. Neither, for different reasons, is the *General Theory*. It is also difficult to say which theory is *more* general than the other. While Keynes dropped several of the classical assumptions, he imposed other restrictive conditions, for instance by assuming a monetary economy. While Keynes made his theory more general with one move, he made it less general with another.

In addition, Keynes did very little to ground his theory upon historically specific economic institutions. Although historically specific institutions – such as the joint stock company and the stock exchange – inevitably protrude into his narrative, he did not start from the specific institutions of capitalist society and then develop a theory that illuminated their principal causal processes and relations. Instead, Keynes (1936: 246–7) appealed repeatedly to 'fundamental psychological factors' as the foundation for his theory. His invocation of alleged psychological factors in his discussion of economic processes is more prominent than any discussion of historically specific institutions. Specific institutions appear in the *General Theory* as the mechanisms through which seemingly ahistorical psychological forces express their power. Again, there is evidence to suggest that Keynes was attempting to develop a 'general theory' that would apply to a number of different types of socioeconomic system. He conceived of this general theory as having a universal and psychological foundation.

A striking piece of further evidence confirms this verdict. As Bertram Schefold (1980) has shown, in his 1936 Preface to the German edition of the *General Theory*, Keynes made the following argument:

> This is one of the reasons which justify my calling my theory a *General* theory. Since it is based on less narrow assumptions than the orthodox theory, it is also more easily applied to a large area of different circumstances.

According to Keynes, his *General Theory* applied not only to the 'Anglo-Saxon countries... where laissez-faire still prevails' but also to countries then with strong 'national leadership' such as Germany. He made this statement on the basis that his analysis was not based on specific institutions but allegedly on 'the theory of psychological laws relating consumption and saving'. Hence Keynes clearly claimed that his theory was not based on historically specific institutions but on general 'psychological laws'.

Furthermore, Keynes did not in fact deliver what he had promised: a general theory. Keynes did make some universal statements. In particular, he stressed aspects of human psychology. But he could not show how psychological propensities worked out in practice except by introducing an explicit or implicit institutional framework. Human psychology had to play out its part on some specific stage. It had to be applied to quite specific institutional structures, such as the stock market, state money and legal contracts. For example, the famous discussion of the psychology of speculation in chapter 12 of the *General Theory* required a specific institutional framework, principally the stock market.

Consider the specific economic phenomena to which Keynes referred in the title of the book. Even here he did not fulfil the promise of a general theory. The work did not provide a general theory of the nature and level of employment in all past, present or possible human societies. What it explored is the quite specific relationship in modern capitalism between the levels of employment, expectations and effective demand. Rather than providing a truly general theory of interest or money, Keynes explored the quite specific, capitalist type of system in which 'money is the drink which stimulates the system to activity' (Keynes 1936: 173). Money has existed for thousands of years but it did not become the elixir of production until the rise of modern capitalism. Keynes favoured the 'general theory' rhetoric but always ended up exploring the particular circumstances of the contemporary capitalist system. Absent in the *General Theory* is a truly general theory of employment, interest or money.

Notably, Keynes did show some awareness of the philosophical basis of the problem of historical specificity. In a letter to Roy Harrod dated 4 July 1938 Keynes (1938 [1973]: 296) wrote:

> Economics is the science of thinking in terms of models joined to the art of choosing models which are relevant to the contemporary world. It is compelled to do this, because, unlike the typical natural science, the

material to which it is applied is, in too many respects, not homogeneous through time.

In the above letter he implied that economic theory must related to historically specific material. Yet the *General Theory* was attempted on the basis of universal 'psychological laws'. If Keynes had tried to develop economics in full awareness that economies are 'not homogeneous through time', then he would have been less likely to attempt an entirely *general* theory.

Any analysis in economics that engages with reality is bound to make some assumptions about the institutional makeup of society. The *General Theory* was no exception. But the striving for generality relegates specific institutions to the background, whereas they ought to occupy the centre of the stage. There is not much discussion in the *General Theory* of specific economic institutions that are, in fact, indispensable to his argument. For example, Keynes was concerned to examine the nature of the wage bargain, and the relation between real and money wages. But the institutions of the labour market and employment are not discussed to any depth. In this respect, Keynes attempted the impossible: to draw quite specific conclusions from a theory that purported to be general.

This pretence of generality has widely afflicted economics for much of the twentieth century. Because of Keynes, many of his followers have attempted general theories as well. On the other hand, some post-Keynesians have stressed the importance of history and specific economic institutions that the rhetoric of general theorising has been implicitly undermined.

In particular, Chick (1986) has showed that standard assumptions of monetary theory are specific to the financial institutions involved. As these institutions evolved through time, different theoretical principles can pertain. In particular, the nature of money itself changes, from precious metal, to bank deposits, to data in computer memories. Chick argued that because of the institutional realities of pre-industrial capitalism, saving necessarily preceded investment. Subsequently, as soon as banks were able to create credit, saving no longer had to precede investment. As the banking system evolved it enhanced the capacity for the banks to create credit. Hence, by the 1920s and the time of Keynes, banking institutions and the credit system had evolved to the point that investment could and would precede saving. This was the quite specific historic period to which the allegedly *General Theory* applied. Today, as Chick pointed out in her paper, financial institutions have developed further, including a huge role for global speculation in a variety of financial assets. This may mean that Keynesian analyses and remedies can to some extent become obsolete.

Chick's argument underlines the fact that the *General Theory* was not, in truth, a general theory but it applied to a historically specific set of capitalist institutions. Like Chick, other post-Keynesians have explicitly centred their analysis on historically specific institutions. What has been largely unnoticed, however, is the implication that the allegedly general theoretical status of the *General Theory* is likely to be undermined as a result.

## 2. Keynes, Schumpeter and economic policy

In his extended and generous obituary of Keynes, Schumpeter (1946: 514) wrote:

> But there is one word in the book that cannot be defended on these lines –
> the word 'general'. Those emphasizing devices – even if quite unexcep-
> tionable in other respects – cannot do more than individuate very special
> cases. Keynesians might hold that these special cases are the actual ones
> of our age. They cannot hold more than that.

Schumpeter thus criticised Keynes for propounding a theory that claimed to be general but in fact was not. Similarly, in his earlier review of the *General Theory*, Schumpeter noted the contrast between Keynes's claim to provide a general theory and his keenness to promote specific economic policies. Schumpeter (1936: 792) claimed that Keynes had adopted the 'Ricardian' practice of claiming highly specific policies from an allegedly general theory:

> In his preface Mr Keynes underlines the significance of the words
> 'General Theory' in his title. ... But ... everywhere he really pleads for a
> definite policy.

In his 1946 obituary of Keynes, Schumpeter (1946: 514n) noted that Oskar Lange in 1938 had 'paid due respect to the only truly general theory ever written – the theory of Léon Walras'. Lange (1938: 20) had argued that 'both the Keynesian and the traditional theory of interest are but two limiting cases of what may be regarded to be the general theory of interest ... the essentials of this general theory are contained already in the work of Walras.' Schumpeter (1954: 1082) also later declared Keynes's *General Theory* to be 'a special case of the genuinely general theory of Walras'. Clearly, Schumpeter too was beguiled by the lure of a general theory. That is one reason why he praised Walras throughout his life. In 1936, Schumpeter's (persuasive) criticism of Keynes was that specific policies could never be properly grounded on a general theory. Later, his (unpersuasive) criticism of Keynes was that the *General Theory* was not general enough.

Schumpeter's invocation of Walras as a general theorist was also questionable. Contrary to Schumpeter, Walrasian theory is not general. It has been admitted by leading practitioners of Walrasian theory – such as Kenneth Arrow (1986) and Frank Hahn (1980) – that it fails to incorporate key phenomena, such as time and money.

The genuine problem that Schumpeter recognised is that Keynes simultane-ously revered a 'general theory' and attempted to derive quite specific policy con-clusions from such an edifice. In this respect, Schumpeter's criticism hit home. It might be possible to regard Keynes's work as a framework for such specific analyses, but Keynes himself did not lay down guidelines for the development of historically specific theories.

## 3. Illustration: Why a general theory of barter would lose money

There are several problems with general theorising in the social sciences. One is of analytical and computational intractability. Facing such computational limits, general theorists typically simplify their models, thus abandoning the generality of the theory. Another related problem is that a general theory is that we are confined to broad principles governing all possible structures within the domain of analysis. In practice, a manageable theory has to confine itself to a relatively tiny subset of all possible structures. Furthermore, the cost of excessive generality is to miss out on key features common to a subset of phenomena.

To illustrate the latter argument, we shall consider two very simple 'models', of respectively a barter and a monetary economy. Robert Clower's (1967) theoretical framework is the starting point. In a barter economy, every commodity can, in principle, be traded for every other commodity. By contrast, in a money economy without barter, commodities are traded for money only. Hence, for Clower (1967: 5–7) in a monetary economy:

> the peculiar feature of money as contrasted with a barter economy is precisely that *some* commodities in a money economy *cannot* be traded directly for all other commodities. … *Money buys goods and goods buy money; but goods do not buy goods.*

Figure 6.1 – taken and amended slightly from Clower (1967) – represents these two contrasting arrangements:

In the figure, $C_1$, $C_2$, $C_3$ and $C_4$ each represent commodities. $M$ is money. The presence of symbol $\times$ indicates that an exchange between two commodities is possible; a '0' indicates that no such exchange normally takes place. This restrictive structure of an exchange economy is a necessary but not sufficient condition

|        | $C_1$ | $C_2$ | $C_3$ | $C_4$ |
|--------|-------|-------|-------|-------|
| $C_1$  | ×     | ×     | ×     | ×     |
| $C_2$  | ×     | ×     | ×     | ×     |
| $C_3$  | ×     | ×     | ×     | ×     |
| $C_4$  | ×     | ×     | ×     | ×     |

Exchange relations in a barter economy

|        | $M$   | $C_2$ | $C_3$ | $C_4$ |
|--------|-------|-------|-------|-------|
| $M$    | ×     | ×     | ×     | ×     |
| $C_2$  | ×     | ×     | 0     | 0     |
| $C_3$  | ×     | 0     | ×     | 0     |
| $C_4$  | ×     | 0     | 0     | ×     |

Exchange relations in a monetary economy

*Figure 6.1* Exchange relations under money and barter.

for the existence of money. In addition, money has other special attributes – such as a store of value and means of dealing with an uncertain future – that are not represented here.[2]

Clearly, a barter economy model in which all exchanges are possible involves *fewer restrictive assumptions* than a model in which there is money. A model of a monetary economy must include *additional* restrictive assumptions in order to obtain the special structure of a monetary economy in Fig. 6.1. At least as far as the adequate representation of a monetary economy is concerned, *more* assumptions are required.

However, which model is 'more general'? Of the two models in Fig. 6.1, in a strong sense the barter economy model is more general. The presence of an '×' in any cell in a matrix in Fig. 6.1 indicates that an exchange is possible, not that the exchange has to take place. In this sense, therefore, a monetary economy is a special case of a barter economy: the barter economy model is more general. However, this gives us a partial and potentially misleading picture and the statement needs to be qualified.

Crucially, the very process of generalisation – from a 'monetary' to a barter model – means that some essential features of a money economy are lost. Because *everything* in a barter economy has the property of being able to exchange with everything else – a necessary feature of money – then *nothing* has the property of money. If all men are kings then there are no kings, because kingship implies the existence of non-regal inferiors. Hence, from this point of view, neither a barter model nor Walrasian theory is an adequate representation of a monetary economy. For a theory to accommodate money, it has to incorporate the special qualities of money; it has to become a special theory.

Paradoxically, general theories lose something and cease to be truly general. Their generality becomes relative rather than absolute. While remaining more general in scope, the barter economy model loses key features of the monetary economy. A common feature of all general theories is that, by embracing a wide range of possible structures, they fail to accentuate the key features pertaining to a particular set of circumstances. Greater generality is typically gained at the cost of an ability to discriminate between and explain concrete particulars. A general theory of exchange, including barter, will overlook some of the important features of a particular type of exchange economy, that is a monetary economy. As a result, if it were possible to construct a more general theory on the basis of the barter model, then it would be inadequate precisely because of its generality.

## 4. Post-Keynesianism commentaries

Keynes (1936: viii) himself wrote of his 'long struggle of escape ... from habitual modes of thought and expression'. Ironically, post-Keynesianism itself has faced a 'long struggle of escape' from the *General Theory* title, its claimed ahistorical foundation in universal psychological laws, and its problematic first chapter.

Nevertheless, several leading post-Keynesians were instinctively aware of institutional and historical specificities. Joan Robinson (1974) repeatedly emphasised the importance of 'historical time'. Paul Davidson (1980) likewise understood that 'the economy is a process in historical time' and economic and political institutions 'play an extremely important role' in determining real-world economic outcomes. Alfred Eichner (1979: 172) clearly argued that post-Keynesian economics must concern itself with 'the behavior of the system as a whole, constituted as a set of historically specific institutions'. Indeed, Eichner had a much better acquaintance than most with institutional economics. However, none of this amounted to an explicit recognition of the problem of historical specificity. Praiseworthy historical and institutional instincts would have been enhanced by an awareness of past debates on the problem.

This methodological failure helped to undermine any focus on 'historically specific institutions'. This was particularly the case when leading post-Keynesians endorsed Keynes's generalist methodology. For example, Davidson (1994: 15) defended the idea that the work of Keynes and his followers provided 'a more general theory of the economy since it requires fewer initial axioms'. But, as argued above, such a general theory would necessarily exclude many assumptions that were grounded on historically specific institutions. Davidson (1996: 52–4) argued for 'the minimum axioms needed for the general theory ... applicable to *all* economic regimes of money-using systems' and for the exclusion of any additional assumptions. Accordingly, the *General Theory* would be so general as it would encompass the 2,000 years or more when money has been in use, and neglect many of the key institutions specific to modern industrial capitalism.

Arguably, the general tension in the post-Keynesian tradition (between the emphasis on general theories, on the one hand, and the stress on the importance of history, on the other) is expressed in the works of both Keynes and Davidson. Keynes, as we have seen, sought an exclusively general theory while recognising that economies were 'not homogeneous through time'. Whereas, in fact, the latter observation undermines the former venture. Likewise, Davidson endorsed Keynes's attempts at general theorising while he repeatedly emphasised the non-ergodic character of economic processes. In a stronger interpretation of his concept of non-ergodicity, reality itself is both changing and mutable (Davis 1998). In which case, general theorising would be highly limited in scope. In the case of both authors, there is an inconsistency of theoretical outlook.

Anna Carabelli (1991: 116) wrote: 'For Keynes, a ... theory which, at the beginning of its analysis, avoided introducing limiting assumptions of independence, was truly general.' This argument suggests that for Keynes, everything must be conceived as depending on everything else. However, as we have seen above, the assumption of a monetary economy rules out a whole set of pairwise and barter interactions. The whole point about institutional specificity is that some interactions are ruled out. A general theory of markets would include a market for slaves. Nevertheless, a theory of a modern market economy without slavery would have to assume that the (persistently zero) supply of slaves was quite independent of the demand for labour in the economy. It is in the nature of institutions, laws and rules that some things are prohibited or unyielding.

Lange and Schumpeter were in error to describe Walras's theory as entirely general, because it included several restrictive assumptions. However, Keynes, Carabelli and Davidson were doubly wrong – in claiming that the *General Theory* was truly general and in claiming that generality is necessarily a positive attribute. Notably, all five of these economists were misled by the lure of a general theory. They all failed to observe that a theory designed to apply to a more particular domain may be more adequate in its analysis of the distinguishing characteristics of the type of economy in question. What Keynesians required was not a general theory but a historically specific theory of a modern, monetary, capitalist economy.

To some extent, the post-Keynesian label itself encouraged attempts to build a new or extended 'general theory', against the warnings, before and after Keynes, of members of the German historical and American institutionalist schools. Hence several post-Keynesians have downplayed the institutional specifics and developed ostensibly general theories, allegedly to enhance the 'general theory' of Keynes.

## 5. Concluding remarks

The intention of this article is not to detract from Keynes's great contribution to economics. It is argued, however, that Keynes was misled by the lure of a general theory. Furthermore, he was largely ignorant of the historical and institutionalist schools and of their critiques of general theorising in economics (Garvy 1975; Hodgson, 2001).

It is clear, however, that not all post-Keynesians have committed this methodological error. While some – such as Davidson – remain with Keynes on this point, others – such as Chick – emphasise the historical specificity of theory. If there are some morals to be drawn here, we must first point to the inherent limits of all general theorising in social science. Second, economists – particularly critical economists – must recognise and attempt to deal with the problem of historical specificity. In this endeavour we can learn from the achievements and mistakes of the past.

## Notes

1 Extensive use is made here of material from Hodgson (2001). The author is also especially grateful to Sheila Dow, Stephen Dunn, Paul Ormerod and Bertram Schefold for detailed conversations and other assistance.
2 Accordingly, Clower (1967: 5) was wrong to suggest that '*a barter economy is one in which all commodities are money commodities*'. On the contrary, commodities under barter do not possess all the characteristics of money.

## References

Arrow, K. J. (1986) 'Rationality of Self and Others in an Economic System', *Journal of Business* 59(4.2): S385–99. Reprinted in Eatwell, J., Milgate, M. and Newman, P. (eds) (1987) *The New Palgrave Dictionary of Economics*, Vol. 2. London: Macmillan.

Carabelli, A. M. (1991) 'The Methodology of the Critique of Classical Theory: Keynes on Organic Interdependence', in B. W. Bateman and J. B. Davis (eds), *Keynes and Philosophy: Essays on the Origin of Keynes's Thought*. Aldershot: Edward Elgar, pp. 104–25.

Chick, V. (1986) 'The Evolution of the Banking System and the Theory of Saving, Investment and Interest', *Economies et societées*, 20, serie Monnaie et Production, pp. 111–26; Reprinted in Chick, V. (1991) In P. Arestis and S. C. Dow (eds.), *On Money, Method and Keynes: Selected Essays by Victoria Chick*. London: Macmillan.

Clower, R. W. (1967) 'A Reconsideration of the Microfoundations of Monetary Theory', *Western Economic Journal* 6: 1–9; Reprinted in Clower, R. W. (ed.) (1969) *Monetary Theory*. Harmondsworth: Penguin.

Davidson, P. (1980) 'Post Keynesian Economics', *Public Interest*, Special Edition, pp. 151–73.

Davidson, P. (1994) *Post Keynesian Macroeconomic Theory: A Foundation for Successful Economic Policies for the Twenty-First Century*. Aldershot: Edward Elgar.

Davidson, P. (1996) 'What Revolution? The Legacy of Keynes', *Journal of Post Keynesian Economics* 19(1): 47–60; Reprinted in Davidson, L. (ed.) (1999) *Uncertainty, International Money, Employment and Theory: The Collected Writings of Paul Davidson, Volume 3*. London: Macmillan.

Davis, J. B. (1998) 'Davidson, Non-Ergodicity and Individuals', in P. Arestis (ed.), *Method, Theory and Policy in Keynes: Essays in Honour of Paul Davidson, Volume Three*. Cheltenham: Edward Elgar, pp. 1–16.

Eichner, A. S. (ed.) (1979) *A Guide to Post-Keynesian Economics*. London, UK and Armonk, NY: Macmillan and Sharpe.

Garvy, G. (1975) 'Keynes and the Economic Activists of Pre-Hitler Germany', *Journal of Political Economy* 83(2): 391–405.

Hahn, F. H. (1980) 'General Equilibrium Theory', *The Public Interest*, Special Issue, pp. 123–38. Reprinted in Hahn, F. H. (ed)(1984) *Equilibrium and Macroeconomics*. Oxford: Basil Blackwell.

Hodgson, G. M. (2001) *How Economics Forgot History: The Problem of Historical Specificity in Social Science*. London and New York: Routledge.

Keynes, J. M. (1936) *The General Theory of Employment, Interest and Money*. London: Macmillan.

Keynes, J. M. (1938)[1973] *The Collected Writings of John Maynard Keynes, Vol. XIV, 'The General Theory and After: Defence and Development'*. London: Macmillan.

Lange, O. R. (1938) 'The Rate of Interest and the Optimum Propensity to Consume', *Economica* 5(1): 12–32.

Robinson, J. (1974) *History versus Equilibrium*. London: Thames Papers in Political Economy.

Schefold, B. (1980) 'The General Theory for a Totalitarian State? A Note on Keynes's Preface to the German Edition of 1936', *Cambridge Journal of Economics* 4(2): 175–6.

Schumpeter, J. A. (1936) 'Review of *The General Theory of Employment, Interest and Money* by John Maynard Keynes', *Journal of the American Statistical Association* 31(196): 791–5.

Schumpeter, J. A. (1946) 'John Maynard Keynes 1883–1946', *American Economic Review* 36(4): 495–518.

Schumpeter, J. A. (1954) *History of Economic Analysis*. New York: Oxford University Press.

# 7

# TIMEFUL THEORIES, TIMEFUL THEORISTS

*Roy J. Rotheim*[1]

Understanding the truth of nonduality allows us to overcome all pain
(Tich Nhat Wanh, 1990, p.9)

In her inspiring speculative essay 'Order Out of Chaos in Economics' (1997), Victoria Chick reports that she:

> ...had long puzzled over an observation which appeared paradoxical: that the people who seem most able to live in the present moment are those who are happiest with 'timeful' theories, and those who displace themselves either forward or backward in time, but who find it most difficult to *be* in the present, are those most attracted to static theory.
>
> (p. 33)

Chick broaches this apparent paradox by referring to Rokeach's notions of open and closed minds (1960), as well as the dual of left-brain/right-brain thinking – the former appearing to be preponderant among mainstream economists – versus what she refers to as 'whole-brained' thinking. With regard to Rokeach's distinction, Chick contends that those with closed minds 'buy into' the external source of authority for their belief mechanisms. The ability to evaluate information cannot occur 'independent of its source and the congruence of that source with [the individual's] own authority/belief system' (ibid.). With regard to the second point, Chick is clear to point out that ego-based consciousness, which has favoured left-brain thinking, has emerged as the result of historically and socially determined forces, not biological natural selection (see p. 35).

In this chapter, I shall elaborate, also in a descriptive and speculative fashion, on these perspicacious observations offered by Victoria Chick. I shall address two broad areas: (1) what can be said about the timeless theory of mainstream economics as opposed to the prerequisites for 'timeful' theory; and (2) what can be said about the individual and socio-psychological implications associated with timeless and timeful theories.

## 1. Timeless theory

Among the most important methodological delineators in economic theory is the role assumed by time. How we think of time helps to define every element in our theoretical framework. If time is considered from a dualist perspective, then entities have unique, independent compositions allowing them to be distinguished from all other entities, to be compared, contrasted, moved, but never organically altered in light of any of those actions. The consumption bundle of an individual may be altered by changes in relative prices and income, but she herself, i.e. her preference orderings, are never affected by any of those aforementioned changes. As such, we can identify her, as she is today, and compare that state to where she might be tomorrow, depending upon possible states of nature.

This limited conceptualization of time *restricts* us to thinking in terms of atomistic individuals directing their lives *only* by the choices they make, irrespective of the real and psychological constraints they may encounter based upon their past interactions and the resultant positions that they now occupy as a consequence of those interactions. Their mental images are thus framed in the dualist conceptualization of me/not me. For the dualist thinker, as Chick points out (p. 37), the opposite of A must always be not-A. The possibility of the organic coexistence of A/not-A where, to use Tony Lawson's phrase 'the existence of each presupposes the other' (1997: 159), is perceptually impossible. As such, the analysis rules out the organically interdependent nature of people or their self-perception based upon those interdependencies. Time, then, is merely a frame of demarcation, allowing differing states to be compared; it does not denote the sense that elements and organisms evolve (or devolve) as a result of actions and interactions that occur in time.

In such a timeless ontology, there is no explanation for how the present came to be, causing (permitting?) theorists to assume that the present moment reflects a confluence of forces, i.e. a stable equilibrium. Our initial points of reference for analysis are where supply equals demand, savings equal investment, $IS = LM$, etc. Such a perspective rules out all questions that inquire as to the forces, tendencies, powers, structures which caused the present moment to be what it is. For the mainstream theorist, the present moment is then simply a benchmark, a point of reference to which all other states may be compared in dualist fashion.

In mainstream economics, there really is no past. The present is always merely one-half of a dual between this present moment and some other time-period called 'the future' which must be independent of, but linked to, the present moment. Constraints, to which individuals make their consumption and production choices, are merely posited, but have no contextual source. This ontological configuration allows the mainstream economist to 'speak' of the future and the relationship between the present moment and the future strictly from the vantage point of the present moment. The future collapses into but never organically affects the fundamental elements that make up the present moment. Thus, when the future occurs, it too must be rational, and therefore it has no relationship to the past. Here, the past does not matter, because, in fact, it does not exist.

The *language* of mainstream analysis is defined strictly by the salient elements of the equilibrium itself. For example, we are accustomed to thinking about the impact that a fall in real wages might have on the level of employment (both for the individual firm and for industry as a whole), by reductions in money wages, as if there were no impact on the change in the structure of money wages on incomes accruing to the individuals receiving the lower money wages, the sales of the firms who relied on a certain level of effective demand to continue normal levels of production, or the prices of the products that are subsequently produced. By not taking into account such possible interdependencies the so-called causal framework between changes in money wages and employment winds up squeezing a time-like heuristical mechanism into a timeless realm. Blaming individual workers or in fact the working class for their own unemployment or for rising inflation expectations, because of excessive wage growth, reflects the insidious side of the mainstream's timeless theoretical framework.

Finally, in a timeless construct, the order imposed by the strictures of the system indicate, as Tony Lawson has so persuasively asserted, that no real purposeful choice exists for the individual, where the individual might choose one or another option (Lawson 1997: 96). Just as the future cannot have any effect on the present, while the past cannot logically exist, it is also true that no individual's actions can have any effect on any other individual's nature or actions: individuals are not *internally* related (see Lawson 1997, chapter 12). Once the rules of optimisation are given, there is but one option for the individual and none other; a single option means the lack of choice.

## 2. Timeful theory

In light of the above observations on 'timeless' theory, how should we consider Chick's reference to 'timeful' theory? Here she gives us a few signposts by which we might direct our inquiry. She observes, initially, that 'time only has significance with the introduction of uncertainty' (p. 28). She then goes on to note that '[i]t must be shown that the timefulness of production *matters to the results* – that time is essential. ... It is essential because the timeless model supposes a direct exchange between inputs and outputs. Thus we have labour paid in "corn": the real wage model.' (p. 31).

With regard to the first, I think it would be just as appropriate to state that 'uncertainty only has significance with the introduction of time'. For in the case of timeless theory, it is necessary for the existence of the present as the only moment in time that the future must be suitably collapsed into that present moment in time. Such an organising principle is clearly outlined in Arrow–Debreu models where the future is mapped onto the present using a spectrum of states of nature all weighted by the relevant risk factors assigned to each. As G. L. S. Shackle always indicated, such propositions constitute *knowledge*, not uncertainty. There is no time; therefore there can be no uncertainty (Shackle 1970).

To introduce time, as Chick suggests, means that all individuals operating in the system must be *timeful*. What, might we say, is a timeful person? A timeful person is one, following the critical realist perspective, who can make choices with intentionality. Here, there is now the possibility that individuals *recognise* that their actions both affect and are affected by others' actions (see Lawson 1997: 64). This recognition implies that the possible outcomes of any individual action may not be identifiable, a priori, let alone predictable, especially by the individual herself: the choice framework reflects ontological as well as epistemological considerations. It is in this sense that we might say that the individual acts in a world of uncertainty, where the future cannot be reduced to the present moment. Here, the organic connectedness of the future to the present (connected, but not directly reducible to the present) implies that the present moment embodies the organically interdependent results of the multitude of actions in the *past*. Unlike timeless theory, where there cannot be any discernible past, in timeful theory there is such a realm as the past, organically linked with the present. Here it is more likely that the person living in the present moment will recognise the past for what it was, rather than needing to rewrite the past as a safe haven from the psychologically uninhabitable present.

While this emergence of the past as an ontological entity adds a rich dimensionality to the present, it would not be correct to say that a careful codification of the components of the past would somehow deterministically reflect on what might be expected in the future. The present moment reflects powers, forces and organic interactions among individuals who have made choices. Any individual choice made in the present moment based on the duplication of the outcome experienced by that individual occurring during the interregnum between the past and the present may very likely be disappointed. For in a social system characterised by internally related individuals, the next set of forces, powers and organic interactions may not have any discernible relationship to what was understood by individuals to have been the previous outcome of those relations. In a timeful world, individuals are required to use both experience *and* their intuition when making choices.

Volitional choices, based on the realisation that the social world is related and uncertain, define a basic sense of openness, even though it must be made clear that relationality, uncertainty and openness do not imply that there are no anchors that allow individuals to function with some sense of cognitive clarity. For the recognition of openness has also necessitated the establishment of social institutions, rules, cultures which are the creations of but not reducible to human action. Consequently, the social world is both structured, because there are rules, customs, mores, power bases, hierarchies, etc. which govern and inform our everyday lives; and it is open to the extent that the multitude of individual actions that occur in the world lead to relative powers and influences that result in the world tending in one direction or the other that cannot be predicted with certainty by any individual (see Lawson 1997; Rotheim 1998). Most importantly, one should not see the two phrases 'structured' and 'open' as separate or mutually exclusive, in a dualist fashion. They are organically bound notions that transcend the dualism by which 'rational' thinkers would normally conceptualise and therefore misinterpret them. They constitute the mind frame, as Chick identifies it, of both/and, rather than either/or (p. 35; see also Dow 1990).

Now to Chick's second point above. As I indicated in an earlier section, the timeless theory of mainstream economics has created an operational linguistic framework emanating from the static position of equilibrium, itself. The mainstream economist feels perfectly comfortable, in fact the mainstream demands such comfort, when speaking of an operational relationship between changes in real wages (brought about by changes in money wages) and changes in the level of employment both for the individual firm and for industry as a whole. At the end of the day (a concept that only has meaning in a timeless theory), one could identify a level of employment, a quantity of output, a money wage, a price of wage goods, and therefore some distribution of that quantity of output going to wage and non-wage earners. Such a snapshot of the economy does not inform us of any of the internal relations that brought about the multitude of interdependent forces culminating in the outcome captured by the snapshot. What we see are timeless juxtapositions, not timeful relationships.

Now let the snapshot come to life. In an open system, production and other resource commitments are made in the present for a prescribed period of time in anticipation of the fruits of those commitments being realised. The internal relatedness of this system informs each participant that they will not know the extent to which those returns will accrue until some period in the future after the totality of commitments have occurred. As such, the production decision is predicated on those structures which individuals and groups *can* set or have at their disposal, a priori, as well as the realisation that there is a mechanism of relatedness and openness which they can neither set nor of which they have knowledge, a priori. Workers possess technical skill levels to varying degrees, organisational skills, social skills regarding work, etc. They are also provided with existing workplace structures, including different degrees of hierarchies, participation expectations, etc. A producer might know how much physical output she can expect to generate in a given period, but unless she makes some arrangements to set her cost structure before the fact, she will not know what it costs her to produce that output and therefore what price she would need to set to make a return that would bring her back another day. How would she know the choice of technique (assuming there are more than one) to employ without knowing how much of the value of her output she will need to devote to various mixes of inputs? Then think of the exposure to which workers would be subjected were they to allow their money wages to be set after all prices were published in the future.

Moreover, neither individual producers nor producers as a whole are able to predict their nominal or real returns on the products they sell based on their production decisions alone, nor on the productivity of the combinations of inputs that they use to generate that output. How much they will sell and at what price will depend upon how many other similar products are being sold at that time and at what price, *and* on the level of income in the community (be it local, national or international) in which those products are sold. The resultant uncertainty would, in fact, prevent any individual from making any decision beyond the immediate moment.

And yet workers do work; producers do hire resources, borrow money and produce; banks and other financial institutions do lend money; etc. These individuals live in a timeful world, and they establish practices, conventions and rules of behaviour which allow them to function in that timeful world. It is for these reasons that current price lists are published which give firms some knowledge of the nominal revenue they can expect per unit of output. Money price lists also contribute information to firms regarding the nominal costs of their non-labour inputs per unit of output. In the same vein, money borrowed today to underwrite capital expenditure is, by and large, contracted for in money rather than in real terms, again because the price index to be determined in the future to compute the *real* rate of interest cannot be predicted today *and* is not independent of the capital expenditures and central bank policies made in the present moment.

In the case of labour, it would be irrational in a world of uncertainty to attempt to bargain in advance for a given real wage. In an uncertain world, which is relational and open, labour would be acting rationally, not irrationally, if it were to fix its wages in terms of something more tractable and observable today than in relation to prices which were only revealed in the future and which they are not in a position to predict, because the levels of those prices are not independent of the decisions labour makes today. The existence of such ontological uncertainty (see Rotheim 1995) is the reason why Keynes observed that labour, which was not in a position to bargain for a given real wage, resorted to the convention of bargaining in money wages relative to others in their firm, industry, etc. (see Keynes 1936, chapter 2).

From the vantage point of the producer, fixing wage contracts in money terms, today, adds to the knowledge base she has, in conjunction with her knowledge of current price lists, and money rates at which she contracts to borrow money. Each of these conventional behaviours that has become a part of the social fabric of our economy, contributes to the structure that allows for commitments to be made in the present for the future. Individuals recognise that the full extent of the returns to those decisions will rely partly on factors beyond their control, owing to th relational and open nature of the economy in which they operate. But they also recognise that historically the amplitudes of the swings in the economy in which they function have not been so severe as to prevent them from entering into those arrangements. All of these points provide some clarity to Chick's salient insight regarding the prerequisites for a timeful theory: the object of inquiry must be characterised, as Keynes called it, as a money-wage as opposed to a real-wage economy (see Rotheim 1981).

Having addressed some of the distinguishing features of timeless and timeful theories from the perspective of the indicators offered by Chick, we now embark on a riskier and more contentious elaboration of her assertions about what we might call timeless and timeful theorists. In the opening quote of this chapter, we saw Chick identifying certain psychological characteristics of individuals who prefer static to more timeful theories. I shall explore, in the next sections, some of these characteristics that she uses to make these distinctions between individuals as they choose between the mainstream and dissenting economic perspectives.

## 3. Timeless and timeful theorists

At the heart of Chick's characterisation of those comfortable with static theories is the observation that they 'displace themselves either forward or backward in time, but ... find it most difficult to *be* in the present'. Later in the essay, she adds to the components of the psychological makeup of what I have called timeless theorists: they tend to reflect a greater comfort with authority; and they tend to have been socialised to favour those attributes of left-brain behaviour. She says, for instance, that the 'acceptance of paradox, even the acceptance of ambiguity, is particularly difficult for the authoritarian personality' (p. 33). And, as was mentioned at the outset of this chapter, she identifies (after Rokeach) the person accepting of static theories as having a closed mind. Such a mind, she asserts: 'relies strongly on authority and "buys the package" offered by his authority. Thus he cannot evaluate information independently of its source and the congruence of that source with his own authority/belief system.' (ibid.).

So, what might Chick mean when she says that those who favour static, timeless theories displace themselves either forward or backward in time, but ... find it most difficult to *be* in the present? Consider the following statement by Jon Kabat-Zinn:

> The habit of ignoring our present moments in favor of others yet to come leads directly to a pervasive lack of awareness of the web of life in which we are embedded.
>
> (Kabat-Zinn 1994: 4–5)

In light of these thoughts, one might infer that the present moment reveals itself to 'timeless theorists' as a moment of insecurity and fear. It is a place where things need to be accomplished in order to get to the future as quickly as possible, where the fears and insecurities of being deprived of the elements that define a good life will be extinguished. Such people more than likely venerate a past that probably never existed, and long for a future that will be different and better than the present. Each gets reduced to the present moment and together they become the sole points of reference that provide definition to the present moment. So rather than living in the present moment for its own sake, timeless theorists live in a present moment that has no connection to the 'greater awareness, clarity, and acceptance of present-moment reality' (Kabat-Zinn, ibid.). In their actual lives the present is not an internally constituted reality, but rather a marker whose points of reference are a reconstructed past and a future that is to be better than what is perceived to be at the present moment.

It is not their inner sense of being that assigns meaning to the good life nor the path by which that good life is attained. Rather the person who does not know how to live in the present moment relies on external sources, especially those whom they consider authorities, to help define those moments. What emerges is thus a duality between the present moment and the future. The path to getting to the future is defined by external circumstances, in our own culture the accumulation of objects and the affirmation by others, the sum of which we have come to consider as constituting the good life.

Not being able to focus on the present moment causes one to lose the ability for generating knowledge from the inside. If one requires an authority (someone or object external to the individual) to provide knowledge and a sense of reality, then it is clear that one would be threatened about not knowing what is to come next. With an internally generated sense of self, purpose, being, etc., coming from the ability to live in the present moment, one has an anchor, roots, home-base which can allow one to have a tether by which to safely experience ambiguity, uncertainty and openness. Living in such a 'timeful' world cannot exist without the grounding that allows the individual to feel relatively safer as she ventures into the uncertain future, where she does not know what will occur, although where she does recognise that her action may affect the extent to which she may act subsequently (see Shackle 1970).

Observe, here, the parallel to the critical realist notion that the social world is both structured and open. The confidence to experience and create the openness in the world comes with the rootedness that one finds in those aspects of the social world that constitute the structures of that world. Were it not for the fact that the world were structured, individuals would not have the ability to function freely, thereby accepting and internalising the openness that also characterises the world. It should be clear that the phrases structure and openness are not duals by which we compare and contrast the outcomes of human actions. Instead, these two phrases only make sense if they are considered in terms of Chick's notion of 'both/and'. The timeless theorist has no room in his life for the ambiguities and uncertainties that the future might bring, anymore than he has room for such possibilities in his theoretical life. One should not be surprised of this symmetry; a contrast of perspective on uncertainty in one's life and one's theory seems quite unlikely.

For the timeful theorist, on the other hand, who is capable of living in the present moment, her conceptualisation of the future is not seen as entirely external to her existence, but rather emerges in part from the way she lives in the present moment and in each subsequent 'present' moment. This timeful theorist can grasp a theoretical framework where the future is a creation of human action in a world that is both structured and open. She does not need to impose or impute rationality on the present moment, based on external objective criteria, as she is capable of living within the present moment, having an internally generated feeling for some relationship between her actions today and the extent to which they help to create the future moment. As such, we see that timeless theories emanate from timeless theorists, while timeful theories emerge from timeful theorists.

Chick's paradox is then explicable to the extent that individuals who cannot psychologically cope with the future and yet are dominated by things external to themselves which are by their very nature constantly changing in the future, must make order of the present (indicating a preference for statics and order, not openness and ambiguity) even though they have been socialised not to have the slightest notion of how to exist in the present moment. They project either to their past or to the future, because it is their past where a sense of stability is perceived – although still external to themselves – or to the future where things will always be better.

And now to the second of Chick's two observations, this one dealing with a conflict of what she calls 'psychic organisation' between those who prefer static theories and those who are not bound by that theoretical position. Her argument is complex and, like the theoretical mind-frame she espouses, open-ended. She notes clearly that modes of psychic organisation or states of consciousness are historically rather than biologically determined: 'The construction of the ego is matter of socialization or conditioning; the ego is not a biological given, though it may appear to be inherited, since its early development occurs in families.' (p. 36). We tend to identify consciousness, according to Chick, with ego-function associated with left-brain dominance, whereas other hidden qualities (emanating from right-brain functions) are seen in classic dualistic fashion to be 'Not-Mind, emotion; beyond conscious control and therefore untrustworthy; indeed unworthy, suitable only for women' (p. 36). Indeed: 'My specific hypothesis is that the ego has typically been constructed by the rejection and denial of certain right-brain functions, resulting in a very partial kind of consciousness.' (p. 38).

Left-hemisphere activity, according to Betty Edwards, involving analysis, abstraction, counting and marking time, planning step-by-step procedures, verbalising, making rational statements about logic (1979: 35) are well suited to the timeless and static configuration of mainstream economics. Right-hemisphere activities on the other hand: 'intuitive, subjective, relational, holistic, time-free …' (1979: 36), have no place in the positive heuristical framework of the mainstream.

Edwards's description of right-hemisphere activities reflects well on our distinction between timeless/timeful theorists and timeless/timeful theories. First to the question of the right hemisphere being 'time-free'. She comments as follows:

> … [T]he right hemisphere hasn't a good sense of time and doesn't seem to comprehend what is meant by the term 'wasting time' as does the good, sensible left hemisphere. The right brain is not good at categorizing and naming. It seems to regard the thing as-it-is, at the present moment; seeing things for what they simply are, in all of their awesome, fascinating complexity (ibid.).

To the extent that as humans we have the potentiality to use either side of our brain, we must at least wonder why it is, at least since the time of the Enlightenment, where matters of individual freedom and rational thinking saw their inception, that left-hemispheric capabilities have been the primary focus of education – in the family and in the schools – and in social thought (reserved for men), whereas right-hemisphere capabilities have been ignored, dismissed or derogated.

Edwards identifies another attribute of right-hemispheric behaviour to be 'relational.' As was observed above, timeful theory requires the theorist to recognise that the social world is both structured, while being relational and open. Not employing the capabilities provided by the right hemisphere, it is no wonder that mainstream theory can only see themselves and those whom they study as 'legal atoms' in nature. No one's perceptions or actions affect or are affected by anyone else's self-perception or actions. This atomism, which is surely the theoretical prerequisite for all of mainstream analysis, cannot embrace the complexity, ambiguity and openness that would result from a mind-filter that allowed one to see things relationally, as it resides on the right hemisphere of the brain.

## 4. Final observations

At the end of her paper, Victoria Chick sees the future of economic, and in fact all social theory as not discarding the employment of left-hemisphere in favour of right-hemisphere thinking (another dual), but rather as progressing to the point where the discipline and individuals practising in the discipline would blend the best of both hemispheres (not either/or, but both/and) in what she calls 'whole-brained man'. To be considered as a timeful theorist would imply not a preference for right-hemisphere as opposed to left-hemisphere characteristics or vice versa, but rather where the individual would know how to use her/his 'whole brain' for describing the economic realm.

Envisioning the economy in whole-brained fashion would, for example, recognise the world to be both structured (left-brained) and relational and open (right-brained) in an organic fashion. Whole-brained individuals would be capable of internalising these three categories, not as separate compartments (dualism), but rather where each presupposed the existence of the other. Then individuals would be perceived as making decisions in an uncertain world combining their sense of the present in light of the past *and* their intuitions about the course that their current actions might take. Prediction, which requires the closed system of the current mainstream, would need to give way to a framework of description cognisant of the myriad of structures existing at any moment in time, the powers and forces acting relationally, and the resultant outcomes of those powers and forces in light of the existing structures giving a sense of the likely direction that the economy at the moment is tending.

Feeling comfortable on both sides of the brain, however, is not something that we have seen in the bulk of the population: it is not something developed in the family; it is not something taught in the schools; and it is surely not something rewarded in the workplace. And at the end of the day, we are a long way from economists and an economic theory that are *timeful* in this fashion. Victoria Chick would agree with this conclusion.

## Note

1 I wish to thank Stephanie Blankenburg, Mary Correa, and Pushi Prasad for their active listening during the drafting of this chapter, and Judy Wyle for the books. The influence of Tony Lawson and his work on critical realism have been profound on my thought processes, as can be evidenced clearly from the text of this chapter.

## References

Chick, V. (1995) ' "Order out of Chaos" in Economics', in S. Dow and J. Hillard (eds), *Keynes, Knowledge, and Uncertainty*. Aldershot: Elgar, pp. 25–41.

Dow, S. (1990) 'Beyond Dualism', *Cambridge Journal of Economics*, June: 143–57.

Hanh, Tich Nhat (1990). *Present Moment, Wonderful Moment*. Berkeley: Parallax.

Kabat-Zinn, J. (1994) *Wherever You Go There You Are*. New York: Hyperion.

Keynes, J. M. (1936) *The General Theory of Employment, Interest, and Money*. Reprinted in JMK VII. London: Macmillan.

Lawson, T. (1997) *Economics and Reality*. London: Routledge.

Rotheim, R. (1981) 'Keynes's Monetary Theory of Value (1933)', *Journal of Post Keynesian Economics*, Summer, Vol 3, no. 4.

Rotheim, R (1995) 'Keynes on Uncertainty and Individual Behaviour in the Theory of Effective Demand,' in S. Dow and J. Hillard (eds.) *Keynes, Knowledge, and Uncertainty* Aldershot: Elgar.

Rotheim, R. (1998) 'On Closed Systems and the Language of Economic Discourse', *Review of Social Economy*, Fall: 324–34, Vol 21, no. 1.

Rotheim, R. (1999) 'Post Keynesian Economics and Critical Realist Philosophy', *Journal of Post Keynesian Economics*, Fall: 71–103, Vol 22, no. 1.

Shackle, G. L. S. (1970) *Uncertainty in Economics*. Cambridge: Cambridge University Press.

# 8

# MATHEMATICAL FORMALISM IN ECONOMICS: WHAT REALLY IS THE PROBLEM?

*Tony Lawson*

Is there a problem with the way mathematics is used in modern economics? The most recently published paper by Victoria Chick with which I am familiar, a contribution to an *Economic Journal* symposium on the topic of 'Formalism in Economics', calls for a debate on this issue (Chick 1998). But is there really an overriding or fundamental difficulty here? And if so, what can be done about it?

I want in this chapter to go over these questions and to suggest answers. The answers I defend are mostly already contained in Vicky's piece. But they are answers, I think, which bear repeating over and again nevertheless, for they are easily misunderstood.

Rather than turn immediately to those problems with formalism I regard as most fundamental, however, I first consider certain related issues sometimes systematised under the heading of problems with formalism (by both critics and advocates of formalism alike), but which are really no such thing. It is my hope that if these latter sorts of 'criticisms' are also, and first, addressed, and then set aside, it will more readily be recognised that there is more to the critique of formalism than these other issues which have tended to receive most of the attention.

## 1. What is *not* really the problem with formalism in economics

In actual fact, of course, contributors to the project of formalising the study of economic phenomena, i.e. the modern mainstream project in economics, mostly avoid all discussion of methodology in economics. Some even support such a stance explicitly. For example, on the occasion of his retirement from Cambridge, Frank Hahn saw fit to contribute a piece to the *Royal Economics Society Newsletter* with the following explicit advice for modern economists:

> avoid discussions of 'mathematics in economics' like the plague and give no thought at all to methodology.
>
> (Hahn 1992)

But not all mainstream economists accept this advice; a very few do broach such matters explicitly. The main shortcomings with the responses of the latter group is not that they are necessarily wrong, but that they tend to ignore the more telling arguments made against the use of formalism in economics (see Lawson 1997b). Certainly, if there is an overriding problem with formalism in economics I believe it is not where its (few) defenders most commonly interpret its critics as supposing it to be. It is some of these less than telling criticisms that I want to dispose of first before turning to others I believe to be rather more serious.

## 2. The content of substantive theory

One example of a 'criticism' of the use of formalism, or anyway of a train of thought sometimes thought to explain the rejection of formalism by critics, is that the use of mathematical techniques produces results that are perceived as unwelcome to these critics. A version of this is raised by Krugman (1998), in a paper which appeared in the same symposium as Vicky's. According to Krugman the real reason formalism is discarded by some critics, and specifically by 'outsiders', is that it often refutes pet doctrines:

> ... when outsiders criticise formalism in economics, their real complaint is often not about method but about content – in particular, they dislike 'formalistic' arguments not because they are formalistic, but because they refute their pet doctrines.
>
> (Krugman 1998: 1829)

Let me then acknowledge straightaway that if critics of formalism do oppose formalistic methods just because the substantive results achieved are unpalatable, because the critics see them as refuting pet theories or whatever, then this opposition is not soundly based. Here we must surely agree with Krugman. I do not doubt that analyses do often find favour in certain quarters just because of their results. But this is a practice that is difficult to defend; ultimately, it is the relevance of the analysis that matters, not whether its results conform with our preferences.

A second criticism seemingly aimed at the use of mathematics to study social phenomena is that the practice is elitist. Critics hold that formalism should be banished in effect because it serves to exclude from the conversation those without the basic mathematical know-how. Krugman (1998) again draws attention to this charge, noting that in 1997 the editor of *Governing* magazine published an op-ed which asserted in particular that '... algebra could not be essential to economic understanding, because if it were this would delegitimise the opinions of people who had not studied algebra when young and were now too old to retool' (Krugman 1998: 1831).

Once more I think we must support Krugman's dismissal of the charge. *If* algebra (or any other specific research approach) is found to be essential to achieving any insight or sensibly formulated project, then it cannot be opposed just because the opinions of those without a sufficient knowledge of algebra (or of the technique, etc., in question) cannot easily get a look in. There *is* a broader issue here about who is admitted to the academy; I personally am in favour of making admission as open as possible. But there is no argument here that applies merely to the mathematising of economics and not to all other branches of study where specific skills, training, experiences and/or know-how are involved.

A further criticism made of the use of formalism, or at least a charge against which modern mathematical modellers like Krugman often see fit to defend themselves, is that formalists do not use empirical data and fail to draw conclusions from their models regarding matters of policy. Krugman (1998: 1830) cites some illustrious exceptions. But to agree with him that the charge is untenable, we need only to look at modern applied econometricians, all of whom use data, and many of whom interpret their models as bearing directly on the policy discussion.

One additional apparent charge often responded to by the modellers is that economics should not even seek to be scientific or in any sense rigorous. In similar fashion modellers often see fit to defend their results as producing clarity and/or consistency. If there are those who rule out on some a priori basis the possibility of social science, or who think the pursuit of clarity is *necessarily* to be avoided, whatever the context, then I myself can be counted against them. Consistency is more problematic. But as long as we do not treat it in static terms, and accept that the best which we often can hope to achieve is developmental consistency (like, say, a tadpole turning into a frog, or initial ideas being transformed into a thesis), then consistency, I believe, can be accepted as an often desirable and feasible goal.

In short, it is my view that not all (or not all aspects) of the defences made of the project of mathematising economics are without content. Certainly, any along the lines of those briefly discussed above appear to fall into this category. The unfortunate fact remains, though, that defences of the sort just discussed do not really bear at all on the more fundamental or telling criticisms that can be levelled against the mathematical project in economics. Two fundamental problems in particular remain. Let me consider each in its turn.

## 3. The real problems with the use of formalistic methods in economics

The first of the two fundamental problems with the use of mathematics in modern economics is simply that formalistic methods appear mostly quite unsuitable to the task of illuminating social phenomena. This result is suggested by our best understanding of the nature of social reality (along with an enquiry into the conditions in which the various methods have relevance), and is borne out by the repeated failures of economics to date. This assessment may be false. But there are grounds for thinking it largely correct. And it is an assessment to which defenders of the mainstream project seem rarely if ever to respond.

Thus, although, as I say, I do agree with Krugman that it would be indefensible to reject formalism simply because it is perceived as refuting pet theories, I believe this is ultimately beside the point. For I doubt in fact that the use of formalism *can* very often refute (or support) pet (or any other kind of) theories about social phenomena, except perhaps in rather trivial instances (such as when identities are involved).[1]

Clearly I must elaborate and defend such a claim. Before doing so, however, I should acknowledge that I am taking it for granted that the primary goal of social research *is* the illumination of social reality. I am here accepting that the central goal is indeed to explain and understand the social world; the aim of pursuing truth is accepted as primary.

Now it is conceivable that an ability to illuminate the social world is not a criterion we all accept. It may well be that some economists prosecute mathematics in economics just because of some merely pragmatic criterion, perhaps because it is elegant or whatever. Some may just be possessed to do mathematical modelling for its own sake, even perhaps because they feel the need to demonstrate they can do it. If so, such individuals do escape the criticisms set out below. But only at the cost of renouncing any claims to relevance at all.

## 4. Mathematical economics and reality

So, to return to my theme, why do I suggest that the refuting of pet doctrines, or of any other theories or hypotheses, is one thing most exercises in formalistic modelling are actually mostly unable to do? I make this claim just because the worlds expressed in such models appear to have little if any connection with the sort of world in which we do or could live. The types of assumptions upon which the models of modern economics are usually based – human beings are omniscient, perfect sighted or possessing of rational expectations, always rational (optimising) in their behaviour, identical, living in two commodity worlds, etc. – are simply (largely) false and widely known to be so.

Notice that under the head of assumptions known or thought to be false here, I do not include statements about states of affairs that, though non-actual, nevertheless appear possible (see Lawson 1997a: 111). It is not that we could really be omniscient or always act rationally (in the sense of optimising), if only we could be bothered or choose to. I include really possible counterfactuals as part of the real, and interpret propositions as unrealistic or (held-to-be) false which make claims that we have every reason to suppose lie outside the bounds of real possibility.

Now if, and once, falsity (in this broad sense) of assumptions is allowed, it is clearly possible to derive any conclusions whatsoever – true ones or false ones – simply by deductive logic. Thus suppose I want to deduce the (apparently true) proposition that 'all ravens are black'. One way I might do it is by including in my assumptions, the propositions: 'all ravens are vegetables' and 'all vegetables are black'. Clearly my desired conclusion follows by deductive logic. In similar fashion if I want to deduce that 'agent $X$ does $Y$', I need only assume (i) that a situation prevails in which it is rational (in a specific sense) for a situated agent $X$ to do $Y$, along with the assumption (ii) that $X$ always acts rationally in the specified sense. The assumptions about the situation and human capabilities and their exercise need not be realistic, merely facilitating of mathematical modelling tractability. What could be more trivial and more pointless? The problem is not the conclusions *per se* of formalistic economic models but the manner in which the conclusions are derived: by way of starting from 'assumptions' known to be descriptively false.

So why use assumptions or specifications already known, or anyway considered, to be significantly and irredeemably false? Is there something about formalistic modelling that necessitates that assumptions adopted are typically false? I think there is. Moreover it is a feature of formalistic modelling identified by Vicky in the paper already noted. Basically the sorts of formalistic modelling methods used by economists require, for their efficacy, that the reality to which they are addressed be closed, when in fact the social world is found to be everywhere open.

By a closed system I mean merely one that supports regularities of the form 'whenever event (or state of affairs) $x$ then event (or state of affairs) $y$'. These regularities can be deterministic or given a probabilistic gloss. They are the sort of result sometimes produced, via human intervention, in well-controlled experiments. Basically, through isolating a stable mechanism of interest from the countervailing effects of all others, a stable correlation between the triggering conditions of the isolated mechanism and its effects can be recorded. These are the sorts of conditions mainstream economists, with their near-exclusive focus on formalistic modelling activities, in effect assume to hold everywhere in the social realm. The problem with the modelling approach, as I say, is just that the social realm is of a nature that such conditions are rarely found. As Vicky expresses matters:

> The economy is clearly an open, evolving system. Both static and conventional dynamic models are closed systems; they are self-contained and predict constant conjunctions of events: whenever $x$ occurs $y$ will follow ... Strictly speaking, closed systems are only applicable to sharply delineated and largely isolated subsystems ... The question of applicability thus rests on finding elements of the economic system which can be harmlessly analysed as isolated components (the operative term is 'harmlessly'). This returns us to the subject of atomism.
>
> (Chick 1998: 1866)

The reference to atomism in this passage is significant. Let me elaborate upon it a little, for there can be confusion over its intended meaning. As noted, to produce an event regularity in a well-controlled experiment (which is where most scientifically interesting event regularities are located), the experimenter has (i)*to isolate* (ii) a *stable* mechanism. The mechanism has to be *isolated* just to prevent other countervailing factors interfering with the results. The (isolated) mechanism has to be *intrinsically stable* just so that, when it is triggered (conditions *x*), predictable effects (outcomes *y*) always follow. Of course, the purpose of the experiment is not the production of an event regularity *per se*, but the empirical identification of the stable mechanism so experimentally isolated.

Now the metaphor of the atom is intended precisely to represent any theoretical claim that posits entities or features that possess the properties of being intrinsically stable and isolated. Of course, real atoms, according to modern scientific understandings, are not necessarily atomistic in this sense. The conception intended, rather, is the familiar one where the atom, much like the billiard ball, responds passively, that is, in a stable predictable way, to the triggering condition of the cue (or being hit by another ball). Of course, if I put my hand on the ball, the result will be affected. The restriction or condition of isolation is intended to prevent this sort of interference.

Thus, just because the guaranteeing of social event regularities requires analogues to the isolated stable mechanisms of controlled experiments, in modern mainstream economics individuals are inevitably treated as atomistic in the noted sense, and formulated as acting in isolated environments. By constructing theoretical conceptions in which (isolated) individual agents are rendered atomistic the latters' behaviour becomes deterministic and predictable. This sort of reductionist theorising is more or less a requirement of formalistic economic modelling. And in the context of a social reality found to be quite different (in fact it is easily demonstrated that social reality is mostly far from atomistic, being highly internally related, open, and of the nature of a process, amongst other things – see Lawson 1997a), this set of restrictions explains both (i) the prevalence,[2] and (ii) the sorts, of known-to-be-false assumptions about human nature and their conditions that modellers are repeatedly forced to make.

The sort of criticism to which I am drawing attention here is not new, of course. And Vicky, a post-Keynesian, is quick to acknowledge parallels with the assessments on formalism in economics made by Keynes more than half a century ago. Consider, for example, Keynes's remarks on the presuppositions of econometrics in particular:

> There is first of all the central question of methodology, – the logic of applying the method of multiple correlation to unanalysed economic material, which we know to be non-homogeneous through time. If we are dealing with the action of numerically measurable, independent forces, adequately analyzed so that we knew we were dealing with independent atomic factors and between them completely comprehensive, acting with fluctuating relative strength on material constant and homogeneous through time, we might be able to use the method of multiple correlation with some confidence for disentangling the laws of their action ...
>
> In fact we know that every one of these conditions is far from being satisfied by the economic material under investigation ...

To proceed to some more detailed comments. The coefficients arrived at are apparently assumed to be constant for 10 years or for a larger period. Yet, surely we know that they are not constant. There is no reason at all why they should not be different every year.

(Keynes 1938 [1973]: 285–6)

## 5. Science and the use of data

Notice, incidentally, that the possibility of social science is not undermined by this discussion. The analysis of experiments, touched upon above, reveals that even in controlled experiments, when tight correlations are sometimes produced, the goal is not the production of these correlations *per se*, but the empirical identification of underlying mechanisms. This is the primary goal of science, and the experimental process is one path to achieving it (Lawson 1997a). Although the opportunities for meaningful experiments, and so scientifically interesting correlations, have been found to be limited in the social realm, the possibilities for identifying the underlying causes of surface phenomena are clearly not. Behind movements in wages, productivity, output and profits, for example, lie systems of industrial relations, labour law, possibly processes of globalisation, and so forth; and social science can go to work uncovering and elaborating these deeper causes.

In other words, economics can yet be scientific in the *sense* of natural science, if not necessarily in the same *way* (methodology) or with respect to the same type of object (ontology). In other words economics can yet be scientific without being scientistic or otherwise reductionist.

Notice, too, that, despite a widespread presumption to the contrary, the use of data *per se* does not protect formalistic modellers from the charge that they are out of touch with reality. Krugman (1998) fails to appreciate this. And I am even aware of professional economists who endeavour to establish that modern mainstream economics is after all in touch with reality, by counting the number of articles in core or 'flagship' journals which make reference to 'empirical facts' or 'draw' policy implications, and announcing that the resulting proportion is reasonably high.

Let us be clear. If economic data record phenomena generated within an open and highly internally related social system, and economists uncritically insist on analysing them using methods which presuppose that they record phenomena generated in closed and atomistic systems, claims to be in touch with reality just because data are involved are not well founded. Similarly, if the whole framework of theoretical modelling is inevitably, and known to be, largely false, it is not obvious that there is any relevance or insight at all to be found in any policy conclusions drawn from it.[3]

To sum up, one quite fundamental criticism that can and must be made against the modern mainstream project in economics is that its formalistic tools appear inappropriate to the task to which they are being put, pure and simple.

## 6. The second fundamental problem with the modern project of mathematising economics

The second fundamental criticism to be made of the modern mainstream project does not concern the nature or relevance of mathematical methods at all. Rather it relates to the manner in which the formalistic modelling project sustains its position of dominance. I refer to the fashion in which those who run economics faculties insist that mathematical formalistic methods are the very stuff of the discipline; that economic courses, or the core ones, reduce to almost nothing except formalistic modelling; that appointments in universities be open, in effect, only to these modellers; that almost nothing but mathematical formalism be permitted in journals regarded as core or prestigious, and so forth.

There is little doubt that the situation is as just described; indeed the insistence that individuals in the economics academy either use formalistic methods or be marginalised is so widespread that I need not dwell on it here. I do, though, think it important that, conceptually at least, the problems with formalism as a viable tool for illuminating social phenomena be separated from the familiar insistence that formalistic methods be more or less everywhere wielded. Perhaps the failings of the formalistic approach do explain the defensiveness revealed by those who seek to impose formalistic methods on all others. But the two problems, though connected, do not necessarily reduce one to the other.

## 7. Rectifying matters

So what is to be done? Let me start my saying what I think is not to be done. Just as defences of the use of mathematical models often miss the more fundamental criticisms levelled, so I think the changes sought by those who so criticise tend also to be misunderstood. The legitimate goal of those who are sceptical of the ability of formalistic methods to illuminate the social world is not to prohibit all such attempts. Certainly I would not support such a response. Rather the acceptable solution can only be to recognise that all proposed approaches have a place, albeit with some onus being placed on the protagonists of each to engage with others, and demonstrate (or at least continually to work to find some justification for) the perceived worth of their favoured strategies, etc., in a pluralist and open conversation.

I have heard it said (usually in discussions when I give seminars or other presentations) that when I argue like this I am being somewhat too liberal, even 'wishy-washy'. After all, have I not argued (over and again) that the conditions of the social realm are such that mathematical methods are unlikely to be of much use in their illumination?

This latter observation, of course, is correct. But it must also be acknowledged that (essentially ontological) arguments of the sort sketched here and elaborated elsewhere (e.g. Lawson 1997a) are somewhat rationalistic, and that this especially always carries dangers. Although such arguments as I defend currently seem (to me) to be at least as sustainable as others with which they compete, they are of course fallible and partial, and may yet turn out to be quite dramatically wrong, at least in certain significant respects. It may be found that, on occasion, aspects of the social world after all approximate a closure, for example. Or new mathematical methods may yet be devised which are found to be (more) appropriate to open systems. Who knows?

No doubt the best way to advance understanding is a combination of rational thought and trial and error. We might expect knowledge, even of fruitful social scientific method, to advance by way of our learning from past mistakes via an evolutionary process; important insights may in this way be achieved more or less by accident. The reason ontological analysis remains so important at this juncture is just that such an evolutionary scientific process is currently blocked. Or rather the environment of selection is so determined that, for the time being, any flourishing (i.e. widespread) practice must be of a mathematical form. In other words, real progress, in social understanding, is, undermined by the pervasive insistence in faculties of economics that the only (or almost only) permitted form of activity involves the wielding of mathematical models. It is this constraint on evolutionary progress in knowledge, that makes the input from (somewhat rationalistic) ontology at this point so important.

So the preferred solution, as I say, is not to place any prohibition on formalistic modelling or indeed on any other type of research practice. Rather the defensible aim can only be to allow supporters of all approaches to justify their projects in any economic forum. The emphasis, then, has to be on interaction and engagement with others (for supporting views, see also Dow 1996; Chick and Dow 2000; Lawson 1999).

So I am bound to conclude that the earlier noted advice from Frank Hahn is quite wrong. Hahn is one of the best, and in my view more courageous, of mainstream economists; he is distinguished in being prepared to say and write in public what most others are willing to say only in private, and yet act upon continuously. But, contra Hahn, the need is not to 'avoid discussions of "mathematics in economics" like the plague and give no thought at all to methodology' but precisely to engage with each other on these matters so much more. We need to demonstrate the (relative) worth of our methods, approaches, theories, and so forth; and, where we are realists, this means demonstrating (at least continually working to discover or justify) their worth with respect to furthering our understanding of social reality.

Thus engagement is fundamental. Of course, we can all make mistakes; approaches yet to justify themselves in any way may yet prove of fundamental worth. So let us also maintain variety; let no approach be ruled out altogether at any stage. But also let demonstrated worth and potential equally play a role. Currently, we seem to have the worst of all worlds. An approach that is found a posteriori to fail in the task of social illumination, and whose failures are easily explained by our best contributions to social theory, is actually everywhere imposed onto the discipline, to the near exclusion of all alternatives. Almost any other arrangement has to be better.

It cannot be repeated enough times, however, that the solution does not turn on replacing one sort of dogma with another. Rather we need to cultivate an open forum of intellectual honesty and respect for others. The point, I believe, is continuously to engage alternative positions, to be both respectful and charitable of opponents' positions, to recognise the fallibility and partiality of even our best (or pet) theories or approaches, and to recognise the value to progress of actively engaging with others on all issues.

In such a forum, the drive to mathematise the study of economics will no doubt find a place. And this brings me back to the paper by Vicky. For the title of Vicky's piece is precisely: 'On Knowing One's Place: The Role of Formalism in Economics'. Basically, I have given my own take on the basic thrust of her contribution. Vicky acknowledges explicitly that the concern to understand social reality does not mean that we necessarily preclude the wielding of conventional formal methods; indeed she seems of a strong opinion that the latter will indeed make a fruitful contribution to understanding (a matter on which I personally wait to be convinced). But she does insist that their place is at best one amongst many, a place whose legitimate boundaries or limits are a matter for informed experiment and discussion. As Vicky puts it: 'Formalism is fine, but it must know its place. Economists need to debate further the boundaries of that place.' (Chick 1998: 1868).

On this I suspect most heterodox economists are agreed. So let the debate continue. Or rather let us instigate a wider ranging conversation that does engage the more fundamental issues, albeit in a way that recognises the fallibility and limits of our own positions. This is the sort of position Vicky has always advocated, so it seems more than appropriate to reemphasise it here in her richly deserved Festschrift.

## Notes

1 Or to the extent that formalistic methods are held to 'support' or 'refute' anything they can be 'found' to support or refute just about everything (according to one's wishes), and so end up again really supporting nothing at all.

2 Of course modellers often seek to 'justify' their claims by asserting that we all need to make unrealistic (i.e. known-to-be-false) assumptions in our analyses. What they fail to realise is that the 'we' in this claim is restricted to formalistic modellers. The rest of us do not 'need' to do so; my claim indeed is that we need not to.

3 Some mainstream economists have recognised all this. Frank Hahn, I believe, is one. And it may be worth repeating some of his reactions explicitly here, if only because other mainstream economists may be persuaded thereby to examine whether there is really much point to the activities in question.

Thus, with respect to any attempts to estimate or test the formal models of economic 'theory' using measured data on actual phenomena, Hahn writes:

> The economists I have been discussing might be taken to be engaged in the following programme: to enquire how far observed events are consistent with an economy which is in continuous Walrasian equilibrium. ... [Even if this programme was successful] ... it would not be true that we understood the events.

For we would not understand how continuous equilibrium is possible in a decentralised economy and we do not understand why a world with Trade Unions and monopolies behaves like a perfectly competitive one. Theorising in economics I have argued is an attempt at understanding and I now add that bad theorising is a premature claim to understand.

(Hahn 1985: 15; see also Hahn 1994: 240)

And elsewhere Hahn reveals, albeit in a somewhat dramatic fashion, what he thinks of the practice of using mathematical models for drawing policy implications:

When policy conclusions are drawn from such models, it is time to reach for one's gun.

(Hahn 1982: 29)

# References

Chick, V. (1998) 'On Knowing One's Place: The Role of Formalism in Economics', *Economic Journal* 108(451): 1829–36.

Chick, V. and Dow, S. C. (2001) 'Formalism, Logic and Reality: a Keynesian analysis', *Cambridge Journal of Economics Volume 25, No. 6, November* (forthcoming).

Dow, S. C. (1996) *The Methodology of Macroeconomic Thought*. Aldershot: Elgar.

Hahn, F. (1982) *Money and Inflation*. Oxford: Basil Blackwell.

Hahn, F. (1985) 'In Praise of Economic Theory', in *1984 Jevons Memorial Fund Lecture*. London: University College.

Hahn, F. (1992) 'Reflections', *Royal Economics Society Newsletter*, No. 77.

Hahn, F. (1994) 'An Intellectual Retrospect', *Banca Nazionale del Lavoro Quarterly Review*: 245–58.

Keynes, J. M. (1938) [1973] 'The Collected Writings of John Maynard Keynes: The General Theory and After: Part II Defense and Development', *Royal Economic Society* XIV.

Krugman, P. (1998) 'Two Cheers for Formalism', *Economic Journal* 108(451): 1859–69.

Lawson, T. (1997a) *Economics and Reality*. London: Routledge.

Lawson, T. (1997b) 'Horses for Courses', in P. Arestis, G. Palma and M. Sawyer (eds), *Markets, Unemployment and Economic Policy: Essays in Honour of Geoff Harcourt (volume two)*. London and New York: Routledge.

Lawson, T. (1999) 'Connections and Distinctions: Post Keynesianism and Critical Realism', *Journal of Post Keynesian Economics,*, Vol 22, No. 1, Fall, pp. 3–14.

# 9

# MATHEMATICS AS NATURAL LAW: AN EPISTEMOLOGICAL CRITIQUE OF FORMALISM IN ECONOMICS

*Jan Toporowski*[1]

'Mathematics is too important
to be left to the mathematicians
they are too sophisticated in their techniques
& too naïve in their way of seeing
the world'
Stefan Themerson *Collected poems* Amsterdam:
Gaberbocchus Press 1998, p. 135

In formalist economics, crucial data on the organisation of production and distribution are excluded from analysis, while intuition and casual observation, and synthetic statistical data, feed a contention of conjectures abstracted from the actual ways in which economies reproduce themselves and develop.

The paper argues that applying the formalism of pure mathematics is a 'natural law' analysis that abstracts from economic processes and causes econometrics cannot transcend the taxonomies used to produce statistics. Formalism in economics is therefore a modern form of metaphysics whose success may be is attributed to the increasing uncertainty and risks attendant upon financial inflation.

## 1. The instrumental approach to scientific investigation

Veblen identified the roots of modern scientific reasoning in our use of machines. This gives us what he called our 'matter-of-fact, cause-and-effect', and materialistic way of thinking about the world:

> The machine technology rests on a knowledge of impersonal, material cause and effect ... the course of things is given mechanically, impersonally, and the resultant discipline is a discipline in the handling of impersonal facts for mechanical effect. It inculcates thinking in terms of opaque, impersonal, cause and effect, to the neglect of those norms of validity which rest on usage and on the conventional standards handed down by usage.
>
> (Veblen 1904: 311–14)

A direct example of machine-inspired science was William Harvey's inference in the seventeenth century of the circulation of blood, and the functions of the heart, from the operations of water-pumps. Veblen's realism is similar to Marxian materialist, historicist philosophy first put forward in Hegelian terms by Marx and Engels in 1845 in *The German Ideology*, and later by Engels in *Ludwig Feuerbach and the End of Classical German Philosophy*. Science arises out of working with nature and machines. The German Marxist philosopher Alfred Sohn-Rethel distinguished practical endeavour, which he regarded as the actual foundation of scientific knowledge, from the search for 'objective' truth by contemplation or manipulation of objects abstracted from practical requirements. Even where the knowledge concerns objects which cannot be directly manipulated, for example the shifting positions of stars, knowledge may still be validated by its practical application, in this case the application of astronomy to navigation (Sohn-Rethel 1978).

In economics, this 'mechanical' approach consists of observing incidents systematically and examining the relationships between them in terms of efficient causes and mechanisms of economic interaction. Phenomena (Veblen's 'matters of fact') are explained by showing how their circumstances and antecedents necessarily give rise to those phenomena, which then feed into the system as circumstances and antecedents of other phenomena in a process over time. Thus in Kalecki's business cycle theory, ebbs and flows in financial accumulation and investment decisions 'cause' successive fluctuations in economic activity (Kalecki 1971, chapter 1). Keynes's analysis of the operations of securities markets shows how investors, or traders, determine market values by a process of anticipating each others' evaluations. The resulting consensus is a temporary convention that feeds into subsequent evaluations (Keynes 1936, chapter 12; see also Kregel 1995).

In this inductive approach, theory emerges from an examination of actual economic processes, and the explanation of events is sought in their actual antecedents and circumstances. Although apparently 'mechanistic', this is different from the 'mechanical' analogies of early neoclassical theories (see Mirowski 1989) or the 'cybernetic' analogies of Oskar Lange's theories of socialist economies (Lange 1938). The early neoclassical writers proceeded by postulating that imagined forces and equilibria, analogous to those with which Newtonian physics sought to 'explain' material phenomena, exist in actual economic processes, while Lange knew that he was describing an imaginary economy.

## 2. Natural law and pure mathematics

Prior to reasoning in terms of material antecedents and circumstances, systematic investigation of phenomena sought their explanation in 'natural laws'. The material universe and living creatures were held to operate spontaneously, or 'naturally', in accordance with 'laws' that transcended the particular events in which the operation of those laws was identified. This was a 'rationalist' reaction to schemes of thought in which divine agency was the ultimate explanation of phenomena. Schumpeter identified the roots of 'natural law' thought in medieval attempts to accommodate otherwise 'pagan' Greek philosophy to Catholic theology. This allowed systematic knowledge of nature that was not drawn from Divine revelation. Thus Thomas Aquinas was able to reconcile reason with religious belief. With the decline of Divine Right as a guide to moral philosophy, 'natural law' was used in the Enlightenment to justify legislative dispositions in, for example, John Locke's political theory. Faith was replaced by introspection, observation and experiment as sources of true knowledge in which perceived regularities became 'natural laws' (Schumpeter 1954: 115–42, 430).

For Adam Smith, such laws questioned the other source of arbitrary authority in the eighteenth century, the reasons of state which justified mercantilist policies. His 'Invisible Hand' theory of market coordination is just such a 'natural law'. In the nineteenth century, political economy sought to discover 'laws' such as diminishing marginal returns, Marx's 'laws' of value, Malthus's 'laws' of population, Say's 'law' of markets, the 'law of one price'. Marshall identified the scientific progress of economics with the development of such 'laws' or tendencies:

> A science progresses by increasing the number and exactness of its laws; by submitting them to tests of ever increasing severity; and by enlarging their scope till a single broad law contains and supersedes a number of narrower laws, which have been shown to be special instances if it.
>
> (Marshall 1938: 30)

'Natural laws' transcend the observed events which they are supposed to determine. They cannot themselves be observed, but what is observed is attributed to their operation. In this way, analysis in terms of 'natural law' regresses causation to the immaterial and unobservable. Most of the natural laws discovered by the physical and natural sciences in the eighteenth and nineteenth centuries, like Newtonian physics, have been superseded in the twentieth century. But these sciences established a tradition of systematic observation which is lost in formalism.

The apparently rapid progress of science in the eighteenth and nineteenth centuries was accompanied by the equally rapid development of mathematics and mathematical techniques. The fact that scientific and mathematical innovations were often made by the same individuals, using mathematical notation as a shorthand and an aid to precision (Marshall's 'exactness'), may suggest, as formalists were to argue, that mathematics was the foundation of scientific understanding. Kant pointed out that mathematics is a metaphysical system of thought that is purely abstract, in the sense that it is a mental construct rather than being inherent in the material world. He saw its domain as the refinement of concepts rather than empirical investigation (Kant 1943: 400). Mathematics is reasoned out, from axioms, assumptions and conventions of notation and argumentation, what Kant called 'intuitions'. Mathematics provides certainty, while empirical perception is always subject to doubt (Kant 1943: 400–3, 469–70).

While mathematics has been used in economics since the seventeenth century, formalism goes beyond quantitative comparisons and the use of algebra in exposition.

Formalism was originally advanced as a programme for the physical sciences by David Hilbert at the International Mathematical Conference in Paris in 1900. He argued that physical sciences in which mathematics plays an important role should be formalised by showing the axioms from which their reasoning is derived, and investigating the consistency of these axioms (Golland 1996). With the pre-eminence in economics of academics such as Paul Samuelson, Kenneth Arrow and Gerard Debreu, who trained as mathematicians and apply to economics the language and procedures of mathematics, formalism has come to be the dominant system of exposition of economic argument (Golland 1996; Backhouse 1998).

Reducing economic arguments to axioms, and investigating deductions from axioms, is the hallmark of formalism in economics. Axioms, like natural laws, are obtained through introspection, intuition, casual observation or experiment. As the starting point for analysis, they have no antecedents in systematic observation. Like 'natural' laws they claim to provide a 'final' (i.e. without antecedent) and transcendent explanation of events, a way of knowing about actual economies before finding anything out about them. When reality falls within the scope of the axioms propounded, then the deductions made must also hold in reality, or form a 'benchmark' for our understanding of reality. Such axioms are nested in congenial ways in which the economy is supposed to operate to realise those axioms. For example, firms that do not maximise their profits are supposed to go out of business.

In methodological formalism mathematics is a form of natural law because mathematical relationships are deemed to reveal actual economic relations. For example, algebraic supply and demand equations supposedly express the essential relationship between buyers and sellers in markets. In demand theory, ratios of marginal utility ostensibly determine consumers' demand for commodities. Second the mathematical relationships transcend the observed instances of their operation, as Newton's Law of Gravity transcended the apple that fell upon him. Methodological formalism advances propositions, theorems and lemmas that are supposed to 'explain' observed situations and events, but do not end with those situations or events. Thus utility maximisation continues beyond any particular purchase or consumption.

Third, mathematics becomes 'natural law' when mathematical deductions are supposed to reveal economic outcomes that occur spontaneously without institutional preconditions or prior arrangements to secure results consistent with the propositions, theorems or lemmas. The deduced outcomes occur 'spontaneously', and therefore are 'natural'. The classic example is the equilibrium when axioms and deductions from them are combined into determinate economic models. Some axioms are mere definitions, for example the system of national accounts. Other axioms are behavioural, such as the so-called 'laws of supply and demand'.

Economics students are taught that the number of equations in a model must equal the number of unknowns to give the highest form of simultaneous determination of all values. Partial methods allow 'exogenous' variables to be set outside the model. Such 'exogenous' variables can then be treated as 'determining' the outcome of the model, and hence as 'causing' that outcome. Exogenous variables may be chosen axiomatically, as in the monetarist view that 'inflation is always and everywhere a monetary phenomenon' and hence that the money supply determines the price level. Or they may be determined by the availability of particular courses of action: in setting discount rates, central banks consider their consequences and therefore attribute to the rate of interest a causal significance that is revealed by the endogenous, axiomatically derived relations in their models.

Whether systems of equations can reveal causal processes has been discussed in economics, from Pareto's criticism of Walras's general equilibrium (Pareto 1909: 246–7), through to contemporary Critical Realism (Lawson 1996) and Keynes's ontological uncertainty (Vercelli 1992). Because of their axiomatic antecedents, systems of equations cannot explain causes but only quantitative outcomes (Vercelli 1992; Chick 1998).

Marshall envisaged economic 'laws' as tendencies in economic affairs. Following Marshall, determining states of equilibrium is justified on the grounds of immanent outcome: when all the consequences of current decisions have worked themselves out, the resulting, putative, equilibrium will be realised (Marshall 1938: 36). According to Friedman the ability to forecast correctly justifies even the most 'unrealistic' axioms (Friedman 1953). Knowledge of immanent states is thereby supposed to make comprehensive knowledge of their antecedents unnecessary, if not redundant. The result is theory without history, or, rather, theory that can be inserted at any point in history to reveal its outcome. If the pace of history is sufficiently fast (see Section 4), the novelty of each day inclines even thoughtful observers to forget the outcomes that were proposed yesterday and concentrate on today's more exciting prospects. Where the axioms include assumptions of rationality and optimisation, the model becomes utopian: an immanent welfare-maximising outcome is revealed without identifying the social arrangements and institutions that will bring about this happy state of affairs. This normative economics is typically put forward as 'positive' economics. Teleological justifications remove methodological formalism further from the investigation of matters of fact, and the cause-and-effect connections that combine, through time, the circumstances and events of actual economies into coherent processes.

## 3. ' ... tests of ever increasing severity'?

The methodological formalism described above has no systematic empirical content. The underlying assumptions or axioms may reflect some isolated observation or intuition. This is presented as a starting point for investigation, rather than an insight with particular antecedents in economic process and circumstances. A recent textbook exposition of the formalistic approach to international finance explicitly gives 'casual empiricism' as the basis of the axioms on which such theory is constructed (Hallwood and MacDonald 2000: 228–9). But this is not how economic processes are observed. Discussing the testing of business cycle theories, Ralph Hawtrey put the matter as follows:

> The Trade Cycle is an empirical discovery. That is to say, experience first showed periodic fluctuations to occur in the state of trade, and then economists set themselves the task of finding a deductive explanation of the phenomenon ... Theories of the trade cycle have, one and all, been invented *to fit the statistical evidence*. That in itself makes a statistical test to discriminate among them difficult. All those theories which palpably conflict with the known statistics have already been rejected or ought to have been.
>
> (Hawtrey 1927)

Statistical testing (as opposed to the investigation of statistics) therefore needs naive, unworldly theory based on axioms, intuitions, or casual observations, to determine which uninformed insight is in 'palpable conflict' with the known statistics. Formalism supplies such theory.

The rapid growth in the scope and detail of economic statistics, and the increasing availability and ease of computing facilities, have removed the constraints of 'common sense' (appeal to personal experience) on the inclination of methodological formalism to abstract itself from reality. The early pioneers of statistics, up to Kuznets in our time, were willing simply to examine statistics for revealed regularities. From the 1970s onwards, econometrics has emerged to rescue methodological formalism from its apparent isolation from empirical reality, without threatening its essential method of deduction from axioms. Typically, many axioms, such as rationality or optimisation, cannot be observed. However, statistical regularities may be deduced from them. The view that a fall in the price of capital relative to other 'factors of production' should give rise to an increase in fixed capital investment, suggests inverse movements of capital price and investment statistics. The predictive power of formalistic 'economic models' is thereby supposed to indicate the realism of their assumptions and axioms.

But statistical testing also needs to presuppose the theoretical innocence of statistics. Unlike the conjectures of methodological formalism, statistics are supposed to emerge from the economic process without any theoretical antecedents, and therefore be capable of validating economic theories in general, and formalist hypotheses in particular. This is most apparent in the notion of Granger Causality, which assumes that direct knowledge of economic processes cannot be conclusive. Instead, lagged correlations of time-series data reveal causal influences by antecedent data series (Granger 1963). However, statistics not only reflect social priorities. (We have lots of financial statistics but relatively poor data on poverty, unemployment or the distribution of income.) They also result from the application of prior economic theory, without which the classification of economic events or transactions is impossible.

Raw economic data may be considered as an array of economic observations, $X$:

$$x_1, x_2, x_3, \ldots x_{\infty-1}, x_{\infty}.$$

The array is infinite and is not complete until the end of time. Although infinite, the array is not random. It is ordered by the historical evolution of the economy, the circulation of money and commodities in it, and the human perception of these processes which arises out of people's involvement in production, distribution and consumption.

The practice of statistics consists of arranging $X$ into finite sets $X^s$ in such a way that the categories of $X^s$ are related by some function $f(s)$ (cf. Morgenstern 1963: 88–92). In creating finite sets, it is obviously necessary to include in $f(s)$ some limiting postulate to exclude observations outside a defined range. $f(s)$ is therefore a taxonomy that is not derived from a consideration of the whole of $X$ but is imposed on it. In this respect, $f(s)$ corresponds to a Kantian metaphysic. Its variables (categories) are those which the statistician deems to provide a comprehensive coverage of observations which he or she wishes to present in a systematic and reduced form.

Whereas the purpose of a statistical model is to present a comprehensive set of data in its range, economic theory is selective. Its purpose is to 'explain' by identifying certain variables (categories) as active, determining variables (cf. Vercelli 1992). For this some kind of causal analysis is necessary. Statistical verification of the theory, whether by casual inspection or by econometrics, consists of testing the model against the statistical representation of the selected variables.

A fundamental problem now arises because of the ambiguity of the relationship between the economic model and $f(s)$. Where the relationship that an economic theory postulates between its selected variables corresponds to $f(s)$, it will be confirmed by the data $X^s$. However, this merely shows that the economic theory and the statistical model are not independent, but that the theory is mathematically implied in the model used to place $X$ into finite sets $X^s$. (cf.'… the System is formulated in terms of the System itself' (Veblen 1898).)

Here the procedure of statistical verification breaks down. Even the most analytical economic theory has its verification reduced to circularity by such testing. At best such testing can show that an economic model is compatible with the statistical taxonomy. As a precaution against this circularity, the principled investigator may go beyond current econometric practice and try to prove that an economic model is independent of the statistical model. Since the two models share the same variables, one way of proving the models' independence would be to compare the variables predicted by the economic model with those obtained from the statistical model. The test of independence then would be the absence of a correlation between predicted values and the statistical values. Unfortunately this would also indicate that the economic model is not verified by the statistical data. Thus it is not possible to verify any economic theory by means of statistics because any compatibility between them could be due to the coincidence of the derived economic model with the statistical taxonomy according to which observed data are arranged. Kalecki's wry remark that 'economics consists of theoretical laws which nobody has verified and empirical laws which nobody can explain' (Steindl 1965: 18) highlights a profound methodological dilemma, first expressed in Kant's distinction between analytic and synthetic propositions.

## 4. Formalism, finance and uncertainty

The rise of formalism in economics may be linked to the emergence of economics as an academic discipline, and the envy with which physics, progenitor of nuclear weapons and space travel, came to be regarded by less mathematically developed disciplines. While the dignity of its profession may be a factor in the ambition and amour propre of academic economists, a more objective influence has been the rise of finance. Increasing financial intermediation, and growing inflows of funds into capital and securities markets have given rise to escalating asset values and rapid financial innovation. Financial inflation encourages formalism by vastly increasing the amount, if not the range, of statistical data which may be the subject of formalistic calculation, and, by augmenting the wealth that depends upon unstable future financial conjunctures, intensifying the uncertainty from which formalism offers psychic relief.

The acceleration of financial innovation is notable in the development of new instruments such as financial futures. Modern information and communications technology facilitates enormously the recording and manipulation of price data on these new instruments, as well as on older financial assets. The very availability of vast amounts of data, and the ease with which they may be manipulated, give enormous scope for apparently rigorous research, reiterating the testing of 'hypotheses' using different data sets and correlation tests. In fact, far from inducing a higher 'rigour' the production each day of more new data offers a new life and new possibilities of testing to all hypotheses. Were data to be demonstrably inconsistent with some hypothesis, new data or some new statistical technique may still support it. In this way, the research life of hypotheses is extended rather than abbreviated by the new rigour. This offers enormous scope for academic economists to span the divide that separates them from practical men, by enslaving themselves to defunct economists.

A second feature of financial inflation is financial instability, as large money inflows into financial markets cause asset price booms and undermine the authorities' control over financial markets. Since conventional opinion determines the optimal distribution of assets in a portfolio, increases in prices of conventionally favoured assets tend to be exaggerated, to the detriment of conventionally disfavoured assets (Keynes 1936, chapter 12). Such disparities in the evolution of asset prices are exacerbated when investment funds mature, and can only increase the proportion of conventionally favoured assets in their portfolios by selling disfavoured assets (Toporowski 2000: 88). Moreover, under the influence of monetarist ideas, the increased frequency and magnitude of changes in short-term interest rates has also enhanced financial instability.

Such volatility of course leads to greater Keynesian uncertainty (lack of complete and certain knowledge of the future), because of the wider range of financial conjunctures that may possibly occur in the future. As financial inflation raises the value of financial claims and liabilities relative to current income, it arouses poignant concerns about future values and the implied portfolio adjustments that should, perhaps, now be made. Will capital gains be sustained, or their increase be sufficiently great and liquid to meet financial liabilities? If not, should assets be immediately liquidated? Will future liabilities rise or fall? These questions, to which there is no certain answer, become more urgent as financial inflation raises the possible gain or loss from ephemeral market conjunctures. The only certainty is that the present conjuncture in the markets will shortly come to an end. Moreover, market efficiency is never perfect so that portfolio and liability adjustments exacerbate instability. Emulatory competition in financial markets increases the impact of such adjustments.

In his *Treatise on Probability*, Keynes was careful to distinguish the calculus of probability from the investigation of causes, even where such causal knowledge forms the basis of 'objective probability' as Cournot had argued (Keynes 1921: 164–6, 302–4). By the 1930s, Keynes had become convinced that the 'weight of arguments' rather than calculated probability was the main factor underpinning 'conventional' expectations in the financial markets (ibid., chapter 6; Keynes 1936: 148–9). By 'weight of argument' Keynes meant that 'one argument has more *weight* than another if it is based upon a greater amount of relevant evidence' (Keynes 1921: 77). The respective weights of the arguments indicate the terms upon which a conventional expectation is determined rationally, in the face of uncertainty.

New financial statistics, new statistical techniques and new results presented as formalistic models of the economy bring evidence that adds weight to the arguments of those models. That added weight gives bankers, fund managers and corporate investors 'confidence' in the future outcomes indicated by those models. Option and futures pricing models are direct uses of formalism in the markets. Another is in the ritual by which the Bank of England's economists present probability distributions of future inflation to the Monetary Policy Committee to bolster its members' confidence in their conjectures. Similarly, hedge fund managers use formalistic models to develop complex portfolio diversification strategies. Allaying financial inflation-induced uncertainty by such apparently 'scientific' predictions, is not a recent practice. During the 1920s stock market boom, senior economists at Harvard established the Harvard Economic Society to provide 'scientific' advice to those participants in the markets who were overawed at the success of those markets. Through the 1929 Crash, and for the next three years as the US economy slid into the Great Depression, the Society published optimistic forecasts, until it finally followed its customers into dissolution (Galbraith 1980: 71, 145–6).

In a perfectly rational world, formalistic models and statistical tests would be carefully analysed for their consistency, insights and comparison of their analytical conclusions with day-to-day developments. Over time each model would be extended and would have its errors corrected. Indeed, the 'monetarist counter-revolution' of the 1970s was followed by considerable debate on the predictive powers of mainframe computer-based Keynesian and monetarist models of the economy. Since then, technological innovation allows models to be set up and tailored to specific requirements on personal computers, so that almost daily, new models, new statistics and new results appear. Moreover, with financial markets destabilised by inflation, everyday brings a new conjuncture with new arguments in search of 'weight' to support them. While an individual economist, or research institute, may, by developing arguments and correcting errors, systematically and cumulatively build up analysis and insight, public and market discussion concentrates on novelties ('news'). Far from enlightening market participants, the most rigorous and well-thought-out formalism loses its literal meaning and appears in the marketplace as 'statsbabble' ('the process by which economic and financial statistics, shorn of their methodological limitations, are propelled around the market by traders using them to arouse speculative intents and desires' (Toporowski 2000: 41)). Fischer Black pointed out that his Black-Scholes model of option pricing was widely used despite its unrealistic assumptions (Black 1989). His more realistic version (ibid.) did not arouse particular interest or use comparable with its predecessor.

In the Babel of modern academic economics, theories are compared in textbooks. But a comparative discussion of the various models, statistics and results reflecting different schools of thought in economics is rarely the starting point of theoretical development (cf. Dow 1996: 19–21; Chick 1995). In any case, any serious comparative discussion can only be ephemeral or marginal to current affairs, because tomorrow will bring a fresh crop of results and economic anxieties to be allayed. In such circumstances, the search for consistency and comprehensively systematic exposition, the hallmark of Victoria Chick's economic thought, appears pedantic and impractical. One expects it from naive, serious-minded Ph.D. students and junior academics with intellectual ambitions, but it is hardly of immediate relevance to today's concerns. Fortunately for the reputation of the profession, the most prestigious academic journals are those giving most 'weight' to today's arguments; and formalism can now supply prodigious evidence for such weight virtually on demand. Publishing pressure and ambition are therefore usually enough to bring those Ph.D. students and junior colleagues into line with what is expected of economists today.

## Note

1  I am grateful to Victoria Chick, for a preliminary discussion of the view presented here and her comments on successive drafts, and to her student Rogerio Studart, with whom I first discussed how financial inflation increases the anguish of uncertainty. Thanks are also due to Stephen Dunn, Alan Freeman, Gary Mongiovi, Warren Samuels and the editors of this volume for pointing out errors and ambiguities.

## References

Backhouse, R. E. (1998) 'If Mathematics is Informal, Then Perhaps We Should Accept That Economics Must Be Informal Too', *Economic Journal* 108(451) pp. 1848–1858.

Black, F. (1989) 'How to Use the Holes in Black-Scholes', *The Continental Bank Journal of Applied Corporate Finance* 1(1).

Chick, V. (1995) ' "Order out of Chaos" in Economics', in S. C. Dow and J. Hillard (eds), *Keynes, Knowledge and Uncertainty*. Aldershot: Edward Elgar.

Chick, V. (1998) 'On Knowing One's Place: The Role of Formalism in Economics', *Economic Journal* 108(451) pp. 1859–1869.

Dow, S. C. (1996) *The Methodology of Macroeconomic Thought: A Conceptual Analysis of Schools of Thought in Economics*. Cheltenham: Edward Elgar.

Friedman, M. (1953) *Essays in Positive Economics*. Chicago: University of Chicago Press.

Galbraith, J. K. (1980) *The Great Crash 1929*. London: André Deutsch.

Golland, L. A. (1996) 'Formalism in Economics', *Journal of the History of Economic Thought*. 18(1) pp. 1–12.

Granger, C. W. J. (1963) 'Testing for Causality: A Personal Viewpoint', *Journal of Economic Dynamics and Control*, No. 2.

Hallwood, C. P. and MacDonald, R. (2000) *International Money and Finance*. Oxford: Blackwell.

Hawtrey, R. G. (1927) 'The Monetary Theory of the Trade Cycle and Its Statistical Test', *Quarterly Journal of Economics*, May pp. 471–486.

Kalecki, M. (1971) *Selected Essays on the Dynamics of the Capitalist Economy 1933–1971*. Cambridge, UK: Cambridge University Press.

Kant, I. (1943) *Critique of Pure Reason*, translated by J. M. D. Meiklejohn. New York: Wiley.

Keynes, J. M. (1921) *Treatise on Probability*. London: Macmillan.

Keynes, J. M. (1936) *The General Theory of Employment, Interest and Money*. London: Macmillan.

Kregel, J. A. (1995) 'Neoclassical Price Theory, Institutions, and the Evolution of Securities Market Organization', *Economic Journal* 105.

Lange, O. (1938) 'On the Economic Theory of Socialism', in B. E. Lippincott (ed.), *On the Economic Theory of Socialism*. Minneapolis: University of Minnesota Press.

Lawson, T. (1996) *Economics and Reality*. London: Routledge.

Marshall, A. (1938) *Principles of Economics*. London: Macmillan.

Mirowski, P. (1989) *More Heat than Light*. New York and Cambridge: Cambridge University Press.

Morgenstern, O. (1963) *On the Accuracy of Economic Observation*. Princeton, NJ, Princeton University Press.

Pareto, V. (1909) *Manuel d'économie Politique*, translated by A. Bonnet. Paris: Giard & Brière.

Schumpeter, J. A. (1954) *History of Economic Analysis*. London: Allen and Unwin.

Sohn-Rethel, A. (1978) *Intellectual and Manual Labour: A Critique of Epistemology*. London: Macmillan.

Steindl, J. (1965) *Random Processes and the Growth of Firms*. London: Charles Griffin.

Toporowski, J. (2000) *The End of Finance: The Theory of Capital Market Inflation, Financial Derivatives and Pension Fund Capitalism*. London: Routledge.

Veblen, T. (1898) 'Why is Economics Not an Evolutionary Science?' *The Quarterly Journal of Economics* Vol. XII, No. 4, July, pp. 373–397.

Veblen, T. (1904) *The Theory of Business Enterprise*. New York: Charles Scribner's Sons.

Vercelli, A. (1992) 'Causality and Economic Analysis: A Survey', in A. Vercelli and N. Dimitri (eds), *Macroeconomics: A Survey of Research Strategies*. Oxford: Oxford University Press.

# 10

# THE ENCOMPASSING PRINCIPLE AS AN EMERGING METHODOLOGY FOR POST-KEYNESIAN ECONOMICS

*Giuseppe Fontana and Bill Gerrard*

## 1. Chick and the coherence debate in post-Keynesian economics

Chick (1995) argues that post-Keynesian economics (PKE) should be viewed '…as a way of thinking, a method of approach, inspired at root by Keynes and Kalecki and their intellectual successors' (p. 22). She maintains that it is the characteristic PK mode of thought that provides coherence to PKE. She identifies three PK methodological principles: realistic abstraction, the economic system as a process in actual historical time and the rejection of individual atomism. Chick concludes that these three principles along with a broad set of theoretical results and policy conclusions constitute PKE.

Chick (1995) helped rekindle the debate on the nature of PKE. Walters and Young (1997) responded to Chick by criticising the notion of PKE as an alternative school of thought. They argue that PKE fails to meet the necessary requisite for an identifiable school of thought, namely, coherence in its methodology, its agenda and its themes. Walters and Young directly contradict Chick by arguing that PKE is characterised by three different and mutually incompatible methodological strategies: critical realism, the Babylonian method and the generalising approach. They conclude that PKE is better seen as a looser association of ideas rather than an alternative (coherent) school of thought. Indeed Walters and Young claim that synthesis is not appropriate for PKE given the fundamental incompatibility of some of its elements.

The question of whether PKE is better viewed as an association or school of thought is not a trivial matter. Walters and Young raise serious issues about the future direction of PKE. The claim that elements of PKE are methodologically inconsistent would seem to fatally undermine the project '…to redevelop the whole of economics along Keynes/Kalecki lines' (Chick 1995: 20). The principal critique of Walters and Young has been provided by Arestis *et al.* (1999). Arestis *et al.* argue that PKE is neither fully coherent nor comprehensive but it does display a clear tendency towards coherence around the central theme of Keynes and

Kalecki that the level of economic activity in a monetary production economy is determined by the level of effective demand. This central theme, in turn, generates the characteristic policy consequence of PKE that maintaining full employment is an institutional problem. Arestis *et al.* contest Walter and Young's claim that PKE lacks coherence at the methodological level. Arestis *et al.* argue that critical realism, the Babylonian method and the generalising approach are just different expressions of the PK commitment to open-systems theorising. The generalising approach is not necessarily incompatible with open-systems theorising as exemplified by Keynes's *General Theory*. The openness of the economic system implies that theories can only be general in an axiomatic sense but not in any historical sense. Theories of open systems are always historically specific and are not universally applicable across economies and over time. 'Good theories are relevant abstractions, and relevance alters as history moves on' (Chick 1983: 2).

Rotheim (1999) also makes the case for the coherence of PKE at both the methodological and theoretical levels. Rotheim specifically argues for critical realism as a viable philosophical foundation for PKE that adds coherence to the PK scientific programme and underpins the body of substantive PK economic doctrines. However, the critical realist interpretation of PKE as developed by Rotheim, following Lawson (1994), tends to reject outright any possibility of constructive engagement between PKE and mainstream economics. Critical realists tend to consider neoclassical economics as methodologically incommensurable with open-systems theorising, because the former uses a priori formal analytical methods.

The arguments of Lawson and Rotheim show a fundamental attachment to the 'PKE-as-*anti-thesis*' view that PKE represents the complete rejection of neoclassical economics, thereby obviating the need for any constructive engagement between PK economists and their neoclassical counterparts. But such a view seems to run counter to Keynes's famous claim in the *General Theory* that classical theory is a special case that comes back into its own at the point that full employment is re-established. Furthermore, the complete rejection of any specific theoretical approach, whether neoclassical or non-mainstream, seems to be inconsistent with an espousal of open-systems theorising. To question the universal relevance of neoclassical economics (as Keynes did regarding its applicability to the problem of involuntary unemployment) does not imply the universal *irrelevance* of neoclassical economics. Indeed a commitment to open-systems theorising represents the rejection of all universal theoretical propositions other than the universal meta-theoretical proposition of non-universality. The arguments of Lawson and Rotheim are representative of an important strand in PKE that rejects any constructive engagement with more mainstream approaches.

The objective of the present contribution to the ongoing coherence debate in PKE is to argue that the encompassing principle provides an appropriate characterisation of the PK way of thought. Furthermore, it is argued that acceptance of the encompassing principle encompasses both the critical realist commitment to open-systems theorising and the scientific imperative to constructively engage with more mainstream approaches to economic theory in order to determine limits to their domains of relevance. Keynes's *General Theory* is seen as providing a classic exemplar of how to encompass existing orthodox theories. Chick's own work, particularly in monetary economics, represents a good modern PK exemplar of encompassing in practice.

## 2. The encompassing principle in abstract

The encompassing principle is the methodological proposition that causal processes are potentially complex and, hence, it follows that progress in the understanding of causal processes requires: (i) the identification of the limits to the domains of relevance of existing theoretical models; and (ii) the development of more general models that encompass the existing models in a synthesis with new models to extend the domains of relevance.

The encompassing principle provides an expression of the two principal methodological characteristics of PKE – realism and open-systems theorising. The encompassing principle is based on a realistic conception of the aim of analysis as the explanation of causal processes. The importance of realistic explanations is a recurrent theme in PK writings as evidenced by Chick's recognition of the principle of realistic abstraction as the first methodological principle of PKE. The encompassing principle is also based on an open-systems approach in that the object of analysis is conceptualised as potentially complex, necessitating the need for general theoretical models to explain the different dimensions of the causal processes. The need for PKE to employ a range of different models has been variously termed 'horses for courses', the Babylonian method and the generalising approach. Lawson (1994) and Rotheim (1999) argue that critical realism provides the appropriate methodological approach for PKE that combines both realism and open-systems theorising. However, in contrast to the encompassing principle, there is a tendency in the critical realism literature to reject outright any constructive engagement between PKE and mainstream economics on grounds of methodological incommensurability.

The theoretical understanding of an open system presupposes a meta-theoretical understanding of the nature of analytical methods when applied to open-systems theorising. Analysis involves the abstract formalisation of a closed theoretical system consisting of a set of axioms and assumptions and the application of logical methods. Analytical methods always involve a set of closure assumptions. Open-systems theorising does not imply the rejection of formal analytical methods such as mathematics and econometrics. Rather open-systems theorising requires that formal analytical methods must only be used with an awareness of the temporary nature of the closure assumptions. Model builders must recognise that the closure assumptions are analytically necessary but temporary and must be relaxed in order to determine the limits to the relevance of any specific theoretical model.

General theoretical models emerge as the synthesis of alternative specific models based on different sets of closure assumptions. The development of a theoretical synthesis may not be a purely logical process of extending and amalgamating existing specific models. A synthesis may require fundamental changes in the conceptualisation of the phenomena under analysis representing a Kuhnian paradigm shift. The intuitive leap will involve the identification of previously tacit closure assumptions incorporated within the basic analytical language of the existing theoretical models.

The term 'encompassing' derives from the LSE approach to econometrics associated with Hendry (Gilbert 1986, 1989). Hendry's econometric methodology is characterised by the search for well-specified, parsimonious empirical models that are grounded in economic theory and provide congruent representations of the underlying data generating processes (DGPs). Given that the 'true' structure of any DGP is unknown, there exists the potential for a multiplicity of empirical models. Encompassing seeks to resolve the proliferation of rival empirical models by requiring any given model to account for the results obtained by other models. Hence Hendry treats encompassing as an additional diagnostic test in the specification search. Hendry's notion of encompassing is usefully termed 'empirical' or 'quantitative' encompassing. It attempts to operationalise the concept of 'scientific progress' in terms of the development of more general empirical models with an ever-increasing range of empirical applicability (Cook 1999). Empirical encompassing is a specific application of the encompassing principle that is consistent with a more general notion of encompassing. Empirical encompassing may be the consequence of a whole spectrum of different types of theoretical developments ranging from relatively minor logical extensions of existing models through to fundamental conceptual changes, paradigm shifts and scientific revolutions.

The exemplar *par excellence* of the encompassing principle in economics is Keynes's *General Theory*. Keynes considered classical theory to be a special case. He sought to determine the limits to its relevance by identifying its fundamental tacit assumptions. Keynes formalised classical theory in terms of two fundamental postulates that provide, respectively, the profit-maximising condition for labour demand by firms and the utility-maximising condition for labour supply by households. Together these two fundamental postulates constitute the demand-and-supply theory of the aggregate labour market and imply an automatic tendency of the economic system to the full-employment equilibrium. As a consequence, classical theory is only concerned with the problem of allocating scarce resources between competing ends. As Keynes recognised, classical theory provides the laws governing the application of, and rewards to, fully employed resources.

Keynes deemed classical theory as a valid and necessary part of the apparatus of thought for understanding the allocative process. But, as Keynes argued, the classical allocative conceptualisation of the economic system could only allow for frictional and voluntary unemployment. Frictional unemployment results from the various imperfections in the allocative process that cause temporary resource misallocation preventing the attainment of the full-employment equilibrium. Voluntary unemployment occurs as a consequence of the labour supply allocation decisions of households (including the effects of any nominal wage rigidity arising from collective bargaining).

For Keynes, the relevance of classical theory is limited to the understanding of allocative (i.e. frictional and voluntary) unemployment. Classical theory could not allow for involuntary unemployment due to non-allocative causes. Hence Keynes attempted to develop a more general theory of the economic system that allowed for both allocative and non-allocative causes of unemployment. Keynes's more general theory encompasses classical theory by relaxing the key closure assumption of Say's Law that supply creates its own demand. Say's Law is the proposition that an allocative economy generates sufficient aggregate demand to sustain the full-employment level of aggregate supply. Classical theory formalised this proposition in the loanable funds theory with the rate of interest as the allocative mechanism ensuring that investment equals savings. Keynes's revolutionary insight is that aggregate demand and, in turn, the aggregate level of resource utilisation are not determined by an allocative process. Rather he proposed the principle of effective demand and the multiplier process as the appropriate utilisation theory of the determination of the aggregate level of employment. This generated the fundamental Keynesian proposition that the economic system could be in equilibrium with involuntary unemployment.

Keynes's method is best described as the encompassing principle (Gerrard 1992, 1997). Keynes did not reject classical theory *per se* but rather rejected its tacit claim to be the only appropriate way of conceptualising economic behaviour. Keynes moved beyond the basic classical allocative conceptualisation of economic analysis to encompass a dualistic conceptualisation of the economic problem as both scarcity and utilisation. Keynes rejected classical theory as a theory of aggregate resource utilisation. But he argued that classical theory comes back into its own when full employment is established. At this point the utilisation problem is resolved and the economic system faces a resource allocation problem only. Indeed Keynes himself adopted the allocative approach to provide an alternative theory of the rate of interest to replace the loanable funds theory. Keynes's liquidity preference theory models the rate of interest as the price mechanism that regulates the financial portfolio allocation process. Keynes's *General Theory* can be viewed as the construction of a *post-classical synthesis* that encompasses classical theory within a more general theory that allows for multiple conceptualisations of economic behaviour (Gerrard 1989). However, mainstream Keynesian economics has retained a purely classical conceptualisation of the economic system. This has resulted in the development of imperfectionist theories of unemployment focusing on the effects of price and wage rigidities. Hence mainstream Keynesian theories of unemployment would be regarded by Keynes as theories of allocative unemployment. In contrast, an appropriate interpretation of PKE is that it is the continuing development of the post-classical synthesis originally outlined by Keynes in the *General Theory* (Gerrard 1995).

PKE is characterised by the belief that Keynes demonstrated the limitations of mainstream theories. PKE emphasises the principle of effective demand and Keynes's analysis of time and uncertainty as representing fundamental departures from neoclassical economics. But there has been a tendency for PKE to deny any relevance to mainstream theories as, for example, in the case of PK advocates of critical realism (e.g. Lawson 1994; Rotheim 1999). But this is not in the spirit of Keynes and represents a repudiation of Keynes's contention that classical theory is relevant for understanding allocative behaviour. The complete rejection of allocative theorising restricts the development of the understanding of economic behaviour. It prevents consideration of the interactions between allocative and non-allocative modes of behaviour. It also tends to be associated with the interpretation of open-systems theorising as a repudiation of formal analytical methods. This could be interpreted as amounting to intellectual nihilism that leads to efforts being concentrated on the negative task of critique and the discussion of methodological alternatives with little in the way of formal development of new, more general and more relevant theories.

The tendency to restrict PKE to methodological critique is apparent in Lawson (1994) when he suggests that critical realism may require PKE to '... jettison (or at least moderate) any claim to being a body of specific substantive economic doctrine at all' (p. 507). For Lawson, critical realism provides a perspective for a better critical interpretation and understanding of economics but does not itself constitute economics. Hence Lawson's critical realism implies that the principal (and possible sole) contribution of PKE is the outright rejection of neoclassical economics *as a method*.

Rotheim (1999) adopts a wider perspective on PKE as both a critical realist methodology and a body of general (not specific) substantive economic doctrines. But this wider perspective leads Rotheim to extend the outright rejection of neoclassical economics at both the methodological and theoretical levels. But the rejection of neoclassical theory is not a necessary implication of the critical realist methodological critique of the neoclassical tendency to treat its character-istic closure assumptions as a priori universals. Rather an open-systems perspec-tive requires that the appropriateness of neoclassical closure assumptions in specific contexts must be critically examined. To deem a priori that neoclassical closure assumptions are never valid is a form of universal closure rejected by crit-ical realism. Indeed Rotheim hints at the potential problems in extending critical realism to substantive theoretical and empirical issues when he recognises that those PK economists concerned with public policy may be forced to part com-pany with the critical realist perspective (p. 101). It is a strange kind of realism that is incompatible with practical policy formulation given the need for effective policy proposals to be grounded on an adequate understanding of the causal structure of the economic system.

Given the close association of critical realism with the complete rejection of neoclassical economics both methodologically and theoretically, it seems more appropriate to use the encompassing principle as the appropriate expression of the methodological basis for PKE. The encompassing principle is consistent with both the critical realist commitment to open-systems theorising and a much more thorough and constructive engagement between PKE and more mainstream approaches at the theoretical level.

## 3. The encompassing principle in practice: Money circulating vs money held

The writings of Chick represent a modern exemplar of the encompassing principle in practice. She uses Keynes's writings (especially the *General Theory*) as a way to develop a general framework that can encompass existing models. From her perspective Keynes provides a base camp from which 'a far richer understanding of the structure of macroeconomic interactions and methods' (Chick 1983: v) can be developed. Chick gives the fullest expression to this methodological approach in her monetary writings.

Chick (1992b) views monetary economics in terms of two main traditions: 'money circulating' and 'money held' approaches. The first tradition is part of the classical paradigm. It emphasises the role of money as medium of exchange and unit of account and seems to have died out in the 1930s. The second tradition is the portfolio-theoretic approach of Hicks (1982), developed by Tobin (1969) and 'capital asset pricing model' theorists. Money is just one of several financial assets in the portfolio of agents. Asset prices adjust to equalise the risk-adjusted returns from money and all other assets held in a diversified portfolio.

Chick laments that, although old and modern contributors to those monetary traditions have proposed interesting arguments to defend their views, little progress has been made because the debate has evolved in a dichotic form. Theories have been proposed on the tacit assumption that money is either continuously changing hands as a medium of exchange or held permanently as a financial asset in the portfolio of agents. She argues that concentration on one or another aspect of money necessarily results in adopting a particular method of analysis. The specific conceptualisation of money as the object of study is inextricably linked with the choice of method of analysis. However, monetary economists have often failed to come to terms with this relationship.

Chick considers the continuing debate between general equilibrium system theorists and their critics on whether or not money can be incorporated into that system. Her answer to is: no, it cannot, and to debate it is a waste of intellectual effort. The formal necessity of the static general equilibrium system requires a commodity numeraire, i.e. the numeraire is accounting rather than actual money. Money as it is known in the real world has no role in the static general equilibrium system. Chick advocates an alternative, more constructive approach:

> Apart from minimising the amount of talk at cross-purposes which so bedevils this field, there is another potential benefit from the explicit concern with deeper structure: if we dismantle the theories carefully, we

stand to gain possession of serviceable building-blocks with which to construct new theories suited to new problems or a changed universe, consciously deciding which pieces to use and which to discard.

(Chick 1992b: 121)

According to the 'money circulating' approach (e.g. the quantity theory), money is a medium of exchange which facilitates the circulation of goods and services. Money is a means to an end. There are two main implications of that view. First, money does not have use value but only exchange value. Second, holdings of money are exclusively represented by the transactions demand for money. As Chick explains those are not trivial implications, especially considering that the transactions demand for money has always been modelled as an end-of-period stock demand, but only makes sense over time (Chick 1992b: 128).

The 'money held' approach has dominated the analysis of monetary policy. Money is a store of wealth, just one of many assets in agents' portfolios. Comparative static analysis shows how asset prices, rates of interest and the composition of agents' portfolios are modified following a change in the money supply. Unfortunately, what is not explained in this literature is how those portfolio adjustments are ever attained. But, as Chick argues, this analysis is seriously flawed by its lack of explanation of the actual portfolio-adjustment process (Chick 1992b: 124). Such an explanation would highlight the problem of treating money held in isolation from money circulating. In any portfolio-adjustment process, money acts as a medium of exchange for buying and selling assets.

Chick's approach to Keynes and the PK school is based on the proposition that Keynes can be seen as a bridge between the two different monetary traditions. Keynes was concerned with money as both medium of exchange and store of wealth. However, in order to understand the particular type of bridge that he represents (one not readily suitable for modern times as she argues), Keynes's theory needs to be carefully 'dismantled' and then reorganised around its building blocks.

One of the main features of Keynes's theory is the interdependence of money and uncertainty. It was clear to Keynes that agents make decisions in a context of incomplete knowledge. Uncertainty is both a cause and an effect of agents holding money as a store of wealth. Similarly, it is again uncertainty that makes money the only medium of exchange that could possibly be used as the final means of payment.

Keynes maintained that economic behaviour is determined by: (i) the probability distribution representing agents' strength of belief in a set of competing hypotheses about the current and future state of the world; and (ii) the degree of confidence of agents as reflected in their assessment of the evidential base from which competing hypotheses and strength of belief are derived. The complex interaction of these two determinants of economic behaviour establishes a general taxonomy of choice situations that includes the analytical case of perfect certainty and risk as well as the alternative analytical case of fundamental uncertainty (Fontana and Gerrard 1999).

In extending the analysis of uncertainty beyond a narrow focus on risk, Keynes demonstrates that agents only possess beliefs about the nature of the world and face difficulties in discerning what the future holds. Viewed as human deficiency, the ignorance of agents about the future remains an insurmountable problem. In the course of making decisions, agents will *always* be in possession of limited knowledge. It is in this sense that Keynes saw uncertainty as a systemic feature of modern economies.

Economic reality is changed by agents through their ongoing engagement in the decision-making process. Viewed as endowed with the ability to be both proactive and reactive, agents simultaneously create and reduce the problem of uncertainty via essentially organic interaction with each other. Reality must be conceptualised as an open system, which may be transformed either partially or completely through the aggregated effects of the decisions of agents.

If uncertainty is such a systematic feature of modern economies, it was Keynes's belief that a general analysis of the effects that uncertainty has on economic behaviour would allow for an understanding of the complex nature and roles of money. Money as medium of exchange facilitates the circulation of goods and services. In an increasingly complex world this is an important role of money. It widens the boundaries of contemporaneous exchange of good and services. Of course, while being a medium of exchange is an essential property of money, it is not unique to money. In fact, it is a property shared by several financial instruments. Any private claim that allows a transaction to go ahead is a medium of exchange. For instance, trade credit can play that role, and in modern economies increasingly does it. But there is an important difference between money and other mediums of exchange such as consumer and trade credit (Chick 1992a,c). While the latter allows a transaction to go ahead, it is only with the former that the completion of an exchange is realised. When sellers receive money in return for goods and services, unlike with other forms of medium of exchange, they know that they now possess a valid claim for current or future commodities.

Money as the means of final payments plays an important role in PKE. Money allows agents to accomplish transactions in the pursuit of their objectives. It is the flow of purchasing power for financing working capital, consumption expenditure and financial transactions (Chick 2000). The monetary analysis of money as means of final payment seeks to uncover the causal sequence that characterises the production and the circulation of commodities. It highlights the nature of the relationship between firms, banks and households (Fontana 2000).

Money is also a store of wealth. It provides the possibility of postponing expenditure decisions, in that way securing agents with some degree of independence between income and consumption. But money is a barren asset. Why should agents wish to hold money as store of wealth, whereas there is practically a multitude of other forms of storing wealth that yield interest or profit? Keynes asked a similar question to his critics in the aftermath of the publication of the *General Theory*. The answer lies in the complex role of money. Money is a store of wealth (as many other assets), but it is also, and distinguishedly, an immediate claim on resources to be used as soon as circumstances prove it profitable. As Hicks used to say, money is liquidity and liquidity is freedom (Hicks 1979: 94). When agents hold assets rather than money, they diminish their freedom. They expose themselves to the risk of being unable to respond to future opportunities. This is a very serious risk for firms, but the general rule about liquidity applies equally well to households.

The prevailing rate of interest is the standard against which firms measure the marginal efficiency of capital. An investment is worth undertaking only if the expected yield is higher than the current rate of interest. But in a world of uncertainty, as time goes on and capital accumulates, there is no guarantee that the rate of interest would fall sufficiently to ensure that there is adequate investment to sustain full employment. The economic system can settle in equilibrium at any level of output and employment. Similarly, households at any time may decide to postpone some of their consumption expenditure until they acquire better knowledge of needs and opportunities. Holding money is a potential demand for commodities. But firms are uncertain about the timing and composition of the actualisation of that demand as future consumer expenditure. Indeed, it may forever remain a potential demand. In short, any increase in the demand for money as a store of wealth brings about a decline in consumption and investment, and hence a negative effect on the level of output and employment.

## 4. Concluding remarks

We have argued that the encompassing principle provides an operational method for developing the PK research project. After years of methodological debate on the proper nature of economic theory, PKE is finally developing a body of substantive theory within a general framework that can constructively engage with mainstream theories. Those PK economists who wish to maintain a scholastic purity untainted by orthodox theories will dismiss such developments as a misguided attempt to gain legitimacy. Nevertheless, it is time to realise that what PKE needs most is substantive theories utilising formal analytical methods but with full awareness of the temporary closure assumptions underpinning specific models. The hope is that the task of developing a more general understanding of actual economic processes is continued by current and future generations of economists with the same flair and enthusiasm as that displayed by Chick over her long and distinguished career.

## References

Arestis, P., Dunn, S. P. and Sawyer, M. (1999) 'Post Keynesian Economics and Its Critics', *Journal of Post Keynesian Economics* 21: 527–49.
Chick, V. (1983) *Macroeconomics After Keynes: A Reconsideration of the General Theory.* Oxford: Philip Allan.

Chick, V. (1992a) 'Unresolved Questions in Monetary Theory: A Critical Review', in P. Arestis and S. Dow (eds), *On Money, Method and Keynes: Selected Essays of Victoria Chick*. London: Macmillan.

Chick, V. (1992b) 'On the Structure of the Theory of Monetary Policy – Part I: Money Circulating v. Money Held', in P. Arestis and S. Dow (eds), *On Money, Method and Keynes: Selected Essays of Victoria Chick*. London: Macmillan.

Chick, V. (1992c) 'Money', in P. Arestis and S. Dow (eds), *On Money, Method and Keynes: Selected Essays of Victoria Chick*. London: Macmillan.

Chick, V. (1995) 'Is There a Case for Post Keynesian Economics?', *Scottish Journal of Political Economy* 42: 20–36.

Chick, V. (2000) 'Money and Effective Demand', in J. Smithin (ed.), *What is Money?* London: Routledge.

Cook, S. (1999) 'Methodological Aspects of the Encompassing Principle', *Journal of Economic Methodology* 6: 61–78.

Fontana, G. (2000) 'Post Keynesians and Circuitists on Money and Uncertainty: An Attempt at Perspective', *Journal of Post Keynesian Economics* 23: 27–48.

Fontana, G. and Gerrard, B. (1999) 'Disequilibrium States and Adjustment Processes: Towards a Historical-Time Analysis of Behaviour Under Uncertainty', in S. Dow and P. Earl (eds), *Contingency, Complexity and the Theory of Firm, Essays in Honour of Brian Loasby*, Vol. 2. Cheltenham: Edward Elgar.

Gerrard, B. (1989) *Theory of the Capitalist Economy: Towards a Post-Classical Synthesis*. Oxford: Blackwell.

Gerrard, B. (1992) 'From *A Treatise on Probability* to the *General Theory*: Continuity or Change in Keynes's Thought?', in B. Gerrard and J. Hillard (eds), *The Philosophy and Economics of J. M. Keynes*. Aldershot: Edward Elgar.

Gerrard, B. (1995) 'Keynes, the Keynesians and the Classics: A Suggested Interpretation', *Economic Journal* 105: 445–58.

Gerrard, B. (1997) 'Method and Methodology in Keynes's *General Theory*', in G. C. Harcourt and P. A. Riach (eds), *A 'Second Edition' of The General Theory*, Vol. 2. London: Routledge.

Gilbert, C. L. (1986) 'Professor Hendry's Methodology', *Oxford Bulletin of Economics and Statistics* 48: 283–307.

Gilbert, C. L. (1989) 'LSE and the British Approach to Time Series Econometrics', *Oxford Economic Papers* 41: 108–28.

Hicks, J. R. (1939) *Value and Capital*. Oxford: Clarendon Press.

Hicks, J. R. (1979) *Causality in Economics*. Oxford: Basil Blackwell.

Hicks, J. R. (1982) 'A Suggestion for Simplifying the Theory of Money', in J. R. Hicks (ed.), *Money, Interest and Wages: Collected Essays on Economic Theory*, Vol. 2. Oxford: Basil Blackwell.

Lawson, T. (1994) 'The Nature of Post Keynesianism and Its Links to Other Traditions: A Realist Perspective', *Journal of Post Keynesian Economics* 16: 503–38.

Rotheim, R. (1999) 'Post Keynesian Economics and Realist Philosophy', *Journal of Post Keynesian Economics* 22: 71–103.

Tobin, J. (1969) 'A General Equilibrium Approach to Monetary Theory', *Journal of Money, Credit and Banking* 1: 15–29.

Walters, B. and Young, D. (1997) 'On the Coherence of Post-Keynesian Economics', *Scottish Journal of Political Economy* 44: 329–49.

# 11

# A NOTE ON NON-WALRASIAN MACROECONOMICS

*Athol Fitzgibbons*

## 1. A brief history of macro-ideas

In the decades after the Second World War, when classical science and big government were most admired, macroeconomic theory meant a set of simultaneous equations that represented the interacting markets. These equations, which were known as the Keynesian synthesis (being a synthesis of Keynes and neoclassical economics), could be econometrically quantified and solved to derive predictions, predictability being one of the admired features of economic science. According to the theory governments were able to adjust such parameters as taxation and the money supply, and thereby attain politically desired levels of national income, employment, interest, etc. Macroeconomic policy, which was called 'fine-tuning', ensured that the capitalist system was a viable alternative to socialism, because deep depressions were no longer a threat.

And yet, there were two dubious assumptions buried in the mathematical fine print of the Keynesian synthesis, which were overlooked so long as the system 'worked'. One assumption was that the markets were irrational, in the sense that they were unable to anticipate a policy-induced inflation, and the other was that government policy makers could precisely exploit this irrational weakness. These assumptions seem somewhat implausible today, but they were no more than good scientific method. Just as the rational scientist could ring the bell and make the irrational dog salivate, so the rational central bank could increase the money supply and make the irrational market drive down the interest rate. Thus science justified the Keynesian policies which, for a quarter of a century, successfully regulated most of the economies of the world.

However, during the 1970s the Keynesian synthesis was faced with a supply-side challenge. Cost pressures from the long postwar technology boom, aggravated by the war in Vietnam, began to substantially increase the prices of labour and resources, including and most spectacularly the price of oil. For the first time high inflation accompanied high unemployment, and the correction of either evil would aggravate the other. At this time the opponents of the Keynesian system, who had

106

hitherto been only a tiny minority of economists, enunciated the methodological flaws upon which the theory depended, namely the above mentioned government infallibility and the money illusion assumptions. To modify these assumptions was to jettison Keynesian theory altogether, and eventually that did happen; Keynesian theory was widely rejected because it lacked credibility. It became evident that, at a time of need, the theory relied *crucially* upon assumptions that were definitely wrong.

For a quarter of a century thereafter the Keynesians wandered in the intellectual wilderness. It was widely accepted that the Keynesian system lacked microfoundations, which meant that it was built on intellectual thin air. But since only Keynesian theory had explained deficient demand – its existence was one of Keynes's main discoveries – deficient demand began to disappear from macroeconomics. New Keynesianism did manage to linger on by emphasising the complexity and detail of the supply side, but the phenomena of aggregate demand, including the business cycle, booms, recessions and crises, were beyond its theoretical scope.

The New Classical economists who supplanted the Keynesians dreamt that if it were possible for everyone to pursue their self-interest, rationally and without interference, then a benevolent Nature would direct their efforts towards the Good. They theorised that the economy was stable of its own accord; that it had a natural rate of unemployment, a natural rate of interest and even – this is my invention, but it does seem to follow from their theory – a natural level of Nasdaq prices. Then as dreams are the precursors to systematic action, the social framework that had supported the Keynesian system was demolished, and steps were taken to create a less regulated and more modern world. Extensive programmes of economic intervention were abandoned, equalitarianism was scaled back, industry assistance was reduced, government enterprises were sold, exchange rates were floated and financial systems were deregulated. At the moral level, self-interest was praised and the virtues that make public life meaningful were devalued; and all this was done with the passion, commitment and feeling of 'rightness' that had once driven the Keynesians.

Unfortunately, excess in one direction encourages excess in the other, and the dream had no basis beyond a semantic confusion. Rational markets (in one sense of the term) would never assume that the markets were rational (in the other sense). Capital markets are mostly driven by self-interest, but they do not have enough information to definitively quantify the future. To put the matter otherwise, and to reply to the New Classical School, ignorance does not cancel out even in the presence of self-interest. Everyone might want to hit the bull's eye and win the prize, but unless the dartboard is clearly visible and stable, the darts will *not* be scattered around a central point.

The New Classical attempt to refute aggregate demand went to an extreme. Just as the Keynesians had assumed that governments could quantify the future, so New Classical theory assumed that the markets could. One exaggeration replaced another, but once again reality came crashing in, all the more so because so many financial markets had been deregulated. All over the globe, deregulated financial markets faithlessly made manifest the errors of the theory that had encouraged their deregulation. They precipitated widespread misery in Eastern Europe, Latin America, Japan and South East Asia, while Western Europe and the US went through a sequence of boom and recession. The more deregulated the economy, the more susceptible it seemed. Just when New Classical theory declared the macroeconomy to be harmonious and tranquil, aggregate demand flew in howling like a banshee in a nightmare.

But now there was no theory of deficient aggregate demand. And since many found that a return to the old Keynesian synthesis and its philosophy of the state was intellectually impossible, the subject of macroeconomics became an intellectual wasteland. The two great macroeconomic systems had both relied on the absolute truth of impossible assumptions, and they had both reached conclusions that were contradicted by everyday experience. New Keynesian theory dominated the textbooks, perhaps because it was a compromise doctrine. But its theory of expectations was incoherent, and it was mostly concerned with the supply side of the product market, whereas the last two decades of the twentieth century were characterised by financial crises. The practical response by macroeconomic policy makers in state treasuries and central banks was to abandon macroeconomic theory, and to rely on 'pragmatism', though this was more as an admission of defeat than a solution. For pragmatism too can mean different things, and pragmatism *without a theory* leaves the policy maker without any systematic way of organising experience and learning from the past.

## 2. The remains of Keynes

The problem today is how to theorise about deficient demand without introducing the government infallibility and money illusion assumptions. It must be possible to explain aggregate demand, and the obvious strategy is to go back to Keynesian theory to the minimum extent possible; the theory need only be whatever the phenomena require and no more. Unfortunately the Keynesian synthesis cannot be separated from its unacceptable knowledge assumptions, and theoretical minimalism involves hiding the evidence.

In his informative and well-written *Return of Depression Economics*, Paul Krugman explained the origin of swings in aggregate demand, and the need for counter cyclical policy, with a parable about a babysitting club. The parable is developed throughout his book. Its members wanted to build up some credit for the future, in case they wanted to go out, but the consequence of this innocent desire was that the demand to babysit exceeded the demand for babysitters. Some members who were driven into deficit were confined to their homes, but eventually the club resolved the crisis by issuing surplus babysitting credits. These cancelled some deficits and satisfied those members who wanted to remain in surplus.

The moral of the parable, which originally concerned a real babysitting club, was that deferred demand could disturb the markets by generating deficient demand or excess supply, even when it arose out of a commendable desire to save and provide for the future. In this case the outcome was a 'recession', which took the form of enforced nights at home, until the club adopted an expansionary 'monetary' policy by issuing purely nominal claims on babysitting in the future.

In theoretical terms the *IS* curve had shifted left because of an increase in the propensity to save, but it could be counteracted by a rightward shift of the *LM* curve which would restore aggregate demand. The parable was advanced to explain macroeconomic crises in Asia and elsewhere.

However, the international capital markets differ in important respects from babysitting clubs. Babysitting clubs tend to be small and manageable enough for the club leadership to know the market, and the warm and fuzzy qualities of babysitting discourage ruthless speculation in babysitting futures. The babysitting parable implicitly invites us to think of rational (knowledgeable) regulators and irrational (not self-interested) markets. But if we take away the warm and fuzzy aspects, the New Classicals could point out that John Stuart Mill explained the fault in the babysitting parable 150 years ago.

Excess demand is a sign of rationing, and the failure to charge market prices. Mill's heirs could respond that the babysitting club did not need a Keynesian monetary policy but a free capital market, which could set a natural rate of interest. In such a market babysitting credits could be exchanged, at a premium or a discount, between those who wanted to babysit now and those who wanted to babysit in the future. If this market were established there would be no deficient demand, because everyone should always be able to babysit, and to get a babysitter, provided only that they were willing to pay the going price.

Furthermore, and to add a New Classical objection to the Keynesian theory of babysitting, the club leadership would not know exactly how many babysitting credits it should issue, and yet if the wrong number were issued there would be serious coordination problems. Too many credits, for example, would lead to a devaluation of the currency, in the sense that more credits would be required to get a babysitter. This would be unfair on those who had painfully acquired their credits and, if there were reason to fear that the club would continue its inflationary policy, everyone would try to spend their credits. In addition there would be a danger of babysitting cronyism, because the club leadership might issue the extra credits to their friends, on the pretext that this was best for the club. In summary the New Classicals could reply that the babysitting club would be best governed by laws, rather than by men and women. The babysitting club could have solved its problems better by relying on the market.

That would not be the end of a real debate, which would continue at much greater length, but it is evident that a Keynesian theory which skims over the question of 'who knows what' is susceptible to attack. The state of knowledge is such a crucial determinant of the stability of the capitalist system that and assumptions about it should be explicit. If there is an important knowledge asymmetry between the government and the capital markets, then it should be justified and explained.

## 3. Non-Walrasian directions

The two reasons why macroeconomic breakdowns occur are that the markets do not have enough information about the future, and that neither do governments.

Milton Friedman (1969) has argued that US macro-failure mostly occurred because of bad government decisions, and (without endorsing his specific argument that the US Federal Reserve was responsible for the Great Depression) it is clear that governments do indeed cause major macroeconomic breakdowns. In my country, in Australia, misconceived government policies have unambiguously caused two recessions, most recently in the early 1990s. However government error is only part of the story, because the late twentieth-century crises in Asia and Latin America were caused by destabilising speculation in the capital markets.

The ultimate cause of macro-breakdowns is neither the market nor the government, but 'future illusion', or the need to make decisions with imperfect knowledge. If someone was omniscient, then it would be profitable for that person to maintain perpetual macro-equilibrium via stabilising speculation, but no one has such omniscience. As for who is the *most* to blame, 'government macro-failure' occurs when the government is in control, whereas 'market macro-failure' occurs when the markets are unregulated and free. Error does not mean that either side is incompetent, and decision makers are usually rational in the sense that they try to make intelligent decisions on the basis of the available information, but that information does not always lead to an optimal and confidently held estimate of the future.

Keynes notwithstanding, the state of radical uncertainty in which there is no information at all must be very rare. The New Classical School notwithstanding, the typical case is that there is *not* enough information to derive a uniquely best estimate of the future. The economy does not act as if there is radical uncertainty, and nor does it act as if there is perfect information – it acts rationally in the common sense, and recognises that there is a mixture of uncertainty and knowledge. However, when financial decisions are supported by nothing more than informed judgements, there will always be potential for volatility. No one is actually irrational when the Indonesian rupiah falls 5 per cent in a day without any change in the underlying situation. Investors do not know the intrinsic value of the rupiah, and so they are free to assume different futures at different times.

Central banks have the same freedom; the same uncertainty that is responsible for inconsistent markets causes government inconsistency as well. Since neither the market nor the authorities can devise a uniquely best strategy, both sets of decisions will reflect judgements of facts and values that can be justified without being really proven. Given the availability of macro-information, the government encounters the same uncertainty that confronts the markets, and whenever the market is most uncertain about the future, so too will the government be. Macro-paradigms *should* concern the behaviour of intelligent people, in both the market and the government, who do not have enough information to make an optimal decision.

If the future could be reduced to a reliable quantitative estimate, there would be no need for a macro-policy, but there would be no need to avoid it either, because it would be completely ineffective. Given a best estimate of the future, everyone would be able to calculate the natural rate of interest, and so changes in the money supply would have only nominal effects. Likewise and for New Classical reasons, fiscal policy would also be ineffective; government deficit spending would fail to have an expansionary effect if it was offset by a perceived increase in future taxes. Nevertheless, monetary policy *will* be effective when the future is not quantifiable (even though information is symmetric), provided only that the central bank is prepared to impose social costs and suffer its own losses. The same can be said of fiscal policy, which will also be effective in the normal case when there is less than complete information. The fact that monetary or fiscal policy would not work if there were perfect information is not an interesting proposition, since if there was perfect information there would be no need for society to have money in the first place.

The macroeconomics of non-quantifiable futures has been called *non-Walrasian theory*, presumably because it dispenses with optimality and market equilibrium. Although I will use that term below, its opposite is not Walrasian economics, but theories that postulate strictly determinate and mechanical behaviour in the markets. (The *macroeconomics of the Third Way* would be a more informative term, because the macro-theory is an applied branch of that political philosophy – see Fitzgibbons 1988, chapter 1.) In any event non-Walrasian theory is a new paradigm in which decision makers have to respond to uncertainty and there is no optimal choice; they want to make rational (perfect knowledge) decisions, but there is missing information. Under these conditions the conventional distinction between market decision making and government decision making loses its meaning and dissolves. When an optimal choice is unavailable everyone is free to act intransitively, which means they can change their decisions even if the external environment is constant. The dichotomous theories of government and the market that characterise normal economic theory rely on a special asymmetry in the state of information, and non-Walrasian theory does not need to assume that special asymmetry. When there is not enough information to logically reduce the future to a single point, it is not 'irrational' (it is consistent with self-interest and other values) to be intransitive. The absence of intrinsic values gives decision makers an extra degree of freedom, and it is this freedom which makes unregulated capitalism a very dynamic, but also a very unstable, system (Fitzgibbons 2000: 14 ff.).

I will comment here on some parallel ideas by Joseph Stiglitz, who has long argued that deficient aggregate demand requires a macroeconomic theory with its microfoundations in partial knowledge. In his *Knowledge for Development* Stiglitz suggested that the capital markets were often 'irrational', and that counter cyclical policy was limited by partial knowledge. I share these ideas and admire Stiglitz's attempts to present them formally, my only criticism being that what is involved is a new paradigm, and not just a new theory. When Stiglitz locates non-Walrasian macroeconomic theory within the political economy of the Keynesian synthesis, he pours new theoretical wine into old political economy bottles. Stiglitz correctly points out that when there is uncertainty, government macro-decision-making must necessarily reflect values – judgements about the future behaviour of the variables will need to be combined with ideas about their importance. Yet that point applies to the market as well as to the government, and for example Keynes's 'constructive impulses', and 'animal spirits', which obviously

*Table 11.1* Political economies of the Keynesian and non-Walrasian systems

|  | *Keynesian synthesis* | *Non-Walrasian theory* |
|---|---|---|
| *Market decisions* | 'Irrational' investors | Logical pursuit of ends, but decisions are intransitive and influenced by values |
| *Government decisions* | Social values guide counter cyclical policy | Logical pursuit of ends, but decisions are intransitive and influenced by values |

reflect values, have played a large role in recent macro-events. Likewise when Stiglitz suggests that uncertainty causes the market to act 'irrationally' (intransitively), he fails to realise that the government too must act 'irrationally', and for the same reason. Government policy will have to be supported by unproven judgements of fact, as in the market, and so there is a problem of policy consistency. As Table 11.1 illustrates, non-Walrasian political economy has a symmetry that the Keynesian synthesis lacks.

Non-Walrasian theory is neutral towards the extent of government macro-intervention, which neutrality some will find frustrating and vague. Keynesian theory says definitively that governments should intervene in the market, and New Classical theory definitively says that it should not, but these theories can only reach their definite answers by abstracting from relevant facts. If we ask whether an entrepreneur, who is just a market decision maker faced by uncertainty, should invest in particular markets, then the answer is sometimes yes, sometimes no, and it depends on the philosophy of the firm. Uncertainty, unfortunately, takes away certainty. Everything depends on situations and minds, and that is also true of macroeconomic policy. Non-Walrasian political economy merely encourages a full and open awareness of the values and the variables. Even though a macro-policy cannot follow from a strict deduction, its supporting reasons, referring to both fact and value, should be available for scrutiny and discussion.

# References

Fitzgibbons, A. (1988) *Keynes's Vision: A New Political Economy.* Oxford: Clarendon Press.

Fitzgibbons, A. (2000) *The Nature of Macroeconomics: Instability and Change in the Capitalist System.* Cheltenham: Edward Elgar.

Friedman, M. (1969) 'The Supply of Money and Changes in Prices and Output', in *The Optimum Quantity of Money and Other Essays.* Macmillan.

Krugman, P. (1999) *The Return of Depression Economics.* New York: Norton.

Stiglitz, J. (1998) 'Knowledge for Development: Economics Sceience, Economic Policy and Economic Advice', *World Bank's Tenth Annual Bank Conference on Development Economics.* Washington, http://www.worldbank.org/html/extdr/extme/jsabcde98/js_abcde98.htm.

# 12

# MARSHALL AND KEYNES ON RATIONAL (ETHICAL) ECONOMIC MAN

*Suzanne W. Helburn*

## 1. Introduction

Whitaker has described Marshall's ethics and world view as a combination of German idealism, evolutionism and utilitarianism. Keynes is variously described as an idealist utilitarian influenced by G. E. Moore, a political utilitarian influenced by Edmund Burke, an idealist with an ethical position similar to that of Plato and/or Aristotle. These characterizations suggest quite different ethical foundations for Marshall's and Keynes's contributions to economic theory and policy. However, the importance each attached to the link between ethical considerations and economic progress suggests a kind of influence on Keynes by Marshall which is worth investigating.

Both men eschewed hedonism and rejected crude nineteenth-century *laissez-faire* liberalism. They both emphasized the role played by spirited, visionary capitalists in promoting capitalist development and maintaining economic stability. Both recognized the limits to the rational use of the hedonic calculus in economic decisions. For both, ethics and economics were interrelated at several levels. The interrelation informed their visions of the human potential and 'progress', both social and economic, and, therefore, influenced their approach to public policy. Ethical presuppositions led them to take seriously public duty and guided their activities and projects as economists. Though politically both Marshall and Keynes can be considered utilitarians, because they took the ultimate aim of public policy to be the well being of the people, neither man considered utilitarianism an adequate ethical theory, because it does not adequately account for human motivation.

This chapter compares Marshall's and Keynes's assumptions about the role of moral functioning of economic agents in promoting economic stability and progress. It investigates the kind of ethical behaviour, particularly on the part of businessmen, each man thought was required to assure steady economic growth. One conclusion is that Marshall discredited the crucial justification for *laissez-faire*, that individuals, acting in their own self-interest, also maximize the general welfare, possibly alerting Keynes to the importance of fallacies of composition in moving from micro- to macro-analysis of economic processes. Although Marshall rejected the *laissez-faire* doctrine, he embraced an evolutionary view of economic/ethical development that he thought would limit the need for public intervention in economic affairs, a proposition Keynes rejected.

## 2. Marshall

The founding fathers of economics relied on the invisible hand and Say's Law to bring economic actions based on self-interest into line with general economic welfare. However, by the end of the nineteenth century we find Marshall asking questions about the fairness of the system, and speculating about the conditions necessary to assure human progress. He argued that 'the economist, like every one else, must concern himself with the ultimate aims of man' (Marshall 1920, book 1, chapter 2, p. 14). He was quite explicit in arguing that normal action by economic actors is not necessarily right morally (chapter 3, p. 29). Although he considered economic freedom a major precondition for the good society, he asked:

> How should we act so as to increase the good and diminish the evil influences of economic freedom, both in its ultimate results and in the course of its progress? If the first are good and the latter evil, but those who suffer the evil, do not reap the good; how far is it right that they should suffer the benefit of others?
>
> (chapter 4, p. 34)

Marshall's hopes for human progress depended on qualitative change in both productivity and human wants which would develop more or less naturally (with some direction from the state and chivalrous elites). Nevertheless, he seemed to separate analysis of secular economic and social progress from the mechanics of economic performance, assuming that economic motives of self-interest operate in his short and long periods. He likened the simple balancing forces of supply and demand to a mechanical equilibrium, but recognized that the mechanism does not necessarily provide a social optimum.

Neither Marshall nor Keynes was interested in developing purely abstract theories of economic rationality. In their theory, both incorporated assumptions they believed to represent crucial traits of economic agents. Although Marshall assumed that people, in their ordinary business lives, are primarily motivated by economic gain, nevertheless, underlying this desire is the full range of higher moral motivations. In *Economics of Industry* Marshall stated:

> economists deal with man as he is: not with an abstract or 'economic' man; but a man of flesh and blood, one who shapes his business life to a

great extent with reference to egoistic motives; but also one who is not above the frailties of vanity or recklessness, and not below the delight of doing his work well for its own sake; who is not below the delight of sacrificing himself for the good of his family, his neighbours, or his country, not below the love of a virtuous life for its own sake.

(Marshall 1912: 26; see a similar statement in Marshall 1920, book 1, chapter 2, p. 22)

In defining economics as the study of men as they act 'in the ordinary business of life', Marshall asserted: 'Everyone who is worth anything carries his higher nature with him into business; ... And it is true that the best energies of the ablest inventors and organizers of improved methods and appliances are stimulated by a noble emulation more than by any love of wealth for its own sake' (Marshall 1920, book 1, chapter 2, p. 12).

Marshall used character traits to explain the great advances in modern life. He was most explicit in his discussions of businessmen, the 'undertakers' whose energy, initiative, enterprise, industry, thrift and foresight make progress happen. In his essay, 'Social Possibilities of Economic Chivalry', Marshall commented that 'the epoch-making discoveries generally come from men who love their work with a chivalrous Love' (Marshall 1925: 332). And he claimed that 'Strong men are getting more and more to recognize that a deep full character is the only true source of happiness, and that it is very seldom formed without the pains of some self-compulsion and some self-repression' (p. 345).

Marshall's materialist, evolutionary, view of human nature is reminiscent of Marx of *The Economic and Philosophic Manuscripts* (devoid, of course, of any dialectical process). On the first page of the *Principles* Marshall noted that 'man's character has been moulded by his every-day work' more than by any other source, except, possibly, religion. He rejected the static view of human nature in favour of a pliable, evolutionary view based on the mutual growth of human wants and human activities (Marshall 1920, book 3, chapter 1, p. 71). In contrast to the pessimistic predictions of stagnation and subsistence living for the masses made by the classical economists, Marshall saw a rosy future for Englishmen based on a mutually reinforcing evolution of economic and human character development:

> Economists have ... learnt to trust that the human will, guided by careful thought, can so modify circumstances as largely to modify character, and thus to bring about new conditions of life still more favourable to character; and therefore to the economic, as well as the moral, well being of the masses of the people.
>
> (Marshall 1920, book 1, chapter 4, p. 40)

Marshall commented that in viewing man as 'a constant quantity', Ricardo and his followers failed to understand the potential for progress in industry and human development, and the negative effect on the efficiency of the poor caused by their poverty. Marshall argued that social science, and economics in particular, would have to change to reflect the rapid change in human nature.

In 'Some Features of American Industry', a paper he read in the fall of 1875, Marshall claimed that ethical progress is closely connected to economic progress. He argued that the ethical condition in any society is mainly controlled by the ethical insight of the masses of the people, by their ability to analyse practical questions, which depends partly on their level of education, but mainly on the nature of their work. This has implications for economics: 'Whereas in other sciences progress depends mainly upon the capacity of a few specialists, the progress of one of the chief factors of ethical science – the knowledge of the capabilities of human nature – is limited by the average capacity of the lowest classes.' (Whitaker 1975: 374–7).

According to Marshall ethical growth depends on two factors: '... the peaceful moulding of character into harmony with the conditions by which it is sur-rounded; so that a man ... will without conscious moral effort be impelled in that course which is in union with the actions, the sympathies, and the interests of the society amid which he spends his life' (Whitaker: 375). These experiences grad-ually become incorporated into the society's moral maxims and customs. Marshall described the second factor affecting ethical growth as 'the education of a firm will through the overcoming of difficulties. This will does not glide care-lessly into conformity with the conditions by which it is surrounded, but submits every particular action to the judgement of reason' (p. 375). When this factor is operative in a society, it can be 'the empire of energy, of strong but subdued enthusiasm, of grand ideals' (p. 376).

Marshall argued that material productive relations are the most important determinants of the relative development of the two factors. Of particular impor-tance are the social cohesion of men who work together, and the existing level of intellectual and moral functioning of the masses. Marshall concluded that under-standing the relation 'in which the industrial phenomena of a country stand to its ethical' is of fundamental importance to 'those who are working their way, as I am, towards that ethical creed which is according to the Doctrine of Evolution' (p. 377).

Understanding Marshall's use of Kantian and Hegelian concepts helps clarify his view of rationality and the sense in which his conception of rationality includes ethical considerations. Winslow argues that both Marshall's metaphysics and theory of history were deeply influenced by Hegel (Winslow 1990), and Chasse emphasizes Marshall's use of Hegel's concept of freedom and self-actualization (Chasse 1984). Whitaker chooses to emphasize the Kantian influence on Marshall (Whitaker 1975: 352; 1977).

Marshall shared with Kant a belief in 'the power of courageous reasoning and in the effectiveness of the reform of institutions' (MacIntyre 1966: 190). Kant can be heard in Marshall's emphasis on individual autonomy and the good will, the good will's motive to do its duty for the sake of doing its duty. In addition, and important to this investigation, is Whitaker's observation that the Kantian categorical imperative shows up in Marshall's insistence that economic agents are antisocial when they take actions which will be harmful to the society if the practice were to be generally adopted (Whitaker 1975: 353). For instance, in 'Fragments on Trades Unions', Marshall stated that it is unreasonable for one union to try to raise its members' wages if the successful adoption of this goal by all unions would cause profits to decline and therefore the capital in the country to decline (p. 347). This is a direct application of Kant's criterion of the categorical imperative, that one can will that it be acted upon universally (and an example of Marshall's identification of a fallacy of composition). This is a demand for logical consistency or rationality (MacIntyre 1966: 193).

Winslow argues that Marshall accepted Hegel's metaphysics – that individual character is variable, dependent on economic and social relations, and subject to a process of organic development which ends in full realization of the human potential for rationality and freedom. Marshall's emphasis on the growing autonomy of humans, the development of objective and subjective freedom – individual autonomy and social responsibility – comes from Hegel.

What is missing from Marshall, however, is Hegel's dialectic, the role of the negative and of conflict in human progress. Marshall gave a particular non-dialectical twist to the notions of objective and subjective freedom. Although he emphasized the power of growing economic freedom in capitalist England, he focused on the positive force of freedom to pursue economic ends, rather than the struggle against oppression or alienation. He recognized the negative consequences of freedom but seemed to attribute this to simple ignorance or crudeness. In contrast, for Hegel freedom always is conceived in terms of the negative in any society; freedom represents an attempt to escape from the bondage of any particular society. Marshall argues that men will gradually learn to censor their decisions by using Kant's criterion to reject antisocial actions. He seems, deliberately, to eliminate negation, suffering, conflict from his analysis and he emphasizes the biological metaphor of slow development of ethical (rational) man which is reflected in slow institutional change.

Marshall reverted to a fairly standard version of calculating economic man in his economic theory in Books III, IV, V and VI of the *Principles*, arguing that economic motives are so regular that they can be predicted. They relate to 'man's conduct under the influence of motives that are measurable by a money price', so that the theoretical conclusions can be verified empirically (Marshall 1920, book 1, chapter 2, p. 22).

Talcott Parsons has argued that Marshall's economic theory and his evolutionary theory of economic and moral development are logically independent and inconsistent, because the economic theory based on maximizing satisfaction depends on fixed wants, whereas the essence of the evolutionary theory is the mutual development of wants and activities (Parsons 1931). Nevertheless, Parsons rightly argues that the evolutionary theory is vital to understanding Marshall's position on a series of problems such as the determinants of the supply of factors of production, *laissez-faire*, social evolution and human nature. Parsons points out, for instance, that Marshall used his evolutionary theory to argue that growth in character and morality make government intervention more likely to work, but less necessary.

Although attempts have been made to integrate Marshall's economic and evolutionary theories (Maloney 1985; Whitaker 1977), Parsons' analysis is important to our argument in emphasizing Marshall's recognition that higher moral functioning must be assumed in order to conclude that economic and human progress proceed together in capitalist society. Marshall, in his economic analysis, proved the inadequacy of the nineteenth century utilitarian defence of capitalism and *laissez-faire*. He proved that the system can produce negative externalities: monopoly, unequal income distribution, overcrowding, inadequate reproduction of the working class therefore inadequate quantities of and qualities in workers, inadequate saving. Marshall needed his evolutionary theory to identify economic progress with total social welfare.

Marshall assumed that capitalist development would encourage rational decision making. The market system and freedom of enterprise would encourage the development of rational business behaviour and cooperative attitudes about work on the part of the masses. The system creates measurable motives, but reliance on marginal calculation does not necessarily imply purely self-centred motivation. It merely implies the existence of a standard of comparison of alternatives based on monetary costs and benefits. The quality of the projects or opportunities being compared depend on underlying values of the economic agents. For Marshall, what was distinctive and progressive about the capitalist system was the incentive provided for material progress, and the rational forms of calculation and foresight it produced for comparing the value of alternative courses of action.

In sum, Marshall believed capitalist development would promote the development of both moral judgement and rational economic decisions (an uneasy alliance) such that the defects of capitalism would diminish as people learned to base action on the Kantian criterion. This would reduce negative externalities, therefore the need for government intervention. Problems intrinsic to the system, such as those related to the unequal distribution of income and the tendency to under invest in the labour force, would, however, have to be solved through collective action.

## 3. Keynes

Keynes did not share Marshall's optimistic view of the evolution of capitalism and he was disparaging of Darwinian social theories, although he did not identify them with Marshall. Granting that in capitalist society competition promotes the survival of the fittest, Keynes commented that the most successful profit makers make it to the top through the 'bankruptcy of the less efficient' or the less lucky (Keynes 1931, 'The End of *Laissez-Faire*'). Keynes emphasized the cost and character of the competitive struggle. Like Marshall, Keynes likened the economy to a mechanism, but he was decidedly more concerned about the painful adjustments which were required if the mechanism had to be relied upon to bring about structural change. In objecting to the restoration of sterling to its prewar value in 1925, which would require a depression in export industries, he argued that the 'vast machine' would 'crash along, with regard only to its equilibrium as a whole, and without attention to the chance consequences of the injury to individual groups'. Those who favour the restoration, he noted, 'sit in the top tier of the machine' (Keynes 1931, 'Economic Consequences of Mr Churchill', p. 224).

Keynes, writing in the interwar period, focused on the fundamental economic instability of modern economies – inflation and depressions and the need to reject the *laissez-faire* doctrine. He attributed the success of capitalist growth before the First World War to enterprising capitalists' pursuit of business projects for their own sake. He agreed with Marshall that the great benefits of capitalist development are dependent on a faith in the system and motives that involve more than pure self-interested monetary gain. Instead of evolutionary progress to nervana, however, Keynes accepted John R. Commons's analysis that the capitalist system was in transition from an age of abundance dominated by economic anarchy to an age of stabilization which required deliberate public intervention to promote social justice and social stability (Keynes 1931, 'Am I a Liberal?'). In Keynes's view twentieth-century economic instability was directly related to the pursuit of narrow self-interest and 'rational' business decisions and the unlikely prospect that individuals acting alone will consider fallacies of composition inherent in the system. He recognized a contradiction immanent in an entrepreneurial system motivated by monetary gain – a tendency for capitalists to substitute speculation for enterprise in unsettled times, possibly an appropriate business strategy for the individual under the circumstances, but one which both increases economic instability and lowers long-run growth.

Did Keynes adopt Marshall's view of the nineteenth-century capitalist? Keynes never seemed to reject his earlier description in *The Economic Consequences of the Peace* of the 'entrepreneur class of capitalists' as the 'active and constructive element in capitalist society' (Keynes 1919: 149). However, there are differences between Marshall's and Keynes's character assessment of capitalists that explain his conclusion in chapter 12 of *The General Theory* that investors in the twentieth century were increasingly attracted to speculation rather than enterprise. Clearly Keynes moved from Marshall's insights to a more complex assessment of the role of businessmen in his own (and our) era.

Keynes was not a Kantian and he did not value purposefulness for its own sake. His valuation of the captains of industry was based, at least partly, on his views of excellence acquired at Cambridge under the influence of G. E. Moore. In his Apostle essay, 'Science and Art' written in 1909, Keynes compared the value of a businessman with that of the artist and the scientist. While the artist is most highly valued, Keynes argued that the scientist should be valued more than the businessman because 'the beauties of argument and the excitement of discovery' are 'not imaginary goods' whereas much of the life of the businessman is 'irksome toil'. Admitting the importance of the work of a businessman, Keynes claimed that the value of the work is quite a different thing from the value of the process.

In 1921, in a dinner speech to the Apostles, remembering a member of the 'brethren' who had died that year, Keynes wondered why Moulton had chosen to become a businessman. Keynes concluded: 'I fancy ... that, rightly judged, his act was one of artistry, not of avarice; and the impulse came, not at all from greed, but from the necessity still to exercise a perfected talent.' Keynes asked, what is a man to do if he is highly intelligent, creative, vital, has the egotism of an artist and the genius, but not the talent? He suggested that Moulton, through his activity as a businessman, may have come as close as he could to the satisfactions of an artist (Keynes 1921, Juvenilia manuscripts). While admiring of the character traits of such a man of action, Keynes seems to be suggesting that the successful businessman is motivated more by the desire for self-actualization than by a disciplined will to do good.

In1927 in a book review of H. G. Wells, *The World of William Clissold*, Keynes clearly veered from Marshall's view of the tandem development of economic and ethical growth in questioning the potential for the great businessmen of the day to lead society into the good life. Although Keynes reiterated his admiration of the creative intellect and energy of the great modern businessmen, he suggested a shallowness of character. He commented that because they lack a creed, 'they fall back on the grand substitute motive, the perfect *ersatz*, the anodyne for those who, in fact, want nothing at all – money ... they flutter about the world seeking for something to which they can attach their abundant *libido*. But they have not found it. ... They remain businessmen' (Keynes 1931, 'Clissold', p. 320).

In the economic turmoil following the First World War, Keynes considered the great captain of industry a tarnished idol (Keynes 1931, 'The End of *Laissez-Faire*', p. 287). With the postwar inflation, business lost 'its genuine character and becomes no better than a speculation in the exchanges, the fluctuations in which entirely obliterate the normal profits of commerce' (Keynes 1919: 154). In chapter 12 of *The General Theory*, Keynes presented a still more critical analysis of business behaviour, attributing the ills of the economy to speculation and the pursuit of short-run monetary gains. Keynes emphasized the effects of the development of stock and other asset markets that made it less risky to invest in securities that could be bought and sold at will, than in long-term investments whose profitability could not really be evaluated at all. The development of capital markets encouraged speculation, buying and selling based on forecasting the psychology of the market. With their increasingly efficient organization, Keynes noted that investment institutions and private individuals preferred to invest in liquid assets. In substituting speculation for long-term investment, businessmen lower the rate of aggregate real investment, therefore aggregate demand, further increasing the instability of the system. Keynes seems to consider speculative investing a reasonable response by individual investors to the circumstances, but antisocial since it detracts from real investment for the community as a whole.

Keynes credited Marx's analysis of the circulation of capital for providing insight about capitalist motivation and the fallacy of Say's Law. Marx described two forms of money circulation: commodity exchange, C–M–C, where individuals exchange a commodity (labour) for money in order to obtain consumer goods of the same value, and capitalist exchange, M–C–M, where capitalists engage in production in order to convert their original money capital into more money. For capitalists, the motive for exchange is not an increase in output but in money capital. To maximize capital accumulation (or to preserve one's capital during periods of crisis), the capitalist will invest his money where it provides the greatest expansion of money capital, whether or not this involves commodity production. Only the expectation of a monetary gain will cause him to increase employment. Asset manipulation is another form of using money to make money. Keynes remarked, 'The entrepreneur is guided ... by the alternative opportunities for using money having regard to the spot and forward price structure taken as a whole' (Keynes 1979: 81–3).

Keynes nevertheless admired the enterprising nature of capitalists as providing the essential source of imagination and initiative. He considered their positive impulses to initiate and carry out long-term projects the motive force for progress. These are beneficial actions that are not based solely, not even primarily, on calculations of their profitability. Rather, they are dependent on 'spontaneous optimism ... whether moral or hedonistic or economic'.

> Most, probably, of our decisions to do something positive, the full consequences of which will be drawn out over many days to come, can only be taken as a result of animal spirits – of a spontaneous urge to action other than inaction, and not as the outcome of a weighted average of quantitative benefits multiplied by quantitative probabilities.
>
> (Keynes 1936, chapter 12, p. 161)

Creating an economic climate congenial to promoting and maintaining this spontaneous optimism, was, of course, a major concern of Keynes. However, Keynes's main message in this section of chapter 12 is to emphasize that decisions about the future cannot depend on mathematical expectations, because under conditions of uncertainty the calculations cannot be made. Rather,

> ... it is our innate urge to activity which makes the wheels go round, our rational selves choosing between the alternatives as best we are able, calculating where we can, but often falling back to our motive on whim or sentiment or chance.
>
> (p. 163)

These passages have been the subject of considerable controversy. Fitzgibbons, who argues that Keynes holds a rational ethic of virtue, claims that the reference to animal spirits comes from Plato, referring to action without reward that reminded Plato of a faithful dog (Fitzgibbons 1988). It implies that long-run investment decisions involve an intuitive judgement supplemented by the logic of means rather than ends. Fitzgibbons argues that the tendency for businessmen to substitute speculation for enterprise involves a kind of self-deception – the assumption that today's conditions will continue in the future. Keynes, he asserts, is arguing that 'a gravitational tendency toward bad faith is ultimately responsible for the instability of the capitalist system' (p. 82). Fitzgibbons argues that Keynes was trying to show that when investors lose their animal spirits, their moral courage, they become subjective and irrational and the economy becomes volatile.

Carabelli claims that Keynes's use of animal spirits comes from Descartes and represents unconscious mental action led by the soul (1988: 214, 298). Applying Keynes's theory of probability, she points out that Keynes had less faith than Marshall in the existence of measurable motives, because, he argued, the future cannot be converted into the same quantifiable status as the present. She argues convincingly that Keynes rejected the dichotomy between rationality and irrationality, preferring to use the criterion of reasonability (p. 219). Economic actors take into account uncertainty, making reasonable choices based on intuition and partial knowledge. This interpretation of rationality seems consistent with the passage quoted above.

## 4. Conclusion

Keynes progressed and diverged from Marshall's view of the upstanding and courageous nineteenth-century industrialist. He did not seem to consider entrepreneurs necessarily virtuous, only spirited (and subject to fits of bad faith when economic conditions deteriorate). Their motive for investing is based on 'whim or sentiment or chance', dependent on 'spontaneous optimism ... whether moral, hedonistic or economic'. Investment decisions, according to Keynes, are based on subjective expectations and often, particularly in good times, non-economic motivations which could involve high-minded goals. Clearly, Keynes rejected the assumption of investor as 'rational economic man' in favour of investor as a reasonable, egotistical man who often is motivated to do good, but tries to protect his capital during bad times. Such men make reasonable decisions, given the circumstances, that is, given their incomplete state of knowledge and the quality of their intuition. At least, for the purposes of understanding investment behaviour, Keynes found it necessary to avoid the abstraction, 'rational economic man'.

Capitalists may or may not act as ethical agents, but they are necessary to continuing economic progress, making it essential to maintain a business climate that encourages their enterprise. The virtuous are among the elites who try to keep the economic system on an even keel while encouraging the 'arts of life' that Keynes considered to be of greater and more permanent significance (Keynes 1931, 'Economic Possibilities for Our Grandchildren', p. 332).

This brings us back to the question of fallacies of composition. Marshall expected economic agents (workers as well as the propertied) to evolve morally to the point where they recognize and take them into account in their own decisions.

Keynes recognized that most people will continue to make decisions more narrowly based on their own self-interest, although not usually based on precise calculations of monetary gain. Thus, it is the function of public officials, aided by economist technicians, to offset the effects when the whole does not equal the sum of the parts. Their job is to control the environment and curb the abuses of the system so that the free play of economic forces can realize the full potential of production, which, in turn, makes more possible the good life:

> Individualism, if it can be purged of its defects and its abuses, is the best safeguard of personal liberty in the sense that, compared with any other system, it greatly widens the field for the exercise of personal choice. It is also the best safeguard of the variety of life, which emerges precisely from this extended field of personal choice ... For this variety ... colours the present with the diversification of its fancy; and, being the handmaid of experiment as well as of tradition and of fancy, it is the most powerful instrument to better the future.
>
> (Keynes 1936, chapter 24, p. 380)

## References

Carabelli, A. (1988) *On Keynes's Method.* London: Macmillan and New York: St Martin's Press.

Chasse, J. D. (1984) 'Marshall, the Human Agent and Economic Growth: Wants and Activities Revisited', *History of Political Economy* 16: 3.

Coats, A. W. (1990) 'Marshall and Ethics', in R. McWilliams (ed.), *Alfred Marshall in Retrospect.* Tullberg: Edward Elgar.

Fitzgibbons, A. J. (1988) *Keynes's Vision: A New Political Economy.* Oxford: Oxford University Press.

Keynes, J. M., Juvenilia manuscripts housed in the Modern Archives at King's College Library, Cambridge. 'Science and Art' (1909). 'Vice President and Brethren', from a dinner speech at the Apostles annual dinner (1921).

Keynes, J. M., in Donald E. Moggridge (ed.), *The Collected Writings of John Maynard Keynes.* Macmillan Cambridge University Press for the Royal Economic Society. Vol. 2, *The Economic Consequences of the Peace (1919).* Vol. 9, *Essays in Persuasion (1931).* Vol. 10, *Essays in Biography (1933).* Vol. 29, *The General Theory and After (1979).*

Keynes, J. M. (1936) *The General Theory of Employment, Interest, and Money.* Harcourt Brace Jovanovich.

MacIntyre, A. (1966) *A Short History of Ethics,* New York Collier Books, New York: Macmillan.

MacIntyre, A. (1984) *After Virtue,* 2nd edn. Notre Dame, Indiana: University of Notre Dame Press.

Maloney, J. (1985) *Orthodoxy and the Professionalization of Economics.* Cambridge: Cambridge University Press.

Marshall, A. (1912) *Elements of Economics of Industry,* 3rd edn. Macmillan.

Marshall, A. (1920) *Principles of Economics,* 8th edn. Philadelphia: Porcupine Press.

Parsons, T. (1931) 'Wants and Activities in Marshall', *Quarterly Journal of Economics.* 46: 101–40.

Pigou, A. (ed.), *Memorials of Alfred Marshall*. London: Macmillan, 1925, for the Royal Economic Society.

Whitaker, J. K. (1975) *The Early Economic Writings of Alfred Marshall, 1867–1890*, Vol. 2. Macmillan for the Royal Economic Society.

Whitaker, J. K. (1977) 'Some Neglected Aspects of Alfred Marshall's Economic and Social Thought', *History of Political Economy* 9: 2.

Winslow, T. (1990) 'Marshall and Hegel: Organicism and Marshall's Accounts of Method and Historical Development', manuscript.

# 13

# COGNITION AND COORDINATION

*Brian J. Loasby*

## 1. Cognition and Uncertainty

Economics is a human and a social science, a study of both individual actions and the behaviour of complex systems; as taught to students, the key concept in the former is optimization and in the latter equilibrium. Although in principle the theoretical procedure purports to explain system behaviour as the result of individual choice, in practice choice within standard models can be explained only in an equilibrium setting, by endowing choosers with expectations about the configuration of the system which will ensure that their *ex ante* choices will turn out *ex post* to be rational. The equilibrium which is deduced is therefore the product not only, as Shackle insisted, of pre-reconciled choice, but also of pre-reconciled expectations. How these expectations are arrived at is not explained; their formation – and even their epistemic possibility – is outside the system, and outside time. As is most clearly seen in the Arrow–Debreu model, time, space and uncertainty become dimensions of the system, and cannot therefore be characteristics of the decision-making process; this is extremely convenient, because the decision-making processes which appear to be envisaged – contracting in more traditional market models, individual yet interdependent ratiocination in game-theoretic analysis – are unable to accommodate them.

As Herbert Simon has frequently observed, the cognitive powers required to make the choices which are deduced to be optimal are utterly incredible. Schumpeter (1934) declared that rational choice was always a fiction, but that in a stable environment its results could be duplicated by an appropriate configuration of routines, established by a lengthy process of trial and error, which made very modest cognitive demands; thus the maintenance of economic coordination in an Arrow–Debreu world, in which equilibrium over all locations, dates and contingencies is determined at a point outside time and cannot be challenged within the model specification, is not a very serious cognitive problem. But neither does it raise any policy issues, since nothing remains to be done; such economics has nothing to contribute either to economic decision making or to policy analysis.

However, Schumpeter added, routines could not cope with novelty; and neither could rational choice – essentially because, in later language, novelty was incompatible with rational expectations. Knight (1921) similarly observed that in an unchanging environment the knowledge required for intelligent choice could be supplanted by routine, but added that 'it is doubtful whether intelligence itself would exist in such a situation' (Knight 1921: 268). The significance of this observation becomes apparent when we consider Knight's distinction between risk, defined as a situation in which there are recognized procedures (or routines) for assigning probabilities across a known set of possible outcomes, and uncertainty, in which no such procedures are available, and in which therefore everyone must invent a way of coping with the difficulty, or follow someone else's way. By using standard theory Knight demonstrated that it is uncertainty which makes possible profit, entrepreneurship and the firm; it is uncertainty that requires intelligence. We may also conjecture that uncertainty provided a selection environment which favoured the development of human intelligence; and if so, it is reasonable to assume that the kind of intelligence most likely to be favoured was not that which facilitated deductive reasoning but that which was most effective in dealing with situations in which there was no reliable basis for such reasoning – and also in creating novelty, for we should not forget, as Shackle never did, that uncertainty is a necessary condition for imagination.

More than sixty years ago, Terence Hutchison (1937) was already, as he has remained, a forceful critic of the expectations that were routinely invoked to underpin the logic of modelling equilibria of optimizing agents. He saw clearly that there was no possibility of moving from static to dynamic analysis, to the study of an economics 'in time', without abandoning what Hayek later called 'the pretence of knowledge'. How, after all, can we improve our knowledge if we already know what it is that we are about to discover? Keynes (1921 [1973]) recognized the importance of uncertainty in his *Treatise on Probability*, which treated numerical assignment of probabilities as a special case and emphasized the importance of acknowledging the limitations of our evidence and the weight that could reasonably be placed on any assessment; and Knight also discussed not only the formation of judgements but also the confidence that people might place in judgements, their own as well as other people's.

It is not surprising that uncertainty infiltrated macroeconomics rather than microeconomics. In microeconomics resources might be misallocated by market failure, which generated inappropriate incentives; but, as Hutchison argued in 1937, proofs of misallocation, as well as proofs of allocative efficiency, relied on successful optimization. Financial crises and business cycles, however, which were associated with wasteful investment and unemployed resources, seemed to exhibit a systematic failure to optimize, and attempts to explain them regularly invoked some lapses of rationality (Hutchison 1937: 636), which could most comfortingly be attributed to some inadequacy of knowledge. A favourite source of this inadequacy was the generation of misleading signals by the financial system; indeed monetary theory has for centuries been associated with the possibility of coordination failure. Hicks had recognized in the 1930s that, in the development of theory, one had to introduce uncertainty before one could introduce money (some economists have not yet caught up with him) and the idea that uncertainty rather than money was the basic cause of macroeconomic problems has a long history; Robertson (1915) anticipated Schumpeter in suggesting that business recessions might be a partly unavoidable consequence of innovation. Since we are frequently told that economics is about trade-offs and that there is no free lunch, we should at least be prepared to entertain the idea that unemployment is a pathology of progress and, more generally, that every method of coordinating economic activity has its particular limitations and its particular ways of generating problems. In the remainder of this chapter we shall consider coordination from the perspective of human cognition, without being constrained by standard assumptions of rationality.

## 2. Cognition and patterns

For many of the decisions of interest to economists, we must rely on 'the effectiveness of the mental processes of the type that can handle contingencies, uncertainties and unknowables' (Barnard 1938: 312). By Knight's argument these decisions must include all those which give rise to profit and entrepreneurship, and provide his basic justification for the firm. Coase's (1937) explanation of the firm is also explicitly dependent on uncertainty, but he chooses to emphasize the costs of acquiring the knowledge and making the contracts needed to achieve efficient coordination through markets, and the relative attractions of a commitment to coordinating future activities within a firm, in ways to be worked out as events unfold. In contrast to contemporary transaction-cost theory, the advantages of Coasian firms lie not in the control of opportunism, made possible by asymmetries of information, but in creating a basis for taking opportunities which cannot be foreseen by anyone.

Experimental findings that people are not particularly good at logical reasoning are therefore less disturbing than those who specialize in logical constructions might believe; indeed these limitations may be opportunity costs of the development of capabilities that are appropriate to the circumstances on which Barnard, Knight and Coase all focus. What is increasingly recognized about the architecture of the human brain is its peculiar suitability, not for the serial processing required for developing logical structures, but for the formation of elaborate networks of connections. Humans are particularly adept at forming and using patterns, to the extent that actions which might be construed as the result of logical reasoning are often produced by the application of patterns; we act in ways which are appropriate to a situation when we can identify that situation as a member of a class with which such actions have become firmly associated. The modelling of macroeconomic phenomena as the result of optimization by economic agents in markets which clear is an example of the reliance on established patterns by economists; that these patterns are more obviously related to their own artificial constructs than to economic phenomena is not without parallels in other spheres. Schumpeter's perception that in a stable environment routines produce an illusion of rationality may be seen as the limiting case of this cognitive process; we shall need to consider the importance of routines later.

As a young man, Hayek worked out a psychological theory that would account for the prevalence of pattern making and pattern using, published much later as *The Sensory Order* (1952); this order emerged as a classification system to be imposed on phenomena, thus economizing on the scarce resource of attention, which has been a theme of Simon's work. It does not correspond closely to the order which has since been created by natural scientists – indeed it was the disparity between these two classification systems that provoked Hayek's enquiry, in a striking illustration of Pounds's (1969) proposition that problems are defined by differences. Since the two kinds of order are used for different purposes such a disparity should not be surprising, for a range of domain-specific patterns can be more closely adapted to particular applications than a unified scheme. The argument that domain-specific patterns are better adapted than rationality for human living, and therefore more likely to have emerged from a selection process during which the size of the human brain grew quite rapidly, has been made by Cosmides and Tooby (1994); the basic idea, in the form of a mechanical analogy, was produced soon after the publication of Darwin's *Origin of Species* by Marshall (1994) who, like Hayek, was attracted to evolutionary psychology early in his career.

Of particular interest in Marshall's model is his conjecture of two stages of pattern formation. The first stage relies exclusively on the clustering of impressions and actions and the selective reinforcement of links between classes of impressions and classes of actions which are apparently effective. These processes are influenced by the characteristics of each machine's environment and the sequence of events and responses, thus providing the basis for the 'tendency to variation' which Marshall subsequently identified as a major factor in economic development. When, and only when, this mechanism is working well enough to ensure satisfactory performance, there may begin to emerge a second category of patterns, based not on impressions and actions but on ideas of impressions and actions. The immediate value of this second category is that it provides a means, consistent with the first, of allowing (fallible) images of the future to influence decisions; its greater cognitive demands imply (on familiar economic principles) that it should be used selectively, leaving most actions to unconscious, but still potentially adaptive, procedures, and drawing on these procedures to orient its own speculation. Here again we can make a connection to Knight's discussion of decision making; since there is no basis for rational expectations in uncertainty, we must create an image of the future, and we cannot do so without assuming that the future will be somewhat like the past, even though the need for decision arises from the belief that it will be somewhat different from the past (Knight 1921: 313). Imagination requires an anchor.

The ability to consider future possibilities as well as past experiences makes possible a new kind of cognition, based on conjectures which are modified or replaced through trial and error, leading to an experimental and evolutionary process for the development of knowledge. The most notable outcomes of this kind of cognition in contemporary society are organized science and organized industry; it is therefore entirely appropriate – and, I believe, not coincidental – that

Adam Smith approached both from what we would now call a cognitive viewpoint. Smith accepted Hume's argument that there was no procedure which could prove the truth of any general empirical proposition, and that logical reasoning about empirical issues, being necessarily based on premises which might be false, therefore offered no guarantee against error. Like Marshall and Hayek later, Smith turned to psychology for an explanation of how people developed what came to be accepted as knowledge; and he anticipated Popper in identifying scientific discovery as a particularly clear and analysable manifestation of a general human process.

Smith (1795 [1980]) begins his analysis of 'the principles which lead and direct philosophical enquiries' with an account of the general human desire for a way of accommodating experience within familiar categories, the discomfort of being unable to account for phenomena, and the pleasure experienced when this discomfort is removed by a plausible and aesthetically appealing system of thought. It is important to note the emotional basis of Smith's analysis. No doubt it would be possible to include these emotions in a suitably enlarged preference system, but that would not be very helpful because the discomfort results from the absence of any credible premises from which to reason, and is relieved only by the construction of a new set of 'connecting principles', which is not a logical process; cognition has an essential emotional component. Smith focuses on astronomical ideas, and traces the succession of cosmological systems, each created to resolve perplexities and eventually failing to accommodate new experience, until we arrive at the Newtonian system – which, Smith is careful to point out, might also eventually prove unsatisfactory. In contrast to Kuhn's (1962, 1970) account of the succession of paradigms, which emphasizes discontinuity, Smith explains how each new system, though clearly a work of imagination, adapts and rearranges elements into what Schumpeter was to call 'new combinations'.

The search for connecting principles encourages the emergence of a distinctive scientific community, and subsequently of subcommunities, each paying increasing attention to the details of particular classes of phenomena, and therefore becoming increasingly demanding in its requirements for a satisfactory theory. This division of labour accelerates the growth of knowledge by increasing the likelihood of experiencing discomfort. More than two centuries later, Shackle (who was unaware of this work of Smith's) reinvented Smith's account in order to explain the 'landslide of invention' in economics between 1926 and 1939 as a consequence of the increasing specialization of economics as a discipline and the attempts to provide it with a precise theoretical structure. 'The question for the scientist is what thought-scheme will best provide him with a sense of...order and coherence' (Shackle 1967: 286), thus holding at bay 'the uneasy consciousness of mystery and a threatening unknown' (Shackle 1967: 288). Smith had cited the restoration of order among 'the noblest works of nature' as Copernicus's explicit motivation and drawn attention to the rhetorical power of Newton's unified explanation of cosmological and terrestrial phenomena.

Because science was for Smith (as for Shackle) a quintessentially human activity, we should not be surprised that Smith subsequently applied the proposition that the division of labour accelerates the growth of knowledge to productive activity, and made it the founding principle of his theory of economic growth (Smith (1776 [1976b]); nevertheless, it remains the greatest single act of intellectual creativity in the history of economics, despite the failure of most present-day economists even to recognize what Smith did, and the failure of those writers on business strategy who emphasize the importance of firm-specific competences without even attempting to explain their emergence to appreciate how much their reasoning would be improved by the incorporation of Smith's principles – as Penrose (1959) has shown.

## 3. The intelligent use of patterns

Smith's unifying conception of the growth of knowledge in science and in the economy would also improve economists' sensitivity to the problems associated with their assumptions about agents' knowledge and the application of theory. As the philosopher A. J. Ayer (1971: 114) observed, a being with unlimited cognitive capacity would have no need of theory, which is a means of economizing on cognition. Simon (1982, Vol. 2, p. 178) has emphasized the value of theory in processing information, but without always acknowledging its limitations. A theory is a device, located in the space of representations, for simplifying complexity by manipulating symbols instead of phenomena (this is a characterization, verging on caricature, of Simon's procedural rationality), but it is prone to error because, in Shackle's (1972: 354) words, 'it exists by sufferance of the things that it has excluded'. Such errors are more likely if there is not a strong experimental tradition, and especially if the internal coherence of the theoretical structure appears to be dependent on the continued exclusion of what may be important in practice. 'The appearance of completeness and precision, secured by laying aside the factors not susceptible of mathematical treatment or of orderly presentation, is deceptive.' (Barnard 1938: 313). It was Marshall's recognition of this danger, impressed on him very early by the observation that Cournot's axiomatic reasoning about increasing returns led inevitably to conclusions which were incompatible with the structure and development of the British economy, that prompted his warnings of the need to surround theory with practical knowledge and the perils of pursuing the logic of abstractions.

Theories, formal or informal, exemplify Knight's (1921: 206) account of what we might now call bounded rationality. 'It is clear that to live intelligently in our world ... we must use the principle that things similar in some respects will behave similarly in certain other respects even when they are very different in still other respects.' We adopt this principle without often knowing why the similarities dominate the differences, and we have even less formal justification for the complementary principle in which differences dominate similarities. That we are sometimes wrong, occasionally in spectacular fashion, does not invalidate either principle, but it does warn us not to expect too much from them, or from any other way of resolving our cognitive problems, though there are ways of sorting out the more reliable propositions from the less reliable (Ziman 1978), and improving our understanding of the range of convenience of particular simplifications. Leijonhufvud's 'corridor hypothesis', that an economic system may be stable within a particular range of variation but suffer serious coordination failure outside that range, is in effect a hypothesis about the range of convenience of an intersecting set of theories (many in the rudimentary form of classification systems) on which people have come to rely in managing their activities; and it is as useful in explaining organizational behaviour, and also individual behaviour (Kelly 1963), as in macroeconomics. The cognitive foundations are common to all three applications.

## 4. Institutions, coordination and change

Because our brains are so effective in creating, modifying and using patterns, it is relatively easy to supplement our own cognitive resources with those of other people who, because of a different sample, or even a different sequence, of experience, have come to employ different but related patterns. Smith explained the diffusion of new astronomical systems by our readiness to adopt other people's remedies for discomforts that we have been unable to overcome on our own account; and the same principle underlies Keynes's (1937: 214) observation that when we do not know what to do we tend to follow the lead of others who we believe – or merely hope – are better informed. It is a principle of very wide application; our readiness to accept guidance, and even instruction, from others is necessary to operate successfully in a complex modern society, and it is driven by emotion rather than by rational choice. It could not be driven by rational choice because we do not have the capacity to make more than a small fraction of our choices by making adequate investigations of the consequences of each choice, though we may, and often do, reflect on the kinds of leads that we are following, and even investigate certain options with considerable care.

This external support for the development of individual knowledge (both 'knowledge that' and 'knowledge how') is the neglected basis for understanding how human activities are coordinated (Choi 1993); it also provides a basis for understanding why, and in what circumstances, coordination may fail. Our shared mental architecture and our reliance on patterns rather than case-specific optimization help us to infer the patterns that guide the behaviour of other people and thus contribute substantially to our ability to behave intelligently both by adopting patterns which seem to work and by using these regularities to predict other people's behaviour (Heiner 1983). They also encourage the development of 'sympathy' in Adam Smith's (1759 [1976a]) sense and the reliance on 'moral sentiments' to help us decide what to do. Though Smith's principal application of his theory of institutions is to argue for a substantial degree of natural social cohesion (in implicit contrast to the pessimism of Hobbes, which pervades most contemporary economic treatment of interpersonal relationships), it is important to note that the origin of these rules of behaviour is not as a guide to interactions but as a means of simplifying the task of individual cognition. The convenience, and mental comfort, of applying familiar principles is probably a major explanation for the persistence of 'moral' behaviour when no interaction with other people is in question.

Schlicht (2000) has reminded us of the importance of aesthetic criteria, which are usually widely shared within particular communities, in providing rules for behaviour, and makes particular reference to their role in the appraisal of scientific theories, which has been acknowledged by reflective scientists. Within economics, aesthetic criteria are often invoked, without comment, in support of particular theoretical constructions or methodological strategems. It is not difficult to appreciate the beauty of the Arrow–Debreu system, especially its elegant finessing of the logical intractability of time and uncertainty, even while deploring the epistemic cost; and the extension of rational choice to include rational expectations perfectly exemplifies Smith's observation of 'how easily the learned give up the evidence of their senses to preserve the coherence of the ideas of their imagination' (Smith 1795 [1980]: 77). The recognition of this motivation does not prove that economists are wrong to behave as they do, but it does imply that their practices cannot be discussed solely in terms of rationality, but require consideration of processes which are non-rational – but not irrational.

The organizational cohesion that we usually witness, imperfect though it is, and the general acceptance of authority, not only from nominal superiors but also from organizational equals and subordinates, rests on this motivation to an extent which is rarely reflected in theories cast in terms of incentive structures. Williamson's references to the importance of 'atmosphere' is a notable exception, though it has not been properly integrated into his explanation of organization. Contracts are useful, and sometimes essential, but cooperation and continuing interaction can achieve what contracts cannot, in the development and application of capabilities through adaptations which are made possible in response to task uncertainty. Knight's principle does not apply only to entrepreneurship, as that is usually understood; every kind of task uncertainty entails the insufficiency of established procedures, and therefore the possibility of developing new skills of understanding or performance, leading initially to competitive advantage and eventually to the diffusion of additional knowledge. Organizational design may encourage particular kinds of learning, and the imaginative conjectures that we call entrepreneurial, by bringing certain activities together and setting them apart from others, thus establishing a protected sphere and a set of rules within which experimentation may be possible. The administrative framework is an essential feature of Penrose's (1959) theory of the development and application of resources which constitute the growth of the firm.

Entrepreneurship depends on thinking differently in some respects – even at some cognitive cost to others. As Lachmann (1986: 5) observed, every entrepreneurial action, even those that tend to improve the overall efficiency of allocation, disrupts some plans that were previously working well. Change is a threat, and a source of discomfort: it may therefore, as Smith showed, be a stimulus to further improvement, but it may also, as Schumpeter (1934) argued, cause the collapse of existing businesses and the abandonment of existing practices without the emergence of any adequate replacements. Schumpeterian employment, like Keynesian employment, grows because people do not know what to do: there are no credible premises for rationality, and no patterns that seem to fit the situation. Even entrepreneurs are baffled, because they have no means of deciding which of their visions is capable of realization. Successful change requires a substantial element of predictability, the principal source of which, as Schumpeter recognized, is the prevalence of routine behaviour. Our cognitive limitations cause us to rely on our own routines to provide space for thinking, and other people's routines to provide an empirical context for our thoughts. Thus the general absence of originality may be said to be a necessary condition for selective innovation.

## 5. Cognition and evolution

An evolutionary approach to questions of cognition, the growth of knowledge and economic change provides a way of thinking which combines the generation of novelty with selection from the resultant variety; and this pattern may be applied at many levels, including an individual, a working group, a firm, an industry, a nation or the world economy. It does not generate a simple overall principle of appraisal to compare with Pareto efficiency (which is often difficult to apply and may even be misleading); but it allows us to consider an aspect of efficiency which does not sit comfortably within the domain of rational choice theorizing, even when that is extended to incorporate option values – for these option values rely on precisely the kind of standard procedure which Knight excluded by his definition of uncertainty.

Options are indeed necessary, but it is perhaps better to think of them in terms of reserves. These can be of many kinds, but we may wish to pay particular attention to capabilities, the analysis of which rests on human cognition, and especially on the human ability to make and modify patterns. This cognitive potential constitutes a reserve for each individual, but because the patterns that are developed within any single brain necessarily exclude many possibilities, the division of labour allows a community to accumulate a reserve of capabilities immeasurably greater than any individual can attain; and differentiated capabilities may (though not always) be effectively organized not only to respond to circumstances but also to create opportunities. Particular examples include industrial districts and national clusters of firms within an industry, both of which have been associated with superior performance. These groupings have three potential advantages: they allow for some diversity across member firms; they preserve sufficient commonality to make the absorption of new ideas relatively straightforward; and they provide alternatives for those who find (sometimes for good reason) that their particular ideas are not accepted within their own organization. However, these advantages impose a limit on diversity, and are unlikely to give protection from Schumpeterian innovation which attacks their networks of cognitive assumptions. Cognitive failure, on a very large scale, cannot be excluded, as has been demonstrated many times in many contexts. It is part of the pathology of human cognition.

# References

Ayer, A. J. (1971) *Language, Truth and Logic*, 2nd edn. Harmondsworth: Penguin.

Barnard, C. I. (1938) *The Functions of the Executive*. Cambridge, MA: Harvard University Press.

Choi, Y. B. (1993) *Paradigms and Conventions: Uncertainty, Decision Making and Entrepreneurship*. Ann Arbor: University of Michigan Press.

Coase, R. H. (1937) 'The Nature of the Firm', *Economica* NS 4: 386–405.

Cosmides, L. and Tooby, J. (1994) 'Better than Rational: Evolutionary Psychology and the Invisible Hand', *American Economic Review* 84: 327–32.

Hayek, F. A. (1952) *The Sensory Order*. Chicago: University of Chicago Press.

Heiner, R. A. (1983) 'The Origin of Predictable Behavior', *American Economic Review* 73: 560–95.

Hutchison, T. W. (1937) 'Expectation and Rational Conduct', *Zeitschrift für Nationalökonomie* 8(5): 636–53.

Kelly, G. A. (1963) *A Theory of Personality*. New York: W. W. Norton.

Keynes, J. M. (1921) [1973] *A Treatise on Probability*, reprinted in D. E. Moggridge (ed.), *Collected Writings*, Vol. 8. London: Macmillan.

Keynes, J. M. (1937) 'The General Theory of Employment', *Quarterly Journal of Economics* 51: 209–23, reprinted in D. E. Moggridge (ed.), *Collected Writings*, Vol. 14.

Knight, F. H. (1921) *Risk, Uncertainty and Profit*. Boston: Houghton Mifflin.

Kuhn, T. S. (1962, 1970) *The Structure of Scientific Revolutions*, 1st and 2nd edns. Chicago: University of Chicago Press.

Lachmann, L. M. (1986) *The Market as an Economic Process*. Oxford: Basil Blackwell.

Marshall, A. (1994) 'Ye Machine', *Research in the History of Economic Thought and Methodology, Archival Supplement 4*. Greenwich, CT: JAI Press, pp. 116–32.

Penrose, E. T. (1959) *The Theory of the Growth of the Firm*. Oxford: Basil Blackwell. 3rd edn. Oxford: Oxford University Press, 1995.

Pounds, W. F. (1969) 'The Process of Problem Finding', *Industrial Management Review* 11: 1–19.

Robertson, D. H. (1915) *A Study of Industrial Fluctuation*. London: P. S. King.

Schlicht, E. (2000) 'Aestheticism in the Theory of Custom', *Journal des Economistes et des Etudes Humaines* 10(1) 33–51.

Schumpeter, J. A. (1934) *The Theory of Economic Development*. Cambridge, MA: Harvard University Press.

Shackle, G. L. S. (1967) *The Years of High Theory*. Cambridge: Cambridge University Press.

Shackle, G. L. S. (1972) *Epistemics and Economics*. Cambridge: Cambridge University Press.

Simon, H. A. (1982) *Models of Bounded Rationality*, 2 volumes. Cambridge, MA and London: MIT Press.

Smith, A. (1759) *The Theory of Moral Sentiments*, reprinted in D. D. Raphael and A. L. Macfie (eds) (1976a), *Glasgow Edition of the Works and Correspondence of Adam Smith*, Vol. 1. Oxford: Oxford University Press.

Smith, A. (1776) *An Inquiry into the Nature and Causes of the Wealth of Nations*, reprinted in R. H. Campbell, A. S. Skinner and W. B. Todd (eds) (1976b), *Glasgow Edition of the Works and Correspondence of Adam Smith*, Vol. 2. Oxford: Oxford University Press.

Smith, A. (1795) 'The Principles Which Lead and Direct Philosophical Enquiries: Illustrated by the History of Astronomy', in *Essays on Philosophical Subjects*, reprinted in W. P. D. Wightman (ed.) (1980), *Glasgow Edition of the Works and Correspondence of Adam Smith*, Vol. 3. Oxford: Oxford University Press, pp. 33–105.

Ziman, J. M. (1978) *Reliable Knowledge*. Cambridge: Cambridge University Press.

# 14

# KEYNES'S NOTION OF *CAUSA CAUSANS* AND ITS APPLICATION TO THE GLOBALISATION PROCESS[1]

*Donald Gillies and Grazia Ietto-Gillies*

## 1. Keynes's explanation of unemployment, and the notion of *causa causans*

In his 1937 article, Keynes made use of causal concepts in expounding his theory of determinants of the level of output and employment. This is how he puts it (1937: 121):

> The theory can be summed up by saying that, given the psychology of the public, the level of output and employment as a whole depends on the amount of investment. I put it in this way, not because this is the only factor on which aggregate output depends, but because it is usual in a complex system to regard as the *causa causans* that factor which is most prone to sudden and wide fluctuation. More comprehensively, aggregate output depends on the propensity to hoard, on the policy of the monetary authority as it affects the quantity of money, on the state of confidence concerning the prospective yield of capital assets, on the propensity to spend and on the social factors which influence the level of the money wage. But of these several factors it is those which determine the rate of investment which are most unreliable, since it is they which are influenced by our views of the future about which we know so little.

Keynes was dealing with a *complex system* in which there are many interacting factors. This is indeed the case in economics and the social sciences. In any complex system it is difficult to go to the heart of the problem and identify what is most important. Keynes suggests a way out of this difficulty, namely that we should try to discover a *causa causans* or dominant cause. This he identified as the factor whose variation produces the largest effect on the system as a whole. The reason for focusing on the factor 'which is most prone to sudden and wide fluctuations' is the fact that his aim was to explain fluctuations in the level of output and employment.

Keynes's theory was devised in order to provide the basis for an understanding of the persistent mass unemployment and in order to devise relevant policies. However, Keynes is very careful to distinguish his economic theory from its possible applications. As he says (1937: 121–2):

> This that I offer is, therefore, a theory of why output and employment are so liable to fluctuation. It does not offer a ready-made remedy as to how to avoid these fluctuations and to maintain output at a steady optimum level. But it is, properly speaking, a theory of employment because it explains *why*, in any given circumstances, employment is what it is. Naturally I am interested not only in the diagnosis, but also in the cure; .... But I consider that my suggestions for a cure, which, avowedly, are not worked out completely, are on a different plane from the diagnosis. They are not meant to be definitive; they are subject to all sorts of special assumptions and are necessarily related to the particular conditions of the time.

This passage makes it clear that, in his analysis, Keynes was looking for a *causa causans* for both diagnostic and curative purposes. He distinguishes carefully between his diagnosis (the isolation of the *causa causans*), and his suggestions for a cure based on that diagnosis. He has great confidence in his diagnosis, but thinks that his suggestions for a cure need further elaboration. Nonetheless, action and policies play a large role in his analysis of *causa causans*.

In the next sections we will attempt to apply a similar causal methodology to a contemporary example: globalisation. We start with a brief analysis of various theses on globalisation and then, following Keynes's approach, we will try to isolate its dominant causes, or *causae causantes*.

## 2. Globalisation theses: Hyperglobalists and sceptics

Globalisation has become an everyday household term, used to characterise, explain and justify many current developments. The term and its common usage convey the impression that it is potentially and actually possible for ordinary people and economic actors to get in touch, interact and do business with other people and communities worldwide. The expression has also increasingly come to be associated with the feeling that economic activities, events, processes, have a pattern and life of their own determined by globalisation and that we cannot – and should not – do much to alter them. Globalisation is a complex phenomenon, which covers much more than the strictly economic sphere (Giddens 1999; Held *et al.* 1999). In spite of this broad scope, there are many attempts to define globalisation (McGrew 1992: 23; Oman 1996: 5; Castells 1996: 92; Held *et al.* 1999: 16).

Globalisation has both quantitative and qualitative dimensions which interact with each other (Kozul-Wright and Rowthorn 1998a; Held *et al.* 1999). Among the more quantitative aspects, the most cited ones are cross-countries flows in relation to trade, foreign direct investment and financial transactions.[2] We should also add the flows of profits, dividends and interests related to international investment, the inter-organisation – particularly inter-firm – collaborative agreements as well as the movements of people across frontiers.[3]

There are some attempts at a broad analysis of the globalisation process and its policy implications. These attempts have been categorised by Held et al. (1999) into various theses. The authors consider three main theses in the globalisation debate.

At one end of the spectrum they put the proponents of what they call the 'Hyperglobalist Thesis', of which the main exponent is Kenichi Ohmae (1991, 1995, 1996). Ohmae sees the brave new world at the turn of the millennium dominated by large successful multinational companies (MNCs).The MNCs are seen as a source of efficiency and progress which can deliver wealth and well-being throughout the world – or at least the developed part of it. Globalisation – largely the outcome of MNCs' activities – is seen as an unstoppable force for progress and efficiency. It is market driven and indeed the logic of the market must be allowed to prevail by pushing forward with deregulation and liberalisation. The constraints still posed by nation states must come down: the era of the *Nation State* is over and it must give way to the *Region State*.

Such a death warrant for the nation state was bound to generate support for its survival. One group has indeed been led to deny (or play down considerably) the very existence of globalisation in order to maintain that news of the death of the nation state are grossly premature. Indeed, the nation states and their governments are alive and kicking and there are calls for them to kick harder and more effectively. Held et al. (1999), as well as Giddens (1999), name this the 'Sceptic Thesis'. It is represented by Carnoy et al. (1993) in the US and by Hirst and Thompson (1996) on the other side of the Atlantic.

Carnoy et al. (1993, chapter 3) examine the growth and development of multinational enterprises (MNEs) since the 1970s. They find that, in spite of considerable qualitative and quantitative changes in their activities, MNEs are still very much embedded in the home country. The majority of their activities and profits – except for a few MNEs – are based in the home country and so is their R&D. Therefore, the contemporary MNEs are strongly dependent on the home-country's infrastructure, business culture and government policies. There is a very strong interaction between home nation state and MNEs. The performance of the home economy is affected by the success of its MNEs; conversely, the MNEs' success worldwide depends on the success and support they have in their home base. In this perspective, national policies in the globalisation era become more, not less, relevant. They affect the level of competitiveness of the economy, as well as the physical and human-capital infrastructure. This, in turn, affects the performance and competitiveness of MNEs.

Hirst and Thompson (1996) question the whole notion of globalisation on the basis that: (a) It is not a new phenomenon. Large international flows of trade, portfolio and direct investment, as well as migration flows, are nothing new. The beginning of this century saw a similar, if not higher, intensity of transactions across borders. (b) Multinational companies are not borderless institutions. They are well embedded in their own home nation state in terms of share of overall activities. (c) Most international flows take place within well-defined regions rather than spread across the globe. (d) Capital mobility is confined within the developed countries and does not produce massive shifts from developed to developing countries. Similar arguments are used by Kozul-Wright and Rowthorn (1998b) to support the view that '... there has been a tendency to exaggerate the extent of truly global production relocations' (p. 78).

Thus, if globalisation is a hyped myth, it follows that the nation state is still the key unit of governance within its own borders and also in terms of establishing appropriate international institutions and securing appropriate and consistent cross-country governance. The sceptics' defence of the nation state is based on the denial or playing down of globalisation.

### 3. Globalisation theses: Transformations

History plays a very strong role in the analysis by Held *et al.* (1999) and in their 'Global Transformations' thesis. Their project is to analyse globalisation in its historical setting and antecedents and for the key domains of social activity. The historical epochs chosen for their analysis are: Pre-modern (up to 1500); Early Modern (1500–1850); Modern (1850–1945) and Contemporary (1945–present). The key domains – among which they see growing global interconnectedness – are economics, politics, migration, the environment, the military and culture. Each domain is characterised by specific technological and institutional infra-structures.

The authors use the following dimensions to assess globalisation: *extensity*, that is the spatial/geographical reach; *intensity*, that is the number and quantity of flows; *velocity*, that is the speed of movement of flows across space; and *impact*, that is the overall effects on society and the economy.

From a historical perspective one might be led to conclude that the present glob-alisation process is nothing new – just another transformation towards outreach in the history of humanity. Yet they conclude that the present transformation is unprecedented. They write in their final chapter:

> What is especially notable about contemporary globalization, however, is the confluence of globalizing tendencies within all key domains of social interaction. Thus, it is the particular conjuncture of developments – within the political, military, economic, migratory, cultural and ecological domains – and the complex interaction among these which reproduce the distinctive form and dynamics of contemporary globalization.
>
> (p. 437)

They reject the hyperglobalist views of the demise and redundancy of the nation state. They see the development of new forces (spatial and social) in the domains of politics and power and the need for a rethinking of democracy in a world of overlapping communities.

> ... a democratic political community for the new millennium necessarily describes a world where citizens enjoy multiple citizenships. Faced with overlapping communities of fate they need to be not only citizens of their own communities, but also of the wider regions in which they live, and of the wider global order. Institutions will certainly need to develop in order to reflect the multiple issues, questions and problems that link people together regardless of the particular nation-states in which they were born or brought up.
>
> (p. 449)

A different perspective and transformation thesis is put forward by Chesnais (1997)[4] who sees the current phase of capitalist development as a new regime in which finance capital dominates everything else ('Un régime d'accumulation mondialisé à dominante financière, chapter 12, p. 287). In his view, since the 1980s, capitalism has undergone systematic changes: the specific forms of capital globalisation unleashed by the liberalisation and deregulation policies have led to the emergence of a world regime of accumulation dominated by finance. He writes (chapter 2, p. 48):

> At the end of the twentieth century, the analysis of globalisation of capital must start with finance. The financial sphere is the one in which the internationalisation of markets is most advanced; the one in which the operations of capital have reached the highest degree of mobility.[5]

Does this mean that there is a conflict or separation of roles and aims of industrial and finance capital? Chesnais's answer is definitely negative because he sees industrial and financial groups as closely interlinked and enmeshed in their working towards more profitable accumulation worldwide.

Chesnais gives detailed empirical support to his thesis with data on the accelerated growth of financial transactions[6] (chapter 2). For example, the daily average transactions on the stock exchanges of the UK, the US and Japan have increased by 100 per cent between 1986 and 1990 and by about 200 per cent between 1990 and 1992 (Graph 10.3, p. 253).

## 4. Why we need an analysis of the dominant causes of globalisation

There is, on the whole, relatively little writing on the causes of globalisation. Ohmae's approach to globalisation seems to imply that no single actor or element can be responsible. Globalisation is a process springing out of market forces and as such there is nothing that can or should be done. Milberg (1998) identifies the driving forces of globalisation as: the transnational corporations; technological change; macroeconomic conditions; liberalisation and privatisation, and other policies in both developed and developing countries.

Held *et al.* (1999) tackle the issue of causation in their concluding chapter in their search for 'principal driving forces underlying contemporary globalization' (p. 436). They write later on the same page:

> Seeking to identify the primary causes of contemporary globalization necessarily involves a recognition that in accounting for processes of social change, the language of causality cannot be the same as that of deductive scientific enquiry. In analysing the driving forces underlying processes of historical change, the emphasis is necessarily on the conjunction of tendencies and the factors which impede or fuel those tendencies. The relevant notion of cause here involves the idea of a conjunction of events. Processes and conditions which together tend to generate a particular type of outcome ... Contemporary globalization is not reducible to a single causal process but involves a complex configuration of causal logics. These ... embrace the expansionary tendencies of political, military, economic, migratory, cultural, and ecological systems. But each is mediated by the late twentieth-century communication and transport revolution ....

This notion of causality is more akin to a statement about the fact that globalisation is a confluence of globalising tendencies in a variety of social, economic, political and cultural domains. These tendencies are mediated and fuelled via specific factors, that is via the technologies of transportation and communication. However, we are not told whether there are dominant or main causes and if so what they are, or whether there are unifying underlying elements that affect globalisation in all the domains. In other words we are told the domains of impact of globalisation and the fact that they reinforce each other, but nothing about the '*causae causantes*', the primary or dominant causes of the whole process. The authors start from the plan to give driving forces but end up by giving us domains of impact of globalisation while assigning a mediation role to the revolution in the technology of transportation and communication.

Can we identify causes and driving forces in the globalisation process? Is it indeed useful to do so and why? Let us start with tackling the latter question. We start from the premise that globalisation is indeed a process which involves many factors interacting often in a cumulative way.

A considerable amount of debate in the various theses on globalisation summarised above develops around the issue of state intervention and power of nation states. It therefore centres around whether and how governments can and should intervene to regulate the economies and the globalisation process itself. The range of views on the extent of government intervention as we saw above is varied.

Moreover, there is a difference between the various authors as to the range of policies they consider. Ohmae and Chesnais want policies directly aimed at the globalisation process: policies to enhance the process in the case of Ohmae, and policies to curtail it in the case of Chesnais. In the cases of Hirst and Thompson, Held *et al.* as well as Chesnais, it is a whole range of policies that are – implicitly or explicitly – referring to, from macro-policies to industrial policies.

If the global process impacts on the effectiveness of such policies (including the direction of the effects), how can we design and tailor the policies to achieve the desired aims? This is very difficult if we have no knowledge of what causes the global process, its scale and directions. This knowledge gap may leave the field open for the Ohmae type of approach in which the liberal political agenda prevails in the approach to globalisation. However, like many economic and social phenomena the globalisation process has an uneven impact on individuals, communities, classes, regions and nation states. Some benefit, some lose out, in patterns which may become cumulative through time. An understanding of the root causes will also help us to understand its uneven impact and take action to affect events in the desired directions. As in the case of Keynes's application to the problem of unemployment, the identification of *causae causantes* has both diagnostic and curative implications.

## 5. The '*causae causantes*' of globalisation

Is the current character and pattern of globalisation the only possible one? Is the erosion of governments' power inevitable and/or desirable? Can we devise and implement policies to enhance the positive effects of globalisation and/or to minimise the negative ones? What governance framework and institutions are necessary to achieve this?

It will help us towards beginning to tackle the above issues and questions if we can identify the dominant causes or *causae causantes* of globalisation. At first this would appear as a hopeless task because so many elements interact in the process. However, we believe that the task can be accomplished if we start from two basic points.

First, the realisation that globalisation is not just another phase in geographical outreach. It is much more, it is a new phase of capitalist development. We are, in fact, witnessing a quantitative and qualitative jump in the development of the productive forces. The scale of change in the productive forces is such as to justify the label of a new phase of capitalism.

The development in the productive forces derives from innovation in two connected directions: (a) technological innovation particularly – but not exclusively – in the field of information and communication technologies (ICTs); and (b) organisational innovation which enables the system to take full advantage of the ICTs. These two types of innovation are closely linked and (b) would not have been possible without (a). They both combine to make it possible to extend the geographical range of operations particularly in the domain of economics and business.

142

However, the spatial reach is not the only dimension affected by these innovations. The combination of technological and organisational innovation has led to the adoption of flexible production systems which have profound effects on many areas of economic and social life including the following ones: the introduction of new products and processes; the range of skills required in the new economy; and the relationship between producers and their suppliers/distributors as well as between producers and consumers. Some of these changes have a spatial dimension, some have not. Some of the changes bring considerable efficiency and/or qualitative gains. Others do not or indeed bring serious problems.[7] None of these elements is new, including the spatial reach (as highlighted by Held *et al.* 1999). However, in the last twenty years all of them have received a considerable boost – in relative terms – because of innovation. The overall result is a qualitatively new system, a new phase in capitalist development.

Second, it is useful to distinguish between the driving forces of the globalisation process and its dominant causes. We consider the driving forces to be all those elements that contribute to the process and help it to take the current shape and patterns. In particular, the following ones: the activities of transnational companies (TNCs) and of financial institutions; the diffusion of information and communication technologies; the macro-policies of many governments; widespread liberalisation and privatisation programmes; and the policies of international institutions such as the IMF.

A subset of the above driving forces, we consider to be dominant causes, those at the root of the globalisation process. We follow Keynes in looking for *causae causantes* in a complex system. However, the test of what is a *causa causans* differ because of the different context to which it is applied. Keynes's main preoccupation was the fluctuations in the level of output and employment, therefore he looked for that factor which fluctuates most. Our main preoccupation is with the analysis of globalisation as a new phase of capitalist development and therefore in terms of the development of productive forces. Hence, we look for those factors that most contribute to the development of the productive forces.

This means that, in identifying the *causae causantes* of globalisation, a different litmus test will be followed compared to Keynes's. Keynes's litmus test was 'fluctuations'. We shall use the following litmus test[8]: (a) The driving forces contribute to the development of the productive forces at the basis of the globalisation process. (b) Given such a contribution, these forces are largely irreversible. (c) It follows also from (a) that, without them, the contemporary globalisation process would be inconceivable.

On the basis of these conditions which form the litmus test, we identify the dominant causes or *causae causantes* of globalisation in the following areas of innovation:

- *Technological innovation.* In particular the revolution in the technology of information and communication[9] coupled with the considerable advances in the technology of transportation.

- *Organisational innovation and specially the cross-border organisation of activities*. In particular: the TNCs' power to organise business activities across countries and their comparative position *vis-à-vis* other actors as participants in the globalisation process.

It would have been tempting to look at the relevance and growth of quantitative flows and to identify the dominant causes of globalisation with the largest or fastest growing ones. Looking at the purely quantitative flows there is no doubt that the largest increases in flows are to be found in the sphere of international finance. We have two objections to this approach. First, it does not consider the contribution of the various driving forces to the development of productive forces. Second, it fails to distinguish between trends which are largely irreversible and those which could be halted or further enhanced by political will and the intervention of governments. Third, it does not lay enough stress on the actors which participate in the process, their relative positions within it and their active or passive participation in it.

The financial explosion across countries was largely fuelled by macro-policies, by liberalisation and privatisation policies, and by deregulation in the cross-country acquisition of assets. It could be reversed by reversing those policies. Of course, while those policies are implemented the finance sector does exercise a very considerable impact on the globalisation process: it affects geographical patterns; it increases divergence between countries and communities and classes within countries; and it changes the economic structure of countries and the social fabric of its communities. However, this process is largely reversible if the political will is there.

The ICTs have a dominant role in the globalisation phase of capitalist development because of the contribution they make to the development of the productive forces. None of the quantitative or qualitative elements could have changed to such a large extent without the adoption and diffusion of ICTs. Moreover, this element is irreversible. We could not possibly conceive of going back to the pre-ICTs era, except as a result of major earth-shaking catastrophes.

The defining characteristic of TNCs is their ability to plan, organise and control business activities across countries. It is a characteristic that, at present, is specific mainly to them, compared to the other major players in the economic and social system such as labour, consumers, uninational companies and governments.

The key role played by TNCs as *causa causans* of globalisation manifests itself in a variety of ways and in particular: (1) Given their size, economic power and technological basis, they are in the best position to use the ICTs and indeed to affect its further development and rate of diffusion. (2) They are the institutions that truly operate across nation states. They own assets across borders and they can plan, organise and control production/activities across countries. They are not just part of the institutional infrastructure; they are the key to the whole process. They participate in the process actively rather than passively like most other actors. In this role they shape the pattern of globalisation rather than bear its consequences. (3) Many international financial flows originate with them.[10] (4) They have a comparative position of power that this gives them *vis-à-vis* other actors in the economics system who do not possess – so far – the same ability to plan, organize and control across borders. These other actors are labour, governments, uninational companies and consumers.

## 6. Policy implications

There are specific long-term policy implications from the analysis developed above. First, the fact that those driving forces of the globalisation process which are not dominant causes can be reversed. Thus, for example, this approach considers the growth of financial transactions to be a driving force though not a dominant cause. Much financial activity, far from contributing to the development of the productive forces, is a hindrance to it and has a purely distributive purpose. Moreover, the financial dominance of domestic and international economies is reversible if the political will is there. Regulation of financial flows will affect most economic actors including the TNCs. However, it will not affect their potential for organising production across countries.

The TNCs play the key role in the development of organisational innovation within and across borders; indeed they are, at present, the only actor who can truly plan, organise and control activities across borders. This puts them in a position of considerable power *vis-à-vis* other actors and in particular labour, national governments, consumers and uninational companies. Here the policy implications are twofold.

First is the development of policies designed to enable other actors to participate fully and actively in the globalisation process, in other words policies designed to develop countervailing transnational power in the other actors, be they workers, smaller companies, consumers or national governments.

Second, we must accept that there are gains to be realised from technological and organisational innovation but that there may also be considerable undesirable effects and social costs. The TNCs' activities and the direction of their innovation are not always in the interest of other groups in society, be they consumers or labour or smaller companies or all of us in relation to our environment. Governments must regain control over strategic direction for the economy and society and support or discourage activities of TNCs accordingly.

Third, in a world in which much activity takes place across borders, there is a need for transnational governance. This can be achieved via the establishment of appropriate supranational institutions with the aim of monitoring transnational activities and encouraging some or deter others on the basis of overall strategies worked out in conjunction with national governments. In this context, we see the latter as having a larger not a smaller role.

There is a need for strengthening industrial policies[11] in order to: deal in a balanced way with the strategies of TNCs; support other actors in developing transnational power; and coordinate with supranational institutions. The national state must strengthen both its coordinating and a conflict-resolution functions (Kozul-Wright and Rowthorn 1998, Introduction). The two functions can be applied to the relationship between state and TNCs, between TNCs and other actors in the economic system, between the national and international community, and between national and international governance.

Finally, there are also wider implications for analysis and policies in other areas of economics. The globalisation process and its *causae causantes* may have to be taken into account in wider theoretical analyses leading to policy recommendations. In a volume dedicated to one of the world's major contributors to the study and interpretation of Keynes, it seems appropriate to ask ourselves how the analysis of the previous sections might be of help in applying Keynes's analytical framework to the present economic system. Keynes developed his analysis in a pre-ICTs and TNCs era. Nonetheless, his analysis is still very relevant as Victoria Chick and other post-Keynesian economists have demonstrated. However, it must be updated to take account of the technological revolution and of the activities of TNCs. In the 1937 paper we quoted above, Keynes concludes that any suggestion of cures must be '… related to the particular conditions of the time' (p. 122). The two main defining characteristics of the contemporary globalisation stage of capitalism are the ICTs and the transnational organisation of production by TNCs.

## Notes

1 The authors have benefited from comments and suggestions on a previous version of this chapter by T. Lawson and V. Chick.
2 Cf. empirical evidence in Held *et al.* (1999, chapters 3 and 4), Hirst and Thompson (1996), Chesnais *et al.* (2000) and UNCTAD, *World Investment Report* (various issues).
3 On cross-countries flows of profits from foreign direct investment cf. Ietto-Gillies (2000); the movements of people is dealt extensively in Held *et al.* (1999, chapter 6); on inter-firm collaborative agreements in technological areas cf. Hagedoorn (1996).
4 Chesnais's thesis is not discussed in Held *et al.* (1999).
5 Translation from French by Grazia Ietto-Gillies. See also Chesnais and Simonetti (2000 p. 11).
6 Evidence on such growth is also in Held *et al.* (1999, chapter 4), Akyuz (1995) and Obstfeld (1998).
7 An example of the latter in the field of organisational 'innovation' can be seen in the UK rail industry following privatisation. The difficulties of coordinating an industry fragmented between many operators and their subcontractors are leading to high social costs in terms of safety as well as government subsidies.
8 We are grateful to Tony Lawson for pointing out to us that this test of what constitutes a *causa causans* differs from Keynes's.
9 Freeman (1992) and Perez (1983) talk of a new technological paradigm. Cf. also Castells (1996, 1997), Dalum *et al.* (1999) and Oliner and Sichel (2000).
10 Chick (1979) discusses the need to take account of TNCs' activities in the reshaping of the international financial system.
11 Cf. various essays in Cowling and Sugden (1990) and Cowling (1999).

## References

Akyuz, Y. (1995) 'Taming International Finance', in J. Michie and J. Grieve Smith (eds), *Managing the Global Economy*, Chapter 3. Oxford: Oxford University Press, pp. 55–90.

Carnoy, M., Castells, M., Cohen, S. S. and Cardoso, F. H. (1993) *The New Global Economy in the Information Age. Reflections on our Changing World*. University Park, Pennsylvania: The Pennsylvania State University Press.

Castells, M. (1996) 'The Information Age: Economy, Society, and Culture', *The Rise of the Network Society*, Vol. 1. Oxford: Blackwell.

Castells, M. (1997) 'The Information Age: Economy, Society and Culture', *The Power of Identity*, Vol. II. Oxford: Blackwell.

Chesnais, F. (1997) *La mondialisation du capital*, Nouvelle édition augmentée. Paris: Syros.

Chesnais, F. and Simonetti, R. (2000) 'Globalisation, Foreign Direct Investment and Innovation: A European Perspective', in F. Chesnais, G. Ietto-Gillies, and R. Simonetti (eds), *European Integration and Global Corporate Strategies*, Chapter 1. London: Routledge, pp. 3–24.

Chesnais, F., Ietto-Gillies, G. and Simonetti, R. (2000) *European Integration and Global Corporate Strategies*. London: Routledge.

Chick, V. (1979) 'Transnational Corporations and the Evolution of the International Monetary System', in G. J. Crough (ed.), *Transnational Banking and the World Economy*, Chapter 5. Sydney: Transnational Corporations Research Project.

Cowling, K. (ed.) (1999) *Industrial Policy in Europe. Theoretical Perspectives and Practical Proposals*. London: Routledge.

Cowling, K. and Sugden, R. (eds) (1990) *A New Economic Policy for Britain. Essays on the Development of Industry*. Manchester: Manchester University Press.

Dalum, B., Freeman, C., Simonetti, R., von Tunzelman, N. and Verspagen, B. (1999) 'Europe and the Information and Communication Technologies Revolution', in J. Fageberger, P. Guerrieri and B. Verspagen (eds), *The Economic Challenge for Europe: Adapting to Innovation-Based Growth*, Chapter 5. London: Edward Elgar, pp. 106–29.

Freeman, C. (1992) *The Economics of Hope: Essays on Technical Change, Economic Growth and the Environment*. London: Pinter Publishers.

Giddens, A. (1999) Reith Lectures 1999. 'Runaway World. Lecture 1: Globalisation', http://news.bbc.co.uk/hi/english/...c/events/reith_99/week1/week1.htm.

Hagedoorn, J. (1996) 'Trends and Patterns in Strategic Technology Partnering since the Early Seventies', *Review of Industrial Organization* 11: 601–16.

Held, D., McGrew, A., Goldblatt, D. and Perraton, J. (1999) *Global Transformations*. Cambridge: Polity Press.

Hirst, P. and Thompson, G. (1996) *Globalisation in Question*. Cambridge: Polity Press.

Ietto-Gillies, G. (2000) 'Profits from Foreign Direct Investment', in F. Chesnais, G. Ietto-Gillies and R. Simonetti (eds), *European Integration and Global Corporate Strategies*. London: Routledge.

Keynes, M. (1937) 'The General Theory of Employment', *The Collected Writings of John Maynard Keynes*, Vol. XIV, 1973. London: MacMillan, pp.109–23.

Kozul-Wright, R. and Rowthorn, R. (eds) (1998a) *Transnational Corporations and the Global Economy*. London: MacMillan.

Kozul-Wright, R. and Rowthorn, R. (1998b) 'Spoilt for Choice? Multinational Corporations and the Geography of International Production', *Oxford Review of Economic Policy* 14(2): 74–92.

McGrew, A. G. (1992) 'Conceptualising Global Politics', in A. G. McGrew and P. G. Lewis (eds), *Global Politics: Globalisation and the Nation-State*. Cambridge: Polity Press, pp. 83–117.

Milberg, W. S. (1998) 'Globalization and its Limits', in R. Kozul-Wright and R. Rowthorn (eds), *Transnational Corporations and the Global Economy*, Chapter 2. London: MacMillan, pp. 69–94.

Obstfeld, M. (1998) 'The Global Capital Market: Benefactor or Menace?', *The Journal of Economic Perspectives* 12(4): 9–30.

Ohmae, K. (1991) *The Borderless World. Power and Strategy in the Interlinked Economy*. London: Fontana.

Ohmae, K. (1995) 'Putting Global Logic First', *Harvard Business Review* Jan–Feb: pp. 119–25.

Ohmae, K. (1996) *The End of the Nation State*, London: Harper Collins Publishers.

Oliner, S. D. and Sichel, D. E. (2000) 'The Resurgence of Growth in the Late 1990's: Is Information Technology the Whole Story?', http://www.sf.frb.org/conf2000/papers/resurgence.

Oman, C. (1996) 'The Policy Changes of Globalization and Regionalization', Policy Brief No. 11 OECD. OECD Development Centre.

Perez, C. (1983) 'Structural Changes and the Assimilation of New Technologies in the Economic and Social System', *Futures* 15(5): 357–75.

UNCTAD, DTCI (various years) *World Investment Report*. Geneva: United Nations.

# 15

# TECHNOLOGY AND THE NEED FOR AN ALTERNATIVE VIEW OF THE FIRM IN POST-KEYNESIAN THEORY

*Fabiana Santos and Marco Crocco*

We first met Victoria in 1995 when we both came to the UK for our Ph.D. As a student and a friend both of us had the privilege to share her companionship. For a younger generation of economist coming from Brazil, struggling against all the difficulties of leaving our country, families and friends, we found in Victoria comfort, friendship, support, and above all guidance and constant stimulation. The passion with which she embraces her convictions and beliefs is a continuous source of strength and inspiration for us.

To honour Victoria we choose to develop a point first raised by her in one of our many conversations. Prompted by Victoria's insightful comments, we set out to write more about technology and post-Keynesian views on the theory of the firm.

## 1. Introduction

There has been a widespread agreement among economists as to technical change as a fundamental factor to explain economic development and its importance for investment behaviour. Despite Keynes's unequivocal acceptance of Schumpeter's explanation of the 'major movements' of investment in capitalist societies (1930: 86), neither Keynes nor the Keynesians followed up this recognition of the crucial role of technical change. Post-Keynesian economists have given little attention to the whole dimension of the technical change phenomenon, for they are concerned with purely quantitative aspects of investment and employment. As a result, they have avoided the analysis of technical change and innovation, by considering it a phenomenon exogenous to the system.[1] However, in the same way as 'money matters', the way technical change is generated and incorporated into the system also 'matters'. Therefore, it is necessary to analyse technical change in its all institutional dimensions, and not only through variations on capital/output and labour/output ratios or shifts in the production function. Also, it should be recognised that the approach to technical change proposed here has some implications for the institutional setup upon which the expected aggregate demand and the supply functions are based. The most important of these implications, which we shall explore in this work, is the fact that the incorporation of technical change into post-Keynesian analysis clearly calls for a new approach to the firm.

It is important to say that we are neither searching for new microfoundations to macrodynamics, nor do we have sympathy for methodological reductionism. However, we believe that there are some interactions, not microfoundations, between the micro- and macro-level of analysis, as we shall see in the following discussion about the relationship between the process of firms' decisions and the determination of the point of effective demand.

## 2. The theory of the firm in the post-Keynesian school

Broadly speaking, one may identify two different approaches to the firm in post-Keynesian literature: the polypolistic firm (Joan Robinson 1933; Chick 1983) and the oligopolistic firm (Eichner 1976, 1991; Shapiro 1992, 1995, 1997).

According to Chick (1983) the concept of a polypolistic market is a very simple one, meaning 'many sellers'. Firms are viewed as an 'institutional embodiment of the profit-maximizing owner-manager' (Kozul-Wright 1995: 14).

To show Keynes's argument she defines the market as composed by many atomistic small sellers, which operate under uncertainty. Chick's characterisation of the firm is based upon the disassociation between size of the firm and the fact that the firm is a *price-taker* or *price-setter*. Following Keynes's approach, Chick puts expectations at the centre of her analysis, making it the relevant concept for the understanding of the behaviour of a small firm that is not a *price-taker*. As she points out:

> The expected position of the demand curve it [the small firm] faces in the near future will determine the price it should set for its product and the quantity it should produce.
>
> (1983: 26)

To understand the advantage of the use of the concept of polypolistic market, it is necessary to have in mind that Chick was interested in showing how the point of effective demand is determined regardless of the structure of the market. A key point here is the understanding of firms' behaviour under uncertainty, by distinguishing three stages in decision making, based respectively on hypothetical, expected and actual levels of demand (Chick 1983: 85). The hypothetical level of demand is essential to the definition of the supply curve, as it indicates the optimum level of production (the criterion of optimality being anyone) and price given various hypothetical levels of demand. The expected level of demand will be one of the various hypothetical demand curves and it will determine the volume of output and employment offered by the firm. Whether the expected level of demand is equal to the actual level of expenditure is another matter. There is no guarantee that they will be equal. If a mismatch occurs, 'then a third stage of decision-making process may be entered into, in which the now past level of actual demand influences the current expectations, causing the producer to choose another hypothetical level of demand as the basis for his decision' (1983: 86). If the expected demand turns out to be equal to the actual demand, equilibrium is achieved and there is no incentive to change the expected level of demand for the following periods.

The megacorp theory, on the other hand, considers a market structure composed of interdependent, growth maximising, large firms. The 'imperfections' of competition in this case endow the business environment with a degree of stability sufficient to make investment decisions possible (Richardson 1972, 1990 [1960]; Shapiro 1997). The behaviour and organisation of the megacorp is based on the managerial theory of the firm, where there is a clear separation between ownership of capital and management of the corporation. Moreover, the scope and scale of megacorp's production requires a professionalised management that is impossible to be observed in the traditional neoclassical firm (Shapiro 1992: 20).

In this framework the objectives of the firm coincide with the objectives of the executives, what Shapiro calls 'managerial firm's dominance'. This understanding grounds Eichner's (1976, 1991) view of the megacorp's behaviour. The modern corporation aims at maximising growth, as it is the main interest of management.

It should be noticed that this does not mean that the megacorp has no interest in making as much profit as possible. The point is that profit will be obtained by its rate of growth. In this sense, all operations inside the megacorp are aimed at facilitating the objective of maximising growth. In Shapiro's words:

> Firm growth is the 'long-run' expression of the profit objective, and while the firm cannot maximize its 'long-run profit' (there is no such profit), it can strive for an ever-increasing profit. It can 'maximise' profit growth.
>
> (1995: 297)

It is according to this framework that the process of pricing and the role of technical change should be analysed. The market power of the megacorp will be used to set a price (through a markup mechanism) that should be sufficient to generate the funds that investment requires. Continuous investment is a precondition for maximising growth and the price mechanism is the instrument that allows the generation of the necessary profits to finance it.

In its turn, technical change is essential to make profits by increasing the competitiveness of the firm, that is to say,

> Just as profit is needed for investment, investment is needed for profit. Firms can make profits only as long as they are competitive, and enterprise competitiveness requires investment... The firm has to meet the technical advances of competitors, and the product and output demand of customers, and it cannot do either without investment in its product and production processes.
>
> (Shapiro 1995: 297)

## 3. A brief assessment of the polypolistic firm and the megacorp

The summary description of both accounts shows the advantages and limitations of each approach. There are two common advantages. In both cases the firm is considered a *price-maker* and the market operates under some 'imperfections' of competition. This means that the firm sets prices in its own interests whatever they are. Second, both accounts incorporate a time dimension on price decisions, through the incorporation of future prospects and expectations on the formation of prices. That is to say, they bring uncertainty into the framework.

Moreover, each approach has its own advantages. The polypoly perspective's main contribution is to show that the size of the firm is not a relevant aspect to determine the capacity of the firm to set its own prices. As Chick has shown, the latter does not change whether we consider many small firms or a few large firms.

In turn, the megacorp can be viewed as a more realistic representation of economic life. Apart from considering that firms can (and do) affect market outcomes, it incorporates many features of a capitalist economy – like the separation between ownership and control, technical change, differentiation of products, distinctive degrees of market power and competitiveness – as well as establishes the link between pricing and funding.

However, there are drawbacks, the most important being that both approaches do not constitute theories of the firm, but instead theories of pricing. According to Sawyer, in the post-Keynesian perspective,

> prices play many roles other than (or in addition to) the allocative/ co-ordinating one. Gerrard (1989) identifies this as conductive, positional, strategic and financial. The conductive role relates to the passing on of costs in to prices through say mark-up pricing, and of prices into wages. The positional role concerns the relativity of the price of one economic agent with another (e.g. the importance of relative wages). The strategic role of prices reflects firms adopting competitive strategies, whilst the financial role is to enable firms to generate sufficient funds to finance expansion.
>
> (1995: 304)

Although the relevance of a theory of pricing should be recognised for explaining macroeconomic phenomena – e.g. income distribution, the determination of the point of effective demand or the dynamism of the system – we need to know more than the cost structure of the firm in order to deal with and have a comprehensive understanding of the real world. The geometric representation of a firm's behaviour through some cost curves is insufficient to generate a theory of the firm that is compatible with the very same macroeconomic phenomena that post-Keynesians are interested in. Among these phenomena, one of the most important is technological change, without doubt a central element to explain the dynamism of the economic system.

In the polypoly approach, technology is considered exogenous to the functioning of the system – it is given – and it is available to everyone. As we shall see, this simplified assumption with respect to technical change does not deal with its all features. Further, to assume the exogeneity of technological knowledge is to ignore the fact that a great deal of it is firm specific.

In its turn, the megacorp approach considers both technical change and R&D activity as important elements of a firm's competitiveness. However, this recognition is not fully explored. Following Schumpeter's tradition, the capacity to innovate is directly related to size of the firm. Market power gives the firm the necessary assurance to invest and to allocate resources in R&D. Moreover, the use of technological knowledge generated by this latter activity is important for sustaining and improving the megacorp's market share. However, they do not explicitly recognise that this process is (partly) firm specific and contingent on the firm's past history. In short, the point is that this understanding deals with just one dimension of innovative activity.

The fact that a great deal of technological knowledge is firm specific (i.e. originated through learning processes) and characterised by cumulativeness, tacitness, technological trajectories, etc., requires a new concept of the firm capable of dealing with all these features. As Kozul-Wright notes:

> ... once innovation is understood, the question of firm size (...) appears far less important than the wider issue of organising and co-ordinating the learning process.
>
> (1995: 10)

Therefore, as far as we admit into our formal reasoning the reality of technical change and innovation, geometric representations of either small or large firms based on cost curves say too little about how firms obtain 'sufficient' knowledge to take an investment decision.

As this is an essential point, let us take a closer look at the discussion of this distinctive concept of the firm for it will be easy to see its implications for some macroeconomic factors.

## 4. The firm as a repository of knowledge[2]

Marshall has already recognised the interdependence between growth of knowledge and economic development and the importance of the firm in 'co-ordinating the generation and testing of novel conjectures' (Loasby 1994: 115). In Marshall's words,

> Capital consists in great part of knowledge and organization ... Knowledge is our most powerful engine of production ... Organisation aids knowledge.
>
> (1961: 115)

As noted by Loasby (1994: 255), the corollary of this proposition is that the lack of appropriate organisation impedes knowledge. The task ahead of an organisation is not to 'make the best of what is known', but instead to find out 'what is at present unknown' and this requires co-ordination. Again, as Marshall puts forward, a firm is a form of organisation that aids knowledge, that is, firms provide the institutional framework and co-ordination needed for 'the generation and testing of new conjectures'. Firms thus undertake knowledge-creating activities, which are the underpinning of economic growth.

A firm should therefore be viewed as a repository of knowledge, which is manifested (or embodied) in its capabilities. Capabilities refer to the ways of organising and getting things done (indirect knowledge) and of doing things (direct knowledge). As defined by Richardson, the capability of a firm is its possession of 'knowledge, experience and skills which enable it to undertake "activities" such as discovery and estimation of future wants, research, development, design, execution and co-ordination of processes of physical transformation, the marketing of goods and so on' (1972: 888). And this 'know-how' can only be fully understood if one keeps in mind that it is the outcome of an interactive process involving all the firm's constituent parts (as well as external organisations, such as suppliers, customers, rivals and financial institutions).

In order to create an environment that allows interactive learning to occur, cooperation between various (and possibly conflicting) groups within the firm and continuity of relations are important. Information sharing, codification of procedures, adaptation of work routines, common language and culture – in short, the creation of 'routinised behaviour' (Nelson and Winter 1982) – cannot be done overnight. Once a set of routines is created, the capabilities of the firms will depend not just on the individuals of whom it is composed but also on the particular pattern of 'intimate connections' between them (Loasby 1994: 254). Thus, external transfer of an individual's knowledge beyond a firm's boundary may be difficult if not impossible, since taken out of the context it may be quite useless (Teece 1982: 45).

As a matter of fact, the knowledge embodied in capabilities contains a significant degree of tacitness, which cannot be codified and transferred, but rather must be acquired through practical experience and learning. We may then say that capabilities are firm specific and 'sticky' in the sense that they cannot be acquired or passed on easily, quickly and at low cost (Penrose 1995 [1959]; Teece et al. 1990).

Penrose (1995 [1959]) has already shown, through the concept of the firm's 'productive opportunities', how a firm's knowledge base conditions its growth and diversification. Internal learning combined with the entrepreneurial vision of where, when and how the acquired learning can be put into use compromises the 'productive opportunities' of a firm. Each success (or failure) will lead to fresh learning and new 'visions'; new knowledge being created from past experience (Loasby 1994: 256).

The firm's knowledge base grows from the knowledge accumulated through learning and experience, contingent on the firm's past history (path dependency).

These knowledge-creating activities underpin dynamic competition and economic growth. In fact, technological change (or innovation) is nothing more than a series of simultaneous knowledge-creating activities undertaken by a number of firms often in close cooperation with external organisations (users of innovation, universities, public research bodies, rivals, etc; see Kozul-Wright (1995)). It is the size and the nature of this 'stock' of knowledge that differentiates one firm from another and inhibits the free transfer of technological knowledge among them.

This privileged knowledge, embodied in firms' capabilities, is used by firms to exert influence on market conditions and profitability. On the one hand, distinctive capabilities are the source of profitability differentials that are, in turn, translated into different rates of accumulation. On the other hand, firms use their privileged knowledge (*and not only their pricing policy*) to affect markets conditions, instead of passively accepting given market conditions.

Summing up, our focus concentrates then on the firm and the knowledge on which it is based. Accordingly, as noted by Kozul-Wright:

> a firm's boundaries are no longer contained by its size but by its knowledge base, and there can be no a priori optimal rule with respect to firm size, industrial structure and economic growth.
>
> (1995: 27)

## 5. The firm's capabilities and its impacts on some macroeconomic phenomena

In our view this approach to the firm may affect some macroeconomic phenomena. Due to lack of space it is impossible to provide an extended discussion, so in what follows we focus on drawing some macroeconomic implications of this approach.

We shall concentrate on one important aspect, the interaction between continuous technical change and the process of decision making. What we have in mind is two kinds of decision: the production decision and the investment decision.

### *Capabilities and the point of effective demand*

As we have argued elsewhere (Crocco 1999), the discussion about the production decision is important as it has some impact on the determination of the point of effective demand. The first point to be addressed here is related to the firm's ease of hiring and dismissing labour. As shown previously, due to the process of building capabilities it takes time for a new employee to learn the routinised behaviour of a firm. Moreover, when an employee is dismissed, the firm gives up not only a unit of labour force, but also part of the firm's tacit knowledge. This latter cannot be replaced by the employment of another worker. The capabilities of the firm are not decomposable into the capabilities of the managers and individual workers, but involve teamwork that must be coordinated and practised. These features imply that there is a cost involved in the process of dismissing and hiring labour force.

Even if the same person that is being dismissed is re-hired in the future some cost will be involved. Moreover, according to Teece and Pisano (1994) there is no market for capabilities, except possibly through the market for businesses (to buy or to sell a whole firm). In other words, capabilities must be built because they cannot be bought. As a consequence, a firm becomes much more cautious when dealing with its labour force, as individual and organisational skills acquired in the learning process demand time and are costly. Hence, these costs become an important element when a firm has to decide about its optimal level of employment.

A second important element to take into account is the fact that firms, according to the approach used here, can affect their own demand. As we are dealing with product innovation, firms know that there is a possibility for their market share to increase due to the novelty of the product. Moreover, it is well recognised that every new successful product has a life cycle. As a result, every firm expects that, whenever it launches a new product into the market, demand for its product will show oscillations similar to those predicted by the product cycle theory.

From a theoretical point of view, the above discussion sheds light on the question of whether or not it is still acceptable to assume that a firm varies the size of its labour force every time its production expectations are not validated. In other words, in the case of considering an institutional framework where the firm regards its capabilities as a valuable asset, is an invalidation of the firm's production expectations sufficient to alter the level of employment it offers?

The claim made here is a negative answer to the last question. Firms will define the amount of labour to hire according to expectations related to the whole life cycle of its products. The implication of this view is that, in the enquiry of the point of effective demand, production expectations are no longer theoretically adequate and should be replaced by what we call 'medium-period expectation' or 'single-product expectation' (Crocco 1999). The latter have been defined as the expectations concerning the quasi-rents arising from the introduction of a new product. It involves many production decisions, although it also involves a shorter perspective of time and less monetary resources than the acquisition of a capital good. In other words, we are claiming that the level of employment at a specific point of time is defined by the medium-period expectations (MPEs hereafter), given the total level of investment.

Two consequences can be derived from the replacement of MPEs by production expectations. First, the variation of employment becomes less frequent because of the longer time involved in the formation of MPEs. Second, as we are assuming that a firm can interfere with its own demand, it is necessary to rethink how present expectations are formed in the face of a possible mismatch between previous expectations and actual demand.

The fulfilment or not of previous expectations certainly will affect expectations about the next product innovation. However, MPEs are concerned with a new product that is, at the same time, a development of the previous one. Holding everything else constant, this means that a firm can affect its own demand by launching a new product in the market. The main implication of this special feature is that there is no one-to-one relationship between the mismatch of previous expectations and the formation of the next one, as in the case of short-period expectations. The disappointment of previous expectations does not necessarily imply a negative revision of expectations for the new product. As the latter has some element of novelty, there is a possibility that the firm's demand will be positively affected. Of course, if disappointment is great, the expectations will have to be revised. The key element in this discussion is that the firm's demand cannot be considered stable when product innovation is considered. Product innovation implies that a firm cannot be seen as passive in relation to its own demand. As we have seen, the concept of competition used here means rivalry, which, in turn, implies an active behaviour of the firm in relation to market conditions.

By the same token, in the case of MPEs, the match of previous expectations and realised outcomes does not necessarily produce an equilibrium that equates the prospective yields of sequential products. As we are dealing with a new product that belongs to a technological trajectory, a successful prediction of the prospective yields of a previous product can positively affect the expectations for the next ones.[3]

### Capabilities and investment decision

The discussion now turns to some implications of the understanding of the firm as a repository of knowledge and its consequences for the process of formation of long-period expectations (LPEs). Attention will be concentrated on one question: what will happen with the investment decision in the post-Keynesian approach if product innovation is allowed. In other words, we have to analyse what the impact on LPEs will be if we assume that there will be future developments in the firm's product.

Keynes and the post-Keynesians have been concerned about the precariousness of the basis upon which investment decisions are made, due to uncertainty related to this kind of decision.

However, as Keynes has already pointed out,

> It would be foolish, in forming our expectations, to attach great weight to matters which are very uncertain. It is reasonable, therefore, to be guided to a considerable degree by the facts about which we feel somewhat confident, even though they may be less decisively relevant to the issue than other facts about which our knowledge is vague and scanty.
>
> (1936 [1973]: 148)

According to the quotation above, one has to be guided by the facts of the present situation when deciding whether to invest or not. The usual approach in this case is to introduce into the framework conventions that are held by investors at the moment of the decision. While this cannot be denied, our previous discussion of capabilities suggests that another element can be introduced into this framework.

Applying Keynes's framework mentioned above to the problem in question, it can be seen that, when an investor forms an expectation of future receipts from the sales of the products produced by the capital asset that is now being bought, he attaches great weight to the prospective yields from the product that will be produced *immediately* by the new equipment. The main point here is to show that when one tries to analyse the firm's investment decision, one has to acknowledge that the firm has been developing a technological trajectory. Because of some features of the technological knowledge possessed by the firm (tacitness, cumulativeness, etc. – expressed through its capabilities), the formation of expectations can be made on stronger grounds as the immediate past outcomes obtained by the firm strongly affect the formation of expectations about the immediate future, even when these expectations are about an investment in a new plant.

A firm knows that the immediate products to be produced usually represent a stage on a technological trajectory that has been developed by the firm. Unless the first type of product to be produced by the new capital good is a completely new product (a change of the technological trajectory), there will be strong connections between the latest products produced with the old capital asset and the first products to be produced with the new capital asset. Thus, the expectation of prospective yields from the first type of products to be produced with the new capital asset are strongly affected by the outcomes obtained by the latest types of products produced with the old equipment.[4] In other words, the formation of LPE becomes *partially* endogenised.

## 6. Conclusion

We tried to show that if technical change is to be understood in all its dimensions, a specific theory of the firm must be considered. As we have discussed, a firm viewed as a repository of knowledge seems to be the best way to deal with technical change. We have argued that post-Keynesian theories of the firm (polypolistic and megacorp) are insufficient to cope with the learning process that is inherent to innovative activity. Moreover, and finally, we have demonstrated that there are some macroeconomic implications of whether we assume a theory of firm to be based upon the concept of capabilities or based upon a pricing mechanism.

## Notes

1 We are not saying that they do not incorporate technical change in their analyses, as the works of Kaldor and Mirrlees (1962), Joan Robinson (1965) and Eichner (1991) have shown. What we are claiming is that their treatment, although functional to the analysis of income distribution, is unable to deal with all the dimensions of technical change. For a review about the way post-Keynesians deal with innovation, see Crocco (1999).

2 We draw on ideas of Marshall, Penrose, Richardson, Nelson and Winter, Loasby and Teece to understand how firms deal with the world of continuous product and process development.

3 What is behind this analysis is the discussion about the development of a technological trajectory and its relation to the weight of argument (Crocco 1999, 2000). The success or failure of the introduction of an innovation changes the weight of argument in relation to the introduction of the next innovation (Crocco 1999). In situations where the previous product innovation has been successfully introduced (expectations were confirmed), there is an increase in the weight of argument related to the introduction of the new one, and so, there is an increase in confidence allowing for higher expectations for the next product.

4 If the latest innovations have been introduced successfully, the confidence about the introduction of the new product innovation increases along with the weight related to this decision (Crocco 1999).

# References

Chick, V. (1983) *Macroeconomics After Keynes: A Reconsideration of the General Theory*. Cambridge, MA: MIT Press.

Crocco, M. (1999) 'Uncertainty, Technical Change and Effective Demand', Ph.D. Thesis, Economics Department, University of London – UCL, London.

Crocco, M. (2000) 'The Future's Unknowability: Keynes's Probability, Probable Knowledge and the Decision to Innovate', in F. Louçã and M. Perlman (eds), *Is Economics an Evolutionary Science?* Aldershot: Edward Elgar.

Eichner, A. (1976) *The Megacorp and the Oligopoly*. Cambridge: Cambridge University Press.

Eichner, A. S. (1991) *The Macrodynamics of Advanced Market Economies*. London: M.E. Sharpe.

Gerrard, B. (1989) *Theory of the Capitalist Economy*. Oxford: Basil Blackwell.

Kaldor, N. and Mirrlees, J. (1962) 'A New Model of Economic Growth', *Review of Economic Studies* 29: 174–92.

Keynes, J. M. (1936) [1973] *The General Theory of employment, Interest and Money, The Collected Writings of John Maynard Keynes*, Vol. VII. London: Macmillan.

Kozul-Wright, Z. (1995) 'The Role of the Firm in the Innovation Process', UNCTAD, Discussion Papers, n. 98.

Loasby, B. (1994) 'Organisational Capabilities and Interfirm Relations', *Metroeconomica* 45: 3.

Marshall, A. (1961) *Principles of Economics*, 9th (variorum) edn. London: Macmillan.

Nelson, R. and Winter, S. (1982) *An Evolutionary Theory of Economic Change*. Cambridge, MA: Harvard University Press.

Penrose, E. (1995) [1959] *The Theory of the Growth of the Firm*. Oxford: Oxford University Press.

Richardson, G. (1972) The Organisation of Industry. *Economic Journal* 82: 883–96.

Richardson, G. (1990) [1960] *Information and Investment: A Study in the Working of the Competitive Economy*. Oxford: Clarendon Press.

Robinson, J. (1933) *The Economics of Imperfect Competition*. London: Macmillan.

Robinson, J. (1965) *The Accumulation of Capital*. London: Macmillan.

Sawyer, M. (1995) 'Comment on Earl and Shapiro', in S. Dow and J. Hillard (eds), *Keynes, Knowledge and Uncertainty*. Brookfield: Edward Elgar.

Shapiro, N. (1992) 'The "Megacorp": Eichener's Contribution to the Theory of the Firm', in W. Milberg (ed.), *The Megacorp and Macrodynamics: Essays in Memory of Alfred Eichner*. London: M.E. Sharp.

Shapiro, N. (1995) 'Markets and Mark-ups: Keynesian Views', in S. Dow and J. Hillard (eds), *Keynes, Knowledge and Uncertainty*. Brookfield: Edward Elgar.

Shapiro, N. (1997) 'Imperfect Competition and Keynes', in G. Harcourt and P. Riach (eds), *A 'Second Edition' of the General Theory*. London: Routledge.

Teece, D. (1982) 'Towards an Economic Theory of the Multiproduct Firm', *Journal of Economic Behaviour and Organization* 3: 39–63.

Teece, D. et al. (1990) 'Firm Capabilities, Resources and the Concept of Strategy', CCC Working Papers, 90–8, University of California, Berkley.

Teece, D. and Pisano, G. (1994) 'The Dynamic Capabilities of Firms: An Introduction', *Industrial and Corporate Change* 3(3): 537–56.

# 16

# CONSUMER BELIEFS AND A POSSIBLE WELFARE 'GAIN' FROM MONOPOLY

*Ian Steedman*[1]

Although this chapter is but brief, it has a twofold purpose. First, a simple example will be used to raise the possibility that a monopolized industry might yield a greater social surplus than a competitive industry, even when the horizontal industry cost curve is the same or, indeed, somewhat higher under monopoly. Discussion of this example will then lead into a far broader topic, that of the treatment of consumer beliefs in social surplus calculations (and, implicitly, other economic analyses). If consumers can be ill-informed about the characteristics of commodities, what does that imply for familiar arguments in welfare economics?

## 1. An example

Our example lies squarely within the now conventional framework for discussing the effects of monopoly on welfare, that exemplified in Harberger (1954). No further reference will be made, for example, to 'Austrian' objections to that framework. (See West (1987) for a convenient introduction.) Nor will any of the powerful objections to consumers' surplus analysis be considered here – which is not to say that we reject them! The analysis is to be interpreted in strictly comparative static terms; one is comparing a permanent situation under competition with a permanent situation under monopoly, there being no reference whatever to any process of change through time. Moreover, the example will be of the simplest kind, with a linear market demand curve and (initially at least) zero marginal, average and total costs of production (as in Cournot's famous example of the production of spring-water).

Let the market inverse demand curve be given by

$$p = a - bq. \tag{1}$$

The standard calculations show that the total surplus (all of it consumers' surplus) under perfect competition will be given by

$$S_c = \frac{a^2}{2b}.$$ (2)

Under monopoly, however, there will be profits of

$$P_m = \frac{a^2}{4b}$$ (3)

and a social surplus of

$$S_m = \frac{3a^2}{8b} < S_c.$$

Suppose, however, that the market demand curve is *not* the same under monopoly because the monopolist finds it profitable to engage in sales expenditure; following Chamberlin (1933), we take sales expenditure to be any expenditure intended to alter the demand curve. Such expenditure will not necessarily be on advertising but it is still to the point here to recall Schmalensee's summary statement (1989: 978) that, 'In broad samples of manufacturing industries producing consumer goods, advertising intensity is positively related to industry-average accounting profitability.' (Schmalensee also notes that, 'Advertising is not the dominant component of selling costs in [producer goods] industries', p. 979.)[2]

Let the monopolist's inverse demand curve be given by

$$p = a(e) - b(e)q,$$ (4)

where $e$ is sales expenditure and the $a$ and $b$ in (1), (2) and (3) should now be thought of as $a(0)$ and $b(0)$. Profit is given by

$$P_M = \left[ \frac{a^2(e)}{4b(e)} \right] - e$$ (5)

and social surplus by

$$S_M = \left[ \frac{3a^2(e)}{8b(e)} \right] - e$$ (6)

for arbitrary $e$. But the profit-maximizing monopolist will of course select $e$ so as to maximize $P_M$ in (5). Define $c(e) \equiv [a^2(e)/b(e)]$ and suppose that $c'(0) > 4$ and $c''(e) < 0$; then $e^* > 0$ will certainly be selected and $P_M(e^*) > P_M(0) = P_m$. Now from (2) and (6), $S_M(e^*)$ will exceed $S_c$ if and only if

$$3c(e^*) - 8e^* > 4c(0).$$ (7)

There is no reason at all why (7) should not hold good and, when it does, the monopolized industry, with the same (zero) production costs, yields a *larger* social surplus than that generated under perfect competition.

We may now modify the example slightly, replacing the common industry average cost curve $C = 0$ by the average cost curve $C = C_0$. It will be obvious from continuity considerations that with small enough $C_0$ the qualitative result of our example would be unchanged. Thus monopoly could yield the greater social surplus even if it involved slightly higher production costs.

## 2. Caveat

Before we begin our discussion of the above example, it will perhaps be as well to guard against some possible misunderstandings as to the nature of that example. It might be objected that consumer surplus arguments are unacceptable, for one reason or another; it might be urged that the partial equilibrium nature of the example may be misleading because conditions in 'other' markets will not be the same in the two (monopoly and perfect competition) situations; or it might be questioned whether perfect competition with zero sales expenditure is the relevant case with which to compare the monopoly situation. The reply to all three 'objections' is the same, namely that whatever their strengths or weaknesses may be, *they apply with equal force to the standard 'Harberger' analysis*, having nothing specifically to do with the particular version of it which is presented here. Our example points to a *further* possible problem with the standard 'Harberger' approach and, in order to do so, inevitably stays as close as possible to that approach. To offer as 'objections' to our example considerations which apply equally to every Harberger-like analysis would be to miss the mark completely.

It must also be insisted that our consideration of sales expenditure and of the consequently higher demand curve in the monopoly situation is not to be conceived of as introducing some extraneous or arbitrary factor into the familiar 'Harberger' account. That account already supposes the monopolist to be a profit maximizer and our example is such that profit-maximizing behaviour on the part of the monopolist *entails* that there be positive sales expenditure. In the context of the example, then, it would be quite meaningless to say that one should only compare the competitive situation with that of an '$e = 0$ monopolist' rather than with that of the '$e > 0$ monopolist'. (Some readers might see here an analogy with the 'Schumpeterian' insistence that it may be meaningless to presuppose equal 'research and development expenditures' when comparing competitive and monopolistic situations; but note that our argument is not in the least reliant on the acceptance of any such analogy.)

Finally, it perhaps bears repetition that our example is of a purely comparative static nature, involving no changes, no learning, no dynamics, no .... Thus if we adopt below the common practice of referring to welfare 'gains' and welfare 'losses', we always really intend 'positive' or 'negative' welfare *differences*.

### 3. A welfare gain?

In the above example the conventionally calculated social surplus under perfect competition is smaller than the conventionally calculated social surplus under monopoly. Does it follow that the monopoly situation is preferable from a welfare point of view? The answer is obviously positive[3] *if* the calculated areas under the demand curves are genuinely comparable – but are they?

(a) Anyone who takes the relevant areas to be comparable must immediately accept that there is a welfare gain from monopoly and hence that the conventionally calculated welfare 'loss' from monopoly can be positive, zero or negative; i.e. that the conventional calculation in fact yields *no* qualitative, a priori result.

(b) It might be objected, however, that the areas in question are not really comparable and hence that no conclusion can properly be drawn about the presence or absence of a welfare gain. Thus it might be suggested that the positive sales expenditure under monopoly can only shift the market demand curve because it implies different preferences of potential consumers and that, because of the difference in preferences, our calculated social surpluses are simply non-comparable. If accepted, this response would naturally avoid the conclusion that monopoly yields a welfare gain. But it would be no less destructive of the conventional argument than is response (a) above, at least for a world in which positive sales expenditure is known often to be an aspect of profit-maximizing behaviour.

While response (a) leads to the conclusion that 'anything can happen', response (b) leads to the conclusion that (in the world we inhabit) 'nothing whatever can be said', because the competitive and monopoly surpluses are non-comparable. Although responses (a) and (b) are diametrically opposed, at one level, they nevertheless lead to a single conclusion: in a world in which a profit-maximizing monopoly may make positive sales expenditures, the conventional, Harberger-like argument that a monopoly always yields a welfare loss just cannot be made. And this for reasons having nothing to do with the rejection of consumers' surplus measures, or with economies of scale, or with the monopoly case involving (for whatever reason) a lower industry cost curve.

### 4. Consumer beliefs

It would certainly be possible at this point to enter into a discussion of whether, in the context of the above example, the monopoly market structure is to be considered the first-best solution[4] – or whether it would be better to have a competitive structure, with government-backed sales expenditure financed in some appropriate manner. One could also consider cases with sub-additive or non-sub-additive cost functions; discuss sustainable equilibrium and entry deterrence; etc. However, with no implied disparagement of such concerns, we turn in a different direction to consider further the response (b) introduced above. For it would not really be correct to say that sales expenditure could give a different market demand curve under monopoly *only* if that expenditure involved changed consumer preferences.

Such expenditure might involve different beliefs rather than different preferences – would that render our calculated areas non-comparable or not? (For a closely related discussion *not* involving sales expenditure, see Currie and Steedman (2000).)

Even without adopting the specific and very rigid framework employed by Lancaster (1966, 1971, 1979), we may certainly accept the general idea that consumer preferences are over the attributes/characteristics/properties/qualities of commodities and not over these latter *per se*. Suppose then that the sales expenditure considered in our example has no effect whatever on consumers' preferences over characteristics but does affect their beliefs about the extent to which the product in question has various (desirable or undesirable) characteristics.[5] By assumption, response (b) cannot now be made, at least in its initial form, for now exactly the same preferences *do* underlie all our calculations. Does the difference in the underlying beliefs about the product nevertheless entail that the areas under the demand curves are still non-comparable, albeit for a new kind of reason?

To be more specific, suppose first that the sales expenditure has brought all the relevant consumers' beliefs about the product's characteristics closer to the objective truth of the matter. In the absence of that expenditure, potential purchasers would have underestimated the product's 'endowment' of (what they regard as) good attributes and/or have overestimated its 'endowment' of (what they regard as) bad attributes. In this case, then, the two market demand curves are underpinned by exactly the same fundamental preferences (over characteristics) but that for monopoly expresses the (market level) demand of better-informed consumers than does that for perfect competition. It seems unlikely that anyone will take this difference in beliefs to mean that the conventional calculations carried out above *over*estimate the welfare gain from monopoly. But some might well respond by saying that the difference in beliefs means that the calculations *under*estimate that welfare gain. Yet others might respond by insisting that the relevant 'areas' simply are not comparable.

Now consider the contrary extreme case, in which the sales expenditure has led all the relevant consumers' beliefs about the product to be further from the truth. That is, potential purchasers have been led to overestimate the product's 'endowment' of 'positive' attributes and to underestimate its 'endowment' of 'negative' ones. In this case, presumably, few if any would take the calculated welfare gain from monopoly to give an underestimate of the true gain. Most would probably respond by saying either that the calculation overestimates the gain, or that the relevant 'areas' are again non-comparable. Finally (and most realistically?) one must consider the non-extreme case in which sales expenditure draws some relevant beliefs closer to the truth but leads others further away from it. What does this case imply for the (non-)comparability of the 'areas' in our calculations?

The most simple basis for a determined 'non-comparability' response to the kind of question raised above would be, presumably, the judgement that the economists' familiar treatment of preferences – that 'they are just whatever they are and the economist *qua* economist has nothing whatever to say about them' – should be extended to their treatment of consumers' beliefs. On such a view, the fact that consumers' beliefs can sometimes be known to be closer to or further from the truth in one situation than they are in another would simply not be a relevant fact (for the welfare economist). An economist adopting this view could, of course, acknowledge the conceptual difference between a changed-preferences basis and a changed-beliefs basis for our different market demand curves but would still draw exactly the same conclusion in either case: the 'areas' under them are simply non-comparable from a welfare standpoint and it is not meaningful to compare our calculated areas, or to make any related statements about welfare gain or loss.[6] As noted above, such an approach destroys the whole 'Harberger' tradition in many, many real world contexts – but that is not our main concern here, which is rather to consider whether this view would be acceptable *per se*.

For present purposes we shall accept without discussion the economists' familiar 'hands-off' stance with respect to preferences, in order to concentrate on the question whether it can plausibly be extended to consumers' beliefs (which is not necessarily to endorse that stance, or to imply that preference issues and belief issues can in the end be kept apart). That such an extension is not immediately plausible follows at once from the fact that the 'hands-off' approach to preferences is based, at least in part, on the claim (justified or not) that there is no independent, autonomous standpoint from which preferences can be commented on, no 'correct' standard which they can be said to approach or to deviate from. By contrast, in many dimensions at least there *is* an independent, autonomous standpoint from which consumers' beliefs can be commented on and there are objective truths which they can be said to approximate or to deviate from. (That this is so is not altered by the fact that there are relevant matters about which, although there is an objective truth to be known, the objective truth is not currently known – e.g. the relation between consumption of some foodstuff F and the probability of contracting a disease D.) And if any university teachers of economics should nevertheless insist that consumers' beliefs must still be treated just as are their preferences, what do they take *teaching* to be about?

However, we do not really suppose that many economic theorists would in fact adopt the strict 'hands-off' approach to consumers' beliefs considered in the preceding paragraph. A more likely – and more reasonable – approach would seem to be that 'willingness to pay' based on given preferences and better-informed beliefs about commodities should *count for more* than such willingness based on the same preferences and less-well-informed beliefs.[7] Or, more cautiously, we may pose a question: *What grounds could be given for denying that that is a more reasonable approach?*

To accept the approach just outlined is not, of course, to know at once how to interpret the kind of calculations made above, even when it is assumed (or known) that sales expenditure has affected only beliefs and not preferences over characteristics. On the contrary, such acceptance implies that no such interpretation can properly be given until it is known *how* sales expenditure has affected beliefs and *how* the change in beliefs is to be evaluated. Has it led potential purchasers to have better or less-well-informed beliefs? Even worse, if the answer should be that it has had a *mixture* of such effects – and a mixture, at that, which is not even close to either extreme case – how then ought one to 'expand' or to 'shrink' (to 'multiply' or to 'discount') the relevant areas under monopoly in order to make them really comparable with those under perfect competition? We have no answer to offer here, so again we may pose questions: Can it really make sense to ignore any differences in relevant beliefs when comparing social surpluses in two alternative situations? If so, why? And if not, how should those differences be 'reckoned into' social surplus calculations? Unless it be seriously denied that we live in a world in which some sales expenditures do affect some relevant beliefs, it would seem that answering these questions is a necessary precondition for making responsible use of at least certain social surplus calculations.

## 5. Concluding remarks

Our example, simple minded as it is, suffices to show that the conventionally calculated social surplus can be greater under monopoly than under perfect competition – and this even when the monopoly actually has a higher cost curve. Although this finding certainly depended on the presence of positive sales expenditure under monopoly, it did not necessarily depend on any resultant difference in preferences (over characteristics) and thus could not be dismissed on the grounds that a difference in preferences made the two calculated surpluses non-comparable. Rejecting any suggestion that differences in beliefs are just as much a source of non-comparability as differences in preferences are often held to be, we have posed a number of questions about how such differences in beliefs ought to be allowed for when alternative situations are compared, as in the standard 'welfare loss (gain?) from monopoly' literature.[8]

## Notes

1 I am grateful to J. Broome, J. M. Currie, J. Kemp, D. Leslie, J. S. Metcalfe, S. Parrinello, M. Sawyer, H. Steiner and participants in a seminar given at Notre Dame, Indiana, for helpful discussion and comments.
2 More generally on advertising, see Schmalensee (1972).
3 'Obviously', that is, given that one is taking the consumer-surplus frame of reference to be adequate for the making of welfare comparisons. For a recent and sustained objection to so taking it, see Hausman and McPherson (1996), especially chapter 6.
4 As J. M. Currie has pointed out, there might be scope here for defining a new concept of 'natural monopoly', which has nothing to do with any reduction in production costs.
5 Whilst not wishing to sully the main text with the controversial distinction between 'persuasive' and 'informative' sales promotion, we may perhaps float the idea that the 'informative' kind may be *more* related to belief changes than to preference changes (but certainly without implying that any persuasive/informative distinction coincides with a preference-/belief-changing distinction). Nelson (1974) argues that many features of advertising can be explained in terms of information provision, without reference to preference changes. (He has a section, pp. 749–51, on 'Deceptive Advertising'.) Of course, for many 'industrial organization' purposes all these distinctions can be left aside, as when Spence (1980: 494), e.g., simply says that 'advertising is designed to

influence demand and prices' and then moves straight on to an inverse demand function. Note though that Telser (1964: 538–9) is an early example of using the commodity/characteristics distinction in relation to advertising. (We do not imply, of course, that advertising by firms is the only type of organized information provision directed to consumers.)

6  But note that Dixit and Norman (1978) forcefully reject the claim that no welfare statements can be made when advertising alters preferences, insisting that one can always try to assess the different situations in terms of *both* no-advertising and with-advertising preferences. After reading our next few paragraphs the reader might wish to consider whether it would be appropriate, by analogy, to assess alternative situations in terms of *both* less-well-informed beliefs and better-informed beliefs; at least some readers, we suppose, will decide that it would not.

7  Cf. 'Social preferences, the *ex-post* school [of Peter Hammond *et alia*] argues, should be based on people's preferences. But it is not so clear that they should be based on people's beliefs. Beliefs are subject to standards of truth and falsity, or at least to standards of rationality and irrationality. And that means people's beliefs should not automatically be accepted as a basis for social preferences. It would be wrong, for instance, to base social preferences on a belief that was mistaken.' (Broome 1991: 161). And, 'Even if policy-makers should in general honour people's preferences, they should not necessarily agree with their beliefs.' (Hausman and McPherson 1996: 76). See also Caven (1993, section 4). Griffen (1986) argues at length the case for giving weight to what he calls 'informed-desire'.

8  It might well be thought that far more attention needs to be given to consumers' beliefs in welfare economics more generally and the reader is encouraged to pursue this idea. All 'positive' consumer theory which refers centrally to beliefs (e.g. Cosgel 1994) is of course likely to have implications for welfare theory. And the relevance of beliefs is not confined to 'actual-preference-satisfaction' theories of welfare; cf. Hausman and McPherson (1996: 123–4) on misleading information as reducing the capacity for autonomy.

# References

Broome, J. (1991) *Weighing Goods*. Oxford: Basil Blackwell.

Caven, T. (1993) 'The Scope and Limits of Preference Sovereignty', *Economics and Philosophy* 9: 253–69.

Chamberlin, E. H. (1933) *The Theory of Monopolistic Competition*, Cambridge, MA: Harvard University Press.

Cosgel, M. M. (1994) 'Audience Effects in Consumption', *Economics and Philosophy* 10, April, pp. 19–30.

Currie, J. M. and Steedman, I. (2000) 'Consumer Perceptions of Commodity Characteristics: Implications for Choice and Welfare', *Manchester School* 68: 516–38.

Dixit, A. and Norman, V. (1978) 'Advertising and Welfare', *Bell Journal of Economics* 9: 1–17.

Griffin, J. (1986) *Well-Being. Its Meaning, Measurement and Moral Importance*. Oxford: Clarendon Press.

Harberger, A. C. (1954) 'Monopoly and Resource Allocation', *American Economic Association, Papers and Proceedings* 44: 77–87.

Hausman, D. M. and McPherson, M. S. (1996) *Economic Analysis and Moral Philosophy*. Cambridge: Cambridge University Press.

Lancaster, K. J. (1966) 'A New Approach to Consumer Theory', *Journal of Political Economy* 74: 132–57.

Lancaster, K. J. (1971) *Consumer Demand: A New Approach.* New York: Columbia University Press.

Lancaster, K. J. (1979) *Variety, Equity and Efficiency.* Oxford: Basil Blackwell.

Nelson, P. (1974) 'Advertising as Information', *Journal of Political Economy* 82: 729–54.

Schmalensee, R. (1972) *The Economics of Advertising.* Amsterdam: North-Holland.

Schmalensee, R. (1989) 'Inter-Industry Studies of Structure and Performance, R. Schmalensee and R. Willig (eds), *Handbook of Industrial Organization* Chapter 16, Amsterdam: North-Holland.

Spence, A. M. (1980) 'Notes on Advertising, Economies of Scale, and Entry Barriers', *Quarterly Journal of Economics* 95: 493–507.

Telser, L. G. (1964) 'Advertising and competition', *Journal of Political Economy* LXXII: 537–62.

West, E. G. (1987) 'Monopoly', Entry in J. Eatwell, M. Milgate and P. Newman (eds), *The New Palgrave. A Dictionary of Economics*, Vol. 3. London: Macmillan, pp. 538–41.

# 17

# THE POLITICAL ECONOMY OF ECONOMIC GROWTH AND ENVIRONMENTAL PROTECTION

*David Pearce*

## 1. Introduction

Thirty years ago the application of economics to environmental problems was a novelty. The first stirrings of real concern about environmental degradation had already occurred, with Rachel Carson's *The Silent Spring* (Carson 1964) being an early warning about the pervasive effects of pesticides. Some of the foundations for an economic approach were set out in Kenneth Boulding's seminal 'spaceship earth' essay (Boulding 1966), in which the Earth was likened to a spaceship with finite resources and fuel and limited waste assimilation capacity. In turn, this led to the 'materials balance' view of economic systems (Ayres and Kneese 1969). The essence of the materials balance approach was that it traced the flows of energy and materials through the economy from resource extraction through the conventional production and consumption sectors to emitted waste and environmental problems. While depicted in materials flow and energy flow terms, the implications for economics were formidable, even if they now seem rather tame. First, endless textbooks on economics ignored both resource extraction and waste emissions, as if they somehow belonged to another discipline. Materials balance showed that economic systems are 'nested' in a wider economic–ecological system. The textbooks were (and many continue to be) ignorant of the environment. Second, the laws of thermodynamics applied. The first law – that matter and energy cannot be created or destroyed – meant that whatever was removed from the natural resources sector had to reappear somewhere else as waste. The tonne of coal extracted reappeared as ash, and as nitrogen, sulphur and carbon gases. For any fixed assimilative capacity of the environment to receive and degrade these wastes, the first law showed the potential for externalities to be pervasive to any economic system. This contrasted dramatically with the early discussions of externality in economic analysis, including that by Pigou, whereby externalities were seen as a modest deviation from the beautiful workings of the competitive economy. The reality was and is that externalities are everywhere and alone justify the characterisation of any economy system as being hopelessly inefficient in the Pareto sense. Third, as Boulding had stated, salvation involved substantial efforts to prevent waste from entering the environment via recycling and efficiency in use, i.e. dramatic changes to the ratio of waste to economic activity. Fourth, and more controversially, many interpreted the materials balance approach as telling us that economic activity had gone beyond 'biophysical' limits and that true salvation would come only via reduced consumption. This was the message of *Limits to Growth* (Meadows *et al.* 1972). The 'anti-growth' phenomenon was born, and remains with us today.

In what follows we first look briefly at the anti-growth arguments in the context of the growth of political elitism – the view that ordinary man is somehow not to be trusted with the fate of the Earth and whose preferences need to be overridden in the name of sustainable futures. We then suggest that the only acceptable, but admittedly still risky, option is to secure the massive changes that are technically feasible in resource efficiency. In turn, those efficiency improvements require much more dramatic change in the use of economic approaches to regulation through the use of economic instruments. Finally, we look very briefly at the reasons why economic instruments have progressed only slowly in the real world of politics.

## 2. Growth and anti-growth

In terms of the materials balance approach, reducing the absolute level of aggregate consumption is one apparent policy for solving the problem of 'too much' resource use and 'too much' pollution. The exact objective function in anti-growth views is not always clear. It could, for example, be maximising the chances of human survival over long periods of time, independently of the quality of life of those populations that do survive. This is 'survivability' rather than 'sustainability' which is about raising per capita levels of well-being over time whilst avoiding the worst of the environmental problems in doing so. Survivability is seen by some as a moral imperative, perhaps because of religious views about the role of humankind in the management of Earth, a kind of stewardship role. Such views could be fairly indifferent to whether or not the stewards themselves have an improving standard of well-being. What matters is that the object of their stewardship survives.

Herman Daly is perhaps one of the best known exponents of the view that there are biophysical limits and that economic systems have to be reorganised and managed so as to reflect those limits (see e.g. Daly 1991). He observes that macroeconomics lacks a concept of 'optimal scale' even though microeconomists would spend significant amounts of time analysing, say, the optimal size of a firm. By 'scale' Daly means the volume of resources per capita multiplied by the size of the population. Here is an example of how terms come to be redefined, since one would normally expect the definition to be in terms of the optimal size of the GNP, for example. This is one of the ambiguities of the anti-growth literature since some of it redefines growth as growth of materials and energy consumption, as if the links between consumption and materials/energy inputs are immutable. But if changes in resource efficiency are possible, this is not necessarily the case. In other words, a clear distinction needs to be made between reducing consumption and reducing the inputs that go into consumption. Daly points out that most of economics is not concerned with optimal scales, but with allocating resources optimally within any given scale.

Moreover, the elegance of the market as a means of allocating resources is confined to optimal allocation within a given scale of resource use. It has nothing to say about optimal scale. But a comparison of costs and benefits, argues Daly, could yield insights on optimal macroeconomic scale. From an anthropocentric point of view, optimal scale would be reached where the marginal benefit of gains in man-made capital just equal the marginal costs arising from losses of environmental capital.

The 'optimal scale' argument can be seen to reflect one of three possible positions:

(a) that the absolute level of consumption should be constrained to fit given biophysical limits such as waste emissions being less than assimilative capacity, renewable resource use being less than regeneration rates, and non-renewable resources being substituted for over time by renewable resources;

(b) the absolute level of consumption should be regarded as being unconstrained, but with biophysical limits being honoured through marked increases in the ratio of consumption to resource inputs (including assimilative capacities as a resource), and investment in assimilative capacity; and

(c) some combination of (a) and (b).

Position (b) appears the most logical because it is comparatively simple to see what the menu of policies would be: policies aimed at materials/energy efficiency, materials recycling, reducing entropy by making products recyclable and more durable and investing in assimilative capacity. Population policy would be consistent with all three positions. Policies aimed at reducing overall consumption (and economic growth) fit (a), depending on the nature of the anti-growth position which, as we have seen, is often confused in terms of what is meant by consumption. Now suppose an anti-growth position of type (a) above was accepted. What policies could be used to reduce aggregate consumption?

Reducing consumption can only come about either (a) by raising the fraction of income that is saved for future consumption (investment), or (b) by reducing incomes generally. The savings fraction is open to manipulation by governments through the taxation system or through control of the incentives to save (e.g. interest rates). It seems clear that the anti-growth school of thought favours income reduction rather than savings increases. But income reductions mean reduced production and reduced production means rising unemployment and social instability. This perhaps explains why 'reduced consumption' arguments are often associated with suggestions for work sharing and investment in improved (forced) leisure activities. Such suggestions are designed to overcome the fact that no-growth societies are 'zero sum' societies, i.e. not everyone can gain and there would therefore have to be losers, establishing the basis for worse, not better disputes over the appropriate distribution of resources. Others argue that any reduced consumption effects on employment would be offset by increases in employment due to spending elsewhere on non-consumer goods. Much depends on how the reduced consumption is brought about. If it is taxed away by government, then this argument is persuasive. The government's tax revenues will be spent somewhere else. But if the consumption simply does not materialise, because, say, people are persuaded to work less hard, there will be no compensating expenditure (although, even here, that depends on what people do with the resulting increase in leisure time).

Now suppose that economic growth is something that can be changed. The modern theory of economic growth says that growth is due mainly to 'endogenous' technical change – technical change embodied in capital – including R&D, education as formation of human capital, and perhaps social capital. If this approach is correct, then to *lower* economic growth means lowering technical change, reducing education, etc. This is a strange way to tackle an environmental problem, not least because there are good reasons to suppose that increasing education is one of the 'best' ways of solving environmental problems. A much simpler option for controlling the level of consumption, if that is desired, is to increase consumption taxes – either income taxes (assuming people respond by reducing consumption rather than saving) or indirect taxes on consumer goods.

Probably the most debated policy for reducing consumption is 'lifestyle change'. This would essentially involve encouragement of increased savings and reduced consumption if the aim is to reduce aggregate consumption, and encouragement of low resource-intensive goods and services if the target is materials and energy throughput. The problem with this requirement is how to bring it about, and especially how to bring it about if it involves overriding human wants and desires, a tendency to totalitarianism at worst, and paternalism at best. Brown and Cameron (2000) argue that these wants and desires of ordinary people are themselves 'socially constructed' by the prevailing socioeconomic system. Change the system and the values will change to become more oriented towards sustainability. Policies of persuasion and information will not work because they exist in a context where individuals' values are already pre-ordained to be hostile to such policies. The difficulty remains of how to create a shift to 'post-materialist' values away from 'egocentric self-enhancement'. Brown and Cameron (2000) suggest that a significant minority of people actually hold both sets of values, so that they might be targeted for information and persuasion campaigns in the expectation that they may then influence the rest. Restricting advertising of consumer goods, changes to educational programmes, 'ecological labelling' of products all appear as part of a menu of measures designed to persuade people to be more environmentally friendly. But campaigns of this kind have not been successful in other spheres without there being either a severe financial or criminal penalty (drink-driving), or a clearly related personal health risk that people can identify with (smoking). It is hard to envisage comparable penalties for 'over-consumption' and the links between consumption, resource use and personal well-being are too tenuous for the 'health warning' approach.

Overall, then, an 'anti-growth' stance is problematic. If the policy implication is that aggregate consumption should be reduced, then the policies needed may provoke ills worse than the one they are designed to correct. If it is the consumption of materials/energy throughputs, anti-growth offers no different a perspective than the 'decoupling' school of thought which argues for strenuous efforts to improve resource efficiency in rich and poor countries alike.

What policies would follow from a focus on a notion of 'maximum sustainable consumption'? A number of policies which could ensure sustainable consumption – investment in education, investment in technology, investment in social capital, reduction of environmental damage through decoupling and, more generally, encouragement of savings via tax-breaks and interest rate changes. The lessons are not new, but they can now be fitted together in a coherent story of sustainable consumption.

## 3. Can the economy be 'decoupled' from the environment?

The previous discussion suggests that focusing on 'lifestyle change' as a means of securing sustainable development is extremely risky because:

- It cannot be a short-term measure and environmental problems may be urgent.
- It is unlikely to succeed: whatever the evidence for changes towards 'post-material' values, there are few examples of those values revealing themselves in lifestyle changes.
- It confuses reducing consumption and changing the relationship between resource use and consumption.
- It could be counterproductive in fostering social unrest .
- It is not necessary: other measures are likely to be more effective, particularly those focusing on decoupling.

But can decoupling succeed? Three factors will determine the likely success of decoupling:

- There must be significant scope for decoupling.
- Decoupling must proceed faster than the expansion of output.
- Effective policy instruments must be available to secure decoupling.

Decoupling means that the resource efficiency ratios $M/GNP$ and $E/GNP$, where $M$ is materials and $E$ is primary energy, decline over time. Such declines are composed of two parts: (a) autonomous resource efficiency and (b) policy-induced resource efficiency. Inspection of UK data suggests that the rate at which $E/GNP$

174

declines over time has been about 0.5 per cent per annum. Are autonomous efficiency changes of 0.5 per cent per annum enough to secure sustainability? This is not an easy question to answer, but to provide a benchmark, suppose we see what rate of efficiency change is required to offset anticipated population change and economic growth in the next fifty years. To see what is required, consider the '*IPAT*' formula (Ehrlich and Holdren 1971):

$$I = P \cdot A \cdot T \tag{1}$$

or

$$\text{Environmental impact} = \text{Population} \times \text{Affluence} \times \text{Technology} \tag{2}$$

or

$$I = \text{POP} \cdot \frac{\text{GNP}}{\text{POP}} \cdot \frac{I}{\text{GNP}}. \tag{3}$$

Equation (3) is in fact an *identity*, not an equation and, as such is devoid of behavioural meaning. More usefully, it can be re-expressed in terms of rates of change. Writing POP as $p$, GNP/POP as $y$, and $I$/GNP as $t$ (for 'technology', which in this case is resource use per unit GNP),

$$\frac{\Delta I}{I} = \frac{\Delta p}{p} + \frac{\Delta y}{y} + \frac{\Delta t}{t}. \tag{4}$$

We require that $\Delta I/I = 0$ to honour the biophysical limit argument that no further damage be done to the environment, so

$$\frac{\Delta p}{p} + \frac{\Delta y}{y} + \frac{\Delta t}{t} = 0,$$

and hence

$$\frac{\Delta t}{t} = \frac{\Delta p}{p} + \frac{\Delta y}{y}. \tag{5}$$

The rate of improvement in resource efficiency must be at least equal to the rate of change in population plus the rate of growth of income per capita.

As a broad check, consider the world as a whole. In 1998 world population was 5.90 billion people and in 2050 it is expected to be 8.91 billion (United Nations 2000). This is a growth rate of 0.8 per cent per annum. The rate of growth in income per capita over the next fifty years or so is obviously more difficult to estimate, not least because eqn (5) assumes this rate is exogenous, i.e. is not affected by population growth, and vice versa, the rate of growth of population is not affected by economic growth. Neither is a tenable position in reality. Available data suggest that the rate of change in world per capita GNP was around 1 per cent per annum from 1975 to1998 (UNDP 2000). If this rate were to continue, then eqn (5) suggests that $\Delta p/p + \Delta y/y = 0.8 + 1.0 = 1.8$ per cent per annum. Thus, globally, resource efficiency must improve by at least 1.8 per cent per annum to offset this potential rising impact from economic growth and population change.

If the UK's past development path could be regarded as typical, we see immediately that autonomous resource efficiency improvements will not be enough. They would account for only $0.8/1.8 = 44$ per cent of the required improvement. This appears to be a pessimistic conclusion, but the rate of resource efficiency improvement in the UK was chosen so as to exclude policy interventions which came after 1970. Studies of 'environmental Kuznets curves' (EKCs) – relationships between income per capita and environmental impact per capita – suggest that policy has a very large potential to shift the EKC downwards, effectively producing the result that pollution per capita can decline even at fairly early stages of economic development. It is more relevant, therefore, to look at recent changes in resource efficiency since these will have been affected by both autonomous improvements and policy measures. The policies in question include efforts to raise energy prices domestically, but it should be recognised that energy prices have also been influenced by political events that have affected world oil markets, such as OPEC's oil price activities. From a policy standpoint, however, these effects are still relevant to the analysis because they help to show just how effective price changes can be in influencing resource efficiency.

Globally, the ratio of energy use to GNP has improved by about 1.3 per cent per annum since 1970. This is much closer to the 'breakeven target' of 1.8 per cent for $\Delta t/t$ above. But even world data are misleading because policies affecting energy and materials efficiency were not undertaken in many parts of the world. What matters is what achievements *can* be secured given aggressive policy initiatives. Catalogues of technological potential abound, probably one of the more famous being 'Factor Four' (von Weizsäcker et al. 1997) which argues that resource efficiency can be improved fourfold. Assuming this occurs over fifty years, the rate of change in efficiency would be 2.7 per cent per annum, more than adequate to meet the $\Delta t/t$ target of 1.8 per cent per annum. Manufacturing energy intensity in advanced economies has improved at rates around 2.2 per cent per annum 1960–94, even when the mix of industrial output is held constant (the mix will change and will generally improve efficiency more) (International Energy Agency 1997). United States transport fuel efficiency improved at 1.6 per cent per annum 1970–95 (International Energy Agency 1997).

## 4. Securing resource efficiency: Economic instruments

How can 'decoupling' or 'dematerialising' the economy–environment relationship be achieved? We have seen that relying on autonomous change is not enough. Decoupling requires strong policy measures and these can achieve the required result. Additionally, the available evidence on the scope for technological change indicates that there are few problems of technological feasibility. The measures in question will include the wide array of policy options open to governments, but special attention needs to be paid to the use of market-based instruments and measures to stimulate technological change and its diffusion through the economy.

Market-based approaches to environmental policy are usually contrasted with command-and-control policies, but it is actually quite difficult to differentiate these two broad categories of regulation. A distinction needs to be made between setting a goal for the sources of a given environmental problem, and telling those sources how to control the problem. Regulatory instruments can then be classified according to what they set out to achieve and how they contribute to achieving it. Prohibitions and bans of certain products and substances would be an example of a command-and-control regulation, as would any emission standard that is combined with a requirement about the technology to use, as would a fishing catch limit combined with a requirement on, say, net mesh size. Most of what are called market-based instruments would belong to the category where the regulator does not state goals and does not say how to respond to the regulatory instrument. Thus, a tax on pollution emissions fits this box because, although the regulator will have some environment target in mind, and may state it, each individual source of pollution does not have a target and each source is free to respond to the tax as they see fit. In terms of response, they might alter their product mix, they might install abatement equipment, change fuel sources, practice material and energy conservation, and so on.

Market-based approaches have particular attractions. They give the individual polluter more choice of the means to reduce pollution. The second feature is that market-based approaches give a greater chance of minimising the overall costs of complying with the environmental objective of the regulator (Baumol and Oates 1988). This feature of market-based approaches, namely compliance cost minimisation, is crucial to the political economy of environmental regulation. If market-based approaches are cheaper, then they will minimise the impacts of regulation on competitiveness, a repeatedly stated concern of governments worldwide in respect of regulatory impact. Cost minimisation will also potentially limit the opposition to future environmental policy and hence serve the goals of environmental efficiency and political feasibility of regulation. The market-based approach could also serve the goal of equity – a concern for the social incidence of regulation – because the costs shifted forwards to consumers could be less.

These are the theoretical attractions of market-based approaches. Yet, in practice, their introduction meets substantial political resistance. It is important to understand why.

In all policy contexts there are always losers or, at least, there are always stakeholders who see themselves as losers. Even if policies have net benefits, the actual compensation of losers very often does not take place. Developments in hypothecated revenues from taxes go some way towards compensating the loser, and it is significant that recent environmental taxes in Denmark and the UK involve hypothecation towards reductions in labour taxes and/or environmental funds.

A critical issue is the baseline, i.e. what would have happened had a market-based instrument not been introduced. As far as the baseline is concerned, opposition to economic instruments can quickly be fused with opposition to *any* regulatory measure. From the standpoint of the regulated, the baseline becomes the *status quo*, not the hypothetical 'worse policy' option. Losers may not be real losers, but they perceive themselves as being such. This latter perspective is easily exaggerated because of a media culture which seeks to 'find the loser': good news is not news, bad news is. And it is further encouraged if the losing party does not believe the alternative 'worse regulation' really is worse. This belief is not necessarily irrational. The loser is being asked to compare two alternatives, a traditional regulatory approach of which he/she already has experience, and a 'new' approach of which he/she has little or no experience. The new approach is therefore uncertain and industry (and perhaps the public) traditionally discounts uncertain benefits at a much higher rate than governments do. Not only is it uncertain in terms of its costs to industry, it has credibility problems.

A credibility problem arises with measures which raise revenues, since this always means that what sets out to be an environmental measure can quickly become yet another tax for central (or local) government. This perception is fostered further by the fact that government motivations for introducing environmental taxes are not always clearly divorced from revenue raising. While this is how those being taxed or charged may see it, the reality, and the accompanying 'message', is, or should be, different. If governments did not raise revenues, they could not support the substantial array of public services which benefit the general public. Raising revenues from taxes on 'bads', such as pollution, thus appears far more sensible than raising revenues from taxes on effort and enterprise. The problem is how to convey the alternative scenario. Those who are taxed see the tax on its own rather than in the context of what would have happened if the tax was not introduced.

Finally, there is suspicion about market-based approaches because command and control lends itself to 'regulatory capture' whereby regulator and regulated form a policy network that can often be independent of government.

How can these problems be overcome? One critical element of policy has to be ensuring that the baseline is not perceived as the *status quo*. There need to be firm and transparent statements about the alternative measures, for example making it clear that the alternative to, say, managed self-regulation is a tax. This has in fact been one strategy adopted by some governments who enter into compacts whereby industry self-regulates but under a shadowy threat of severe action if it fails. There need to be firm statements and arguments underlining the need for action and more transparency and public information on why policy is being introduced. Countries vary in the degree of public information provided on regulations. The USA publishes cost-benefit studies, regulatory impact statements, and reasons for rejecting advice or contrary opinion. There is an emerging trend towards this stance in Europe but it remains far less developed. Government also needs to make it harder for polluters to establish the *status quo* baseline by encouraging corporate environmentalism so that firms secure corporate 'green image'. As noted above, hypothecating taxes helps to establish taxes as 'pure' environmental measures and secures some compensation for losers. It is also possible to encourage countervailing power through public information. Highly successful efforts have been made in Sweden and the USA to release information on the release of pollutants or uses of harmful substances such as fertilisers. More complex is the need to reduce the attractions of regulatory capture by changes in the culture and perhaps the organisation of regulators, away from policy networks that encourage industry/regulator fraternisation towards separation of operational and regulatory functions.

On fears that market-based approaches will harm equity, it is necessary to carry out 'incidence studies' as part of regulatory impact assessment, something that is rarely done in practice. The reality is that it is often difficult to tell who is being harmed by regulatory measures, and whether they would be better or worse off under traditional regulation. What matters is the net incidence of the policy measure. The baseline issue arises again because the social incidence may be worse under some other form of regulation than with market-based approaches, even where regulations are targeted to industry and the domestic sector is 'ring fenced' to avoid the direct impacts of the measure. Moreover, the regressivity of policy measures can easily be exaggerated by the media and by vocal pressure groups. The 'academic' truth is that tackling equity concerns instrument-by-instrument is inefficient and it is better to address such concerns in the context of overall policy packages. The political difficulties of relying on this overall assessment alone are acknowledged, since the 'loser syndrome' makes it difficult to persuade losers that they are better off when all measures are accounted for. But if equity impacts are genuine, or even if they are perceived to be genuine, there are actions that can be taken, for example lifeline tariffs, compensation via special allowances for the targeted source of pollution (e.g. pensioners' winter fuel allowances), compensation not directly targeted at the source of the pollution (e.g. lump sum payments via social security), and the hypothecation of revenues from policy instruments to fund compensation measures.

## 5. Conclusions

The 'growth–anti-growth' debate of the 1970s has resurfaced in the 1990s and the new millennium under various guises: 'sustainable consumption', 'sustainable development', 'biophysical limits', etc. A persistent confusion in the popular and political literature equates the requisite policy measures to achieve 'sustainability' with actions to reduce consumption in rich countries. More enlightened contributions note the distinction between consumption and the resource inputs into consumption, a distinction that should be clear from the materials balance characterisation of the economic system. Reducing consumption is neither a politically feasible nor an economically sensible strategy, even if governments were in control of long-run economic development. Changing the ratio of inputs to consumption outputs is very much a realistic policy option. The technological scope for reductions in such ratios is enormous. The means of achieving it are problematic, however. Continued use of command-and-control regulations designed to 'decouple' the economy and environment appear doomed to failure because of the regulatory cost of compliance. Even if there is evidence that such costs are not large, they are perceived as being large and governments have usually failed to demonstrate otherwise. Hence the regulatory stance has to be based on compliance cost minimisation and that points towards market-based instruments. Yet progress with environmental taxes, tradable permits and the like has been painfully slow. Analysing the reasons for the slow progress thus becomes an important dimension in the political economy of environmental regulation. The reasons are complex and often reduce to the complexity of demonstrating the counterfactual: what would have happened if a particular action had not been taken. Counterfactuals do not sit easily with political communication: what is perceived is the impact of the measure under consideration, not some measure of relief that a worse alternative has not been adopted. There is therefore a long way to go in understanding the politics of regulation, an understanding that will require as much input from psychologists and political scientists as it does from economists.

# References

Ayres, R. and Kneese, A. V. (1969) 'Production, Consumption and Externalities', *American Economic Review* 59(3): 282–97.

Baumol, W. and Oates, W. (1988) *The Theory of Environmental Policy*, 2nd edn. Cambridge: Cambridge University Press.

Boulding, K. (1966) 'The Economics of the Coming Spaceship Earth', in H. Jarrett (ed.), *Environmental Quality in a Growing Economy*. Baltimore: Johns Hopkins University Press, pp. 3–14.

Brown, P. and Cameron, L. (2000) 'What Can be Done to Reduce Overconsumption?', *Ecological Economics* 32: 27–41.

Carson, R. (1964) *The Silent Spring*. New York: Houghton Mifflin.

Daly, H. (1991) 'Towards an Environmental Macroeconomics', *Land Economics* 67(2): 255–9.

Ehrlich, P. and Holdren, J. (1971) 'Impact of Population Growth', *Science* 171(3977): 1212–19.

International Energy Agency (1997) *Indicators of Energy Use and Efficiency*. Paris: Organisation for Economic Co-operation and Development.

Meadows, D.H., Meadow, D.L., Randers, J., and Behrens, W. (1972) *Limits to Growth*. London: Earth Island.

United Nations (1997) *Critical Trends: Global Changes and Sustainable Development* Department for Policy Co-ordination and Sustainable Development. New York: United Nations.

United Nations, Population Division, Department of Social and Economic Affairs (2000) *World Population Projections 1998*, available at www.popin.org/pop1998.

United Nations Development Programme (UNDP) (2000) *The Human Development Report 2000*. Oxford: Oxford University Press.

von Weizsäcker, E., Lovins, A. and Lovins, L. (1997) *Factor Four: Doubling Wealth, Halving Resource Use*. London: Earthscan.

# 18

# FIRMS AND BANKS INTERACTING IN A MONETARY PRODUCTION ECONOMY

*Carmen Aparecida Feijó*

The micro–macro relation has always been a main research subject in macroeconomics, and post-Keynesian theorists deal with this interaction in a very distinctive way. Their concern is not to develop the microfoundations of macro-economics or even the macrofoundations of microeconomics, but of searching to identify the mutual influences of both fields, using microeconomics to shed light on motives, choices and strategies and macroeconomics to understand possibilities, constraints and actual developments. Professor Chick's work has been among the leading post-Keynesian contributions to share this view. In her *Macroeconomics after Keynes*, for instance, she states:

> The relationship of the observed behaviour of an aggregate like Firms or Households is not easily related to the plans or actions of its component agents. One problem arises from the potential conflicts between agents within an aggregate, for obviously, the behaviour of the aggregate will depend on the manner in which those conflicts are resolved.
>
> (Chick 1983: 37)

In this chapter we deal with some issues that are raised when we focus our attention on the accommodation at the macroeconomic level of the actions of individual agents. We pay special attention to the generation of profits by the firm and itspossibilities in the aggregate to explain economic growth. We are interested in exploiting two main aspects. One concerns the interaction between the firm and its environment, which limits present choices of courses of action and supplies elements on which firms form expectations about the future. The other one, as proposed by post-Keynesian theory, deals with the interaction of firms with other firms and other economic agents, including banks and the State. The success of plans depends not only on the appropriateness of a firm's decision, but also on the decisions and behaviours of other economic agents. In this context modern market economies tend to develop fragile financial structures and it is up to macroeconomic theory to provide the tools to interpret its short- and long-run path of growth.

In this chapter we discuss the importance of profit generation and the interaction of firms and banks for sustaining stable aggregate growth. We develop this subject, presenting in the next section the main well-known fallacies of composition, among them profits generation and profits distribution in market economies. In Section 2 we discuss the relation between the profits of a firm and aggregate profits. The interaction of firms and banks is introduced in Section 3, and in Section 4 we discuss the generation of profits and validation of debts. We finalise our discussion with Minsky's financial instability hypothesis in Section 5. A summing up is in Section 6.

## 1. Fallacies of composition

The assumption of uncertainty in the post-Keynesian model does not imply the absence of rules of economic behaviour or established standards of rational economic behaviour. On the contrary, in a world of uncertainty, institutions, rules and conventions emerge to support decisions. In this sense, as noted by Dow (1985: 100), post-Keynesians try to combine the acknowledgement of individual freedom from deterministic rules with the recognition that in reality there are standards of behaviour that have their origin in society rather than in the individual itself.

Macroeconomics emerges as a field of study when it is recognised that the logic of aggregate behaviour is not simply given by the sum of individual actions. It assumes that there is a logic of a system's behaviour that both transcends and limits the possible courses of actions of its elements. In other words, macroeconomics is created when 'fallacies of composition' are identified and shown to be theoretically significant.[1]

Fallacies of composition emerge from the fact that external restrictions on individual choices and actions are, in many cases, endogenous to an aggregate approach of the economy. Budget constraints and the size of markets, for example, are given to an individual decision maker but are really determined by the action of agents as a whole.

The best-known fallacies of composition in macroeconomics are those related to the effects of an increase in the propensity to save on the rate of capital accumulation and of a reduction in money wages on the level of employment.

In the firm's case, it can be shown that an act of saving unaccompanied by an act of new investment, rather than stimulating capital accumulation is more likely to lead to a reduction in the level of employment. While it is reasonable to suppose an individual can get wealthier by saving increasing proportions of his income, if everybody does the same society will end up impoverished; aggregate demand will be reduced, and employment will fall.

Keynes emphasised that it is possible for an individual to increase his saving by buying either a newly created asset or an old asset. If a new asset is created, investment is taking place, and this is what really counts for capital accumulation.

Otherwise, the savings of that individual equals the dissaving of somebody else who is selling an old asset.

This happens because income is created when saleable production takes place. If saving increases beyond the non-consumable share of production, markets will shrink and with it aggregate income, forcing some people to dissave. Therefore, if it is possible for any individual to save as much as he wants from his income, for the economy as a whole it is not possible to save more than is being invested. An increase in the propensity to save, without an increase in net investment, can only be equivalent to the losses of firms with unsold production or unused capacity. According to Chick, for the economy as a whole, it may be better to eliminate the propensity to save function and keep the concept only at the micro-level where such a choice is possible (Chick 1983, chapter 9).

Something similar takes place in the second case. As emphasised by both Keynes and Kalecki, a reduction in the money wages of the workers of a given firm may improve the latter's profitability. However, a general reduction of money wages will lead to a contraction of aggregate demand. Prices will go down, and profits will be reduced.[2]

What these cases point to is the necessity to verify the implicit requirements for a given plan, at the macro-level, to be successful. Aggregate results must be explainable in terms of the decisions and acts of the agents that actually caused them. On the other hand, atomistic individualism misses the essential point that goals and methods are not only historically and institutionally specific but also that they are restrictions on individual behaviour explainable only at the macro-level.

To the well-known fallacies of composition mentioned above we add another one. Profits are the goal and fuel of economic expansion in a monetary economy in which production is organised by private firms. Profits, however, depend directly on income distribution and so on what accrues to firms to accumulate. Income distribution, therefore, is a subject that requires an integrated micro–macro treatment. In the remainder of the chapter we will address this question, examining the macro-restrictions on the formation and accumulation of profits by firms.

## 2. The profits of a firm and aggregate profits

Growth is explained in the context of a monetary economy as the result of accumulation decisions made by a particular social group, capitalists. Therefore, as classical political economy has stressed, income distribution and growth are essentially connected subjects. On the other hand, income distribution, particularly the share of income retained by firms, depends, as post-Keynesians have emphasised, on the profile of aggregate demand.

Let us suppose that firms set profit targets when making their pricing decisions aiming to generate internal funds for expansion. Those profits are attained when firms are successful in selling the volumes they expected. Thus, the confirmation or disappointment of profit expectations (and planned means of financing investment) depends on correctly estimating the behaviour of sales during the relevant period.

For an individual firm to see its sales plans confirmed it is sufficient that its own demand be sustained. But the demand for any specific good or service depends on its buyers being able to implement their purchase plans of which that good or service is an element. In a specific market, of course, it may be largely a question of chance, that is to say, about how many buyers a firm attracts. The deeper in detail one delves, the more arbitrary becomes the distribution of demand. In what follows, we will assume that the demand for each market is related in a stable way to aggregate demand, given the relevant income-elasticities, and that the distribution of demand within a given market is such as to keep market shares constant. On these assumptions, then, both aggregate and individual profits are dependent on the level of aggregate demand.[3] Following Kalecki (1971, chapter 8), for a closed economy without government, the confirmation of profit expectations by firms depends, at least partially, on the consumption expenditures of capitalists and on the investment expenditures of firms themselves. There is then a complex interconnection between the micro- and macro-levels of analysis at this point: firms, at the micro-level, form expectations of sales to obtain target profits; the confirmation of these expectations depends, on the other hand, on the firms themselves spending the amount necessary to validate the sales expectations.

The point is that aggregate profits are generated by aggregate demand, not by the markup decision of the firm. Pricing determines the distribution among firms of aggregate profits, but not their generation. The actual generation of profits thus depends on enough acts of spending on consumption goods and on investment goods taking place. As long as the marginal propensity to consume is smaller than one, growth becomes a condition of survival of firms also in this sense.

If firms entertain optimistic expectations as to the possibility of earning profits from their activities, they will issue liabilities to absorb funds and extend their scale of operations. This introduces a crucial requirement of stability operating in the economy related to the validation of expectations. Capitalist firms issue liabilities on the expectation of future cash inflows. If these flows do not materialise, insolvency may follow.[4]

In sum, for firms to be able to obtain the receipts that will allow them to validate their debts and to earn the profits they expected it is necessary that the right volume and structure of aggregate demand be generated. We can consider, with Keynes and Kalecki, that consumption expenditures are induced by income. This means that, in a closed economy without government, aggregate profits depend on investment. If investments are not realised, not only do some firms have losses but also, through the financial linkages, suppliers of funds are hurt.

Investment expenditures perform a strategic role, then, not only because on them depends the validation of profit expectations by firms, but also because they are autonomous with respect to current income. In Keynesian theory, to be autonomous means that investment decisions are independent of current income, both because investment is induced by expectations of future profits and because it is sustained largely by discretionary funds, accumulated assets and external funds obtained from credit institutions. According to Keynes (1973, Vol. 14, pp. 215–23), banks perform a crucial role in making investment possible.[5]

## 3. The role of banks

Banks and other financial institutions are connected to fluctuations in output and employment as they 'hold the key position' to stimulate business. For Keynes credit is a necessary condition, although not the only one, for firms to implement their production and investment plans, as it creates the purchasing power firms need to start their activities. In order to explain the demand for money, Keynes introduces a fourth motive (besides the transaction, precautionary and speculative motives as defined in *The General Theory*, chapter 15), the 'finance' motive, which allows him to discuss the role of the banking system in generating liquidity.[6] It is also through this discussion that Keynes makes his position clear about the dissociation between changes in the level of current activity and the level of *ex ante* savings, that is to say, the process of financing investment decisions.[7] According to his view, the interregnum between the decision to invest and its achievement is bridged by 'Credit, in the sense of "finance", [which ] looks after a flow of investment. It is a revolving fund which can be used over and over again.'(ibid., p. 209).

In this sense, in order that the entrepreneur may feel himself sufficiently liquid to be able to embark on the transaction (a new investment), someone else has to agree to become, for the time being at least, more illiquid than before (ibid., p. 218), and so banks and other financial institutions are in a position of regulating the pace of new investment.

In considering the supply of finance Keynes writes:

> The entrepreneur when he decides to invest has to be satisfied on two points: firstly, that he can obtain sufficient short-term finance during the period of producing the investment; and secondly, that he can eventually fund his short-term obligations by a long-term issue on satisfactory conditions ... Thus the terms of supply of the finance required by *ex ante* investment depend on the *existing* state of liquidity preferences (together with some element of forecast on the part of the entrepreneur as to the terms on which he can fund his finance when the time comes), in conjunction with the supply of money as governed by the policy of the banking system.
>
> (ibid., p. 217, emphasis in original)

To the need for funding we will return later. To provide finance, according to Keynes, is a function of banks. Banking institutions fix their policy of lending money according to, at least, two main factors. One is the amount of reserves in cash thought to be 'safe' in relation to their liabilities. The second factor is that banks will provide loans depending on the margins of safety they can guarantee for their application. Banks cannot know how their loan is being used, and so this is a sort of risk always involved in the operation. But the main risk incurred by banks concerns the liquidity of their loan. As Keynes puts it 'a loan may be liquid from the point of view of an individual banker, because he knows he can get his money back if he wants, although the proceeds of it are being employed in fixed forms' (Keynes 1973, Vol. 13, p. 7).

Uncertainty about future prospective yields may erode the safety margins, causing a contraction in the supply of loans. Banks, then, in order to avoid a devaluation of the market value of their assets, will try to recover their position, and a way of doing this is by refusing to provide new loans, either absolutely or, more likely, in relative terms, raising interest rates of safety margins requirements. So, although banks can create credit, there is a limit to the process given by their own liquidity preference. To take banks' liquidity preference into account also implies that credit is not offered in an indiscriminate way; customers are selected according to the evaluation by the bank of the future profitability of the business or, secondarily, the liquidity of the assets it can offer as collateral. Moreover, the disposition to expand or contract credit depends on expectations about the performance of the whole economy.

This argument about the position of banks to expand credit at their will suggests that the supply of money is, at least in part, endogenously created (Chick 1983, chapter 12).[8] So, being firms, banks make their decisions based on expectations and the assumption that money is endogenously created becomes an additional element to amplify the potential instability of the economic system.[9]

## 4. Aggregate profits and the validation of debts

Since decisions are made under uncertainty, entrepreneurs must take risks when engaged in productive activity. Firms will try to bring risks to a minimum by gathering as much information as they can from their environment. Stability of business will then depend on the degree of confidence entrepreneurs attach to their choices and confidence is built based on the validation of previous plans and expectations. Two sorts of risk are actually incurred by entrepreneurs when deciding to invest. One deals with the behaviour of their markets that will or will not allow them to validate their production and pricing decisions. Another one deals with the validation of their debts, that is to say, with the ability of the firm to keep the value of its assets balanced with that of its liabilities.

The way that this balance can be assured is through the maintenance of an equilibrated cash flow at each stage. That is to say that the extent to which firms will be able to keep their business running in equilibrium will depend first on their ability to generate a cash inflow that is enough to meet their debt commitments, and, second, on their ability to maintain their borrowing capacity in the financial market. At each moment in time the degree of vulnerability of the business will be given by the financial situation of the firm that will allow it to have more or less room for manoeuvre and keep its commitments updated in case production or sales expectations are disappointed.

So, the point is that in a monetary production economy even if individual profit expectations are not promptly validated by demand, firms may survive as long as the financial system is able to meet their demands for cash. This is Minsky's assumption that the financial system in modern economies amplifies the movements of aggregate output as it provides resources to firms to produce and invest. As Minsky puts it, 'A fundamental attribute of our economy is that the ownership of assets is typically financed by debts and debts imply payment commitments.' (Minsky 1986: 42).

At the macro-level then, the extension to which aggregate profits are sufficient to validate aggregate debts is a crucial factor to give stability to the growth of the economic system. Minsky postulates that market economies are by nature unstable. Uncertainty about the unknown future is the ground for instability. But what allows uncertainty to spread over the economic system, generating instability, is the financial links economic agents make among them. Once investment in long-lived assets relies on external finance to be carried out, a synchronisation between payment on debts and receipts of income must occur to keep the functioning of the system on a smooth basis.

All this means that, in discussing macroeconomic stability, one should pay attention not only to indebtedness, but also to the temporal profile of debt payment commitments for they are crucial to determine the nature of financial pressures a firm may suffer. At the firm level the financial postures that may be adopted – hedge, speculative or Ponzi – determine the health of the business. In the macro-level, 'The mixture of hedge, speculative and Ponzi finance in an economy is a major determinant of its stability.' (Minsky 1986: 209). The changes in the aggregate temporal profiles of payments are at the root of the financial fragility and instability post-Keynesian economists attribute to modern capitalism.

## 5. Financial instability

In a period of prosperity, the degree of confidence attached to expectations is increased as decisions undertaken in the past prove to be correct. Entrepreneurs become more willing to take risks as they wish to expand their business. More ambitious investment projects are pursued. Financial institutions in such a context play their role of supporting this greater ambition of the private sector by expanding the supply of credit.

A period of prosperity may begin with hedge units being dominant, and so liquidity is plentiful as the asset structure is heavily weighted by money or liquid assets and the quasi-rents yields by current expenditure on capital assets are high. The degree of indebtedness is low, as the debt commitments are low in relation to the expected yields of capital assets. The interest rate structure is such that it encourages investment in fixed assets as 'short-term interest rates on secure instruments will be significantly lower than the yields from owning capital'(Minsky 1986: 211). The confirmation of expectations about sales revenues and the robustness of the balance sheet of firms encourage them to make more ambitious investment plans.

The passage from a situation where hedge units dominate to a situation where speculative units dominate occurs because capitalists and bankers are seeking more profit opportunities to be exploited.

As long as this process of 'money now in exchange for money later' continues, the margins of safety involved in financial contracts (the proportion of money and other easily negotiable financial instruments to the necessity of cash to fulfil contract obligations) are being reduced. At the same time the demand for funds tends to become more inelastic, because investment in capital assets is a time-consuming activity and, before an investment project is completed, it has no value as determined by the future streams of profits. Because of that, a rigidity in the demand for funds is likely to occur and so an increase in the cost of finance (an increase in interest rates) diminishes (or even eliminates) the margins of safety.

But, while an investment boom is taking place, further credit can be found, however, at a higher cost. An increase in the cost of finance leads firms to commit larger portions of their expected cash flow to debt servicing. This means that portfolios become more speculative and more fragile. As long as profits are rising, increasing indebtedness will be stimulated and lower margins of safety will be accepted. For speculative finance to continue it must be expected that financial resources will remain available so firms engaged in speculative and Ponzi finance can refinance their debts.

This trend changes when the degree of confidence in the ongoing situation decreases. In general this means a decline in the net expected cash inflow and eventually a shortfall of cash and an increase in demand for liquid assets (liquidity preference rises). An unexpected shortfall of cash, an increase in the interest rate together with a change in the degree of confidence about the future behaviour of business will make speculative units review their desired degree of indebtedness. As Dow writes, 'Mistaken expectations are costly when financing is highly geared.' (Dow 1986–7: 246). This will lead firms with high indebtedness to reduce their investment expenditure in an attempt to reduce their dependence on external finance.

This attempt of individual firms to improve their degree of indebtedness may, as suggested by Steindl (1976),

> not put matters right. Assuming that outside savings are relatively inelastic, the further drop in the accumulation of real capital will not be accompanied by a corresponding drop in the accumulation of outside savings, and consequently internal accumulation must drop more than total capital accumulation, and the entrepreneurs will find that their relative indebtedness (gearing ratio) continues to grow. In other words, the impact of any reduction in investment owning to the inelasticity of outside saving must be mainly on internal accumulation.
>
> (p. 114)

So, a reduction in the rate of investment of individual firms slows down the growth of aggregate demand, which implies slower growth of aggregate profits.

Furthermore, a shortfall of profits in face of the needs for cash to validate debts and a decrease in confidence in business, increases furthermore the cost of additional debt (as demand for liquidity increases) and the weight of speculative and Ponzi units in the economic system. The consequence of portfolios becoming more speculative is that the economic system becomes more vulnerable to shocks or to the disappointment of expectations. These will have an amplified negative effect on further economic decisions. This is an environment propitious to a recession or depression.

The growth path to be followed by the system as a whole will then depend on how financial institutions and economic policy react to changes in the degree of confidence. The dynamics of the system depend not only on how much entrepreneurs decide to spend in new capital equipment, but also on how they finance new investment plans. In other words, it is not only the rate of investment that matters, but also how portfolios change to accommodate different rates of growth of aggregate demand. One should notice that the preceding discussion, based on the well-known concepts proposed by Minsky, suggests an approach alternative to Keynes's distinction between finance and funding, referred to in discussing the role of banks. Instead of two clear-cut sequentially defined procedures as suggested by Keynes in an approach that sharply distinguishes the role of banks from that of other financial institutions, Minsky opts for a more general approach in which many types of financial procedures are possible.

## 6. Summing up

In this chapter we turned our attention to some issues trespassing over the borders between micro- and macroeconomic analysis. For post-Keynesians, under the non-probabilistic uncertainty assumption, the validation of individual expectations is not a priori secured, and some accommodation of plans at the macro-level must probably take place. The study of his process of accommodation is in the core of macrodynamics.

The main variable to explain growth is the rate of investment in fixed assets, which is autonomous in relation to current income and governed by long-term profit expectations of individual firms. The confirmation of profit expectations, in turn, depends on the volume and structure of aggregate demand being generated, according to the expenditure plans of economic agents. In this sense we identified a complex interconnection between the micro- and macro-levels of analysis, and post-Keynesian theory pays particular attention to the links between capitalist firms and other economic agents (in special banks and financial institutions) and capitalist firms among themselves.

Investment expenditures made by individual capitalists will determine how fast the economic system will grow, but for post-Keynesian theory it is also relevant to discuss the stability of the growth path. This discussion touches an important crossing between micro and macro – how investment in fixed assets is financed. The interrelation between firms and financial institutions is expressed in the conditions in which finance on fixed assets is agreed.

Capitalist firms issue liabilities on the expectation of future cash inflow. Banks, because they can create money, have the flexibility of accommodating demand for funds by firms. Bankers are, like businessmen, subject to the same expectational climate when making their decisions and, as they are profit seeking institutions, modern market economies tend to be unstable.

A period of high expectations and high liquidity is propitious for more aggressive financing practices to develop. This will lead to more speculative financing, that is to say, using short-term debts to finance long-term positions. Margins of safety deteriorate and changes in expectations lead to new demands for funds being rejected. A phase of more conservative financial practices then follows. So banking practices can be 'highly disruptive', but in economic systems with long-lived capital assets they are needed to make it dynamic.

## Notes

1 According to Dow, 'The fallacy of composition is a central feature of any discussion of microfoundations; according to this fallacy, individual actions, if common to a large number of individuals, will generate an outcome different from what was intended by each.' (Dow 1985: 82).
2 See Keynes (1936, chapter 2) and Kalecki (1971, chapter 14).
3 The assumption of given market shares may be seen as a variant of the procedure of Keynes in the *General Theory*, who assumes a fixed production structure.
4 Insolvency, nevertheless, need not be the only possible outcome. Steindl (1976: 112–14) described an adjustment of balance sheet on the liabilities side that may be necessary when expectations of cash inflows are disappointed. An increase in indebtedness may avoid the curtailment of the firm's current expenditures. The same factor, however, may depress plans for future expenditures.
5 Chick (1992a,b, chapter 12) describes the evolutions of the banking system, connecting its behaviour with changes in the theory of saving, investment and interest rate.
6 See also Chick (1992a,b, chapter 10).
7 After the publishing of *The General Theory*, Keynes wrote two articles where he made clear his point about the irrelevance of *ex ante* saving in financing investment. These articles are reprinted in volume 14 of his *Collected Writings* (pp. 201–23). As already mentioned, this point is developed by Chick (1983, chapter 9).
8 An interesting discussion about the relevance of liquidity for the determination of aggregate demand is in Chick (1979, chapter 4).
9 Anything that increases the elasticity of the credit system increases potential instability. This potential instability is further increased by the role of the central bank in modern market economies.

## References

Chick, V. (1979) *The Theory of Monetary Policy*, revised edition. Oxford: Basil Blackwell.
Chick, V. (1983) *Macroeconomics after Keynes: A Reconstruction of the General Theory*. Cambridge, MA: MIT Press.
Chick, V. (1992a) 'Monetary Increases and Their Consequences: Streams, Backwaters and Floods', in P. Arestis and S. Dow (eds), *On Money, Method and Keynes: Selected Essays by Victoria Chick*, Chapter 10. London: Macmillan.

Chick, V. (1992b) 'The Evolution of the Banking System and the Theory of Saving, Investment and Interest', in P. Arestis and S. Dow (eds), *On Money, Method and Keynes: Selected Essays by Victoria Chick*, Chapter 12. London: Macmillan.

Collected Writings of John Maynard Keynes, *The General Theory and after. Part I: Preparation*, Vol. 13. London: Macmillan.

Collected Writings of John Maynard Keynes, *The General Theory and after. Part II: Defense and Development*, Vol. 14. London: Macmillan.

Dow, S. (1985) *Macroeconomic Thought: A Methodological Approach*. Oxford: Basil Blackwell.

Dow, S. (1986–7) 'Post Keynesian Monetary Theory for an Open Economy', *Journal of Post Keynesian Economics* 9(2): 237–57.

Kalecki, M. (1971) *Selected Essays in the Dynamics of the Capitalist Economy*. Cambridge: Cambridge University Press.

Keynes, J. M. (1936) *The General Theory of Employment Interest and Money*. New York: Harcourt Brace and World.

Minsky, H. (1986) *Stabilizing an Unstable Economy*. New Haven and London: Yale University Press.

Steindl, J. (1976) *Maturity and Stagnation in American Capitalism*, 2nd edn. New York: Monthly Review Press.

# 19

# THE REGIONAL IMPACT OF THE INTERNATIONALIZATION OF THE FINANCIAL SYSTEM: THE CASE OF MERCOSUL

*Adriana M. Amado*[1]

## 1. Introduction

The economic debate of the 1990s was largely based on issues relating to the role of markets in leading the economy toward stability at full employment. The focus of the contemporary debate was a matter of whether or not to give support to the two interlinked processes of economic liberalization and globalization that became increasingly embedded during this decade, at the national and international levels. On the one hand, the orthodoxy pointed out the main benefits of markets, and the disturbances caused by the state and by the frictions created artificially by certain institutions (see Silva and Andrade 1998). Globalization and liberalization enlarged the operating space of markets and approximated real economies to the assumptions that their models were based on. On the other hand, the heterodoxy was pointing out the problems inherent to market mechanisms that, instead of leading to stability and full employment, tended to create instability and involuntary unemployment.

The processes of globalization and liberalization did not occur without some tension in the 1990s, and a certain degree of protection of the national economies that were involved in them. Countering globalization there was a strong tendency towards the formation and intensification of economic blocs. This period was marked by the negotiation towards European Monetary Union, the deepening of the relations of Mercosul,[2] the negotiations on NAFTA, etc. All these processes were in one way or another a reaction by national governments to the globalization process and an attempt to promote a better, strongly positioning in the world economy. Nevertheless, while economic integration was in one sense a movement contrary to globalization, inside the economic blocs the two processes created a strong movement towards the breaking down of the economic barriers that different nations represented. In this way, when the economic integration of different nations reaches the stage of monetary union, the concept of national economies virtually disappears and is substituted by the notion of an economic bloc, which becomes the relevant unit of analysis.

This chapter is concerned mainly with the internal consequences of processes of economic integration, especially with aspects associated with the financial and monetary spheres. It points out that economic integration mainly transforms the international dynamic into something very close to the regional dynamic, and so the proper reference space is no more nations but regions, mainly defined economically. Another important issue focused on here is the distinction between central and peripheral economies which are integrating with each other, and the possible outcomes for these economies of the two processes of liberalization and globalization. In order to do this, we consider first the position of the orthodoxy on the convergence of growth trends between regions, demonstrating that their case for convergence rests mainly on the assumption of decreasing marginal returns to capital. Moreover, this is the result of a certain conception of money in which it is a 'mere convenience' which cannot have real consequences. This is because they assume a that allows agents to know the future, and so they are able to predict the state of the world through the theory of probability and thus operate under risk and not true uncertainty.

We will then analyse the heterodox position, that the outcome of the two processes of globalization and liberalization is the divergence of growth trends, and demonstrate that this divergence is more rapid in regional terms than in national terms as a consequence of the absence of economic frontiers to regions. However, this framework does not adequately analyse the role of money at the regional level.

The emphasis on real variables identified in these theories will be argued to be a consequence of the absence of an adequate monetary theory that takes into account the characteristics of a monetary production economy, that is, an economy which is in historical time and in which crucial events are fundamental. If the relevant notion of time is historical time and so there are crucial events, these economies are subject to true uncertainty and agents cannot use probability theory as a base for their decision-making process. So, they have to use conventions to guide their decisions. Finally, this kind of economy has an asset with some peculiarities that can 'rule the roost' in the accumulation process. This asset is money. In this general environment, it is perfectly rational to demand it in particular circumstances (Keynes 1936).

As will be pointed out, Chick and Dow (1988, 1997) include money in theoretical models that deal with regional trends of growth, basing their case precisely on the notion of the non-neutrality of money at the general level. Regional non-neutrality of money in turn requires the concept of a monetary production economy.

This general theoretical framework will be developed here in order to highlight some important aspects of the possibility of monetary integration of Mercosul, a hypothesis that is sometimes discussed by the policy makers of the countries that form the economic bloc. It will be pointed out that, contrary to other international experiences where financial integration was a sovereign process led by national economies, in the case of this peripheral bloc, Mercosul, financial integration has been led by market mechanisms specially associated with the rapid process of internationalization of the domestic financial system of the countries of the bloc. This process was conducted taking the bloc as a whole, not only the national economies separately, and this will have important consequences for the regional economic organization of those countries.

## 2. Regional and national economies

The new international order raises some questions as to the relevant notion of economic space to be dealt with. In a context of globalization, nations, in economic terms, lose part of their significance to the economic dynamic, since some of the barriers that are one of the main features of those spaces are significantly reduced. However, as some of these barriers persist, especially differences with respect to monetary variables, they continue to be a significant element. Nevertheless, the intensification of the economic process of integration inside economic blocs, which tends to lead to monetary unions, challenges the economic idea of a nation and jeopardizes analysis developed on these grounds. It seems clear that in this context the relevant analytical category is the region, defined in economic terms (Lipietz 1988).

Therefore, it is necessary to differentiate between regional and national economies. Nations are politically independent units. This has important economic consequences. As nations are different political spaces, there are some legal frictions that impede economic relations between those separate units. The first barrier is the existence of different currencies. Another element to be observed is the restriction to flows of productive factors: capital and labour. And, finally, there are restrictions to the free movement of goods. Therefore, economic relations between two regions are much less constrained than those between countries. This makes market mechanisms, and the general tendencies implicit in them, act much more intensively and rapidly in the first group than in the second one.

Thus, the regional space is much closer to the liberal idea of a world without friction where the market can play its role free from political barriers, than the international economy. Thus, if the theory concludes that market mechanisms lead to convergence of patterns of growth, this would happen more rapidly in regional economies than at the international level. On the other hand, if theory suggests instead the divergence of patterns of growth, the regional dynamic, obviously, would lead to a more rapid and more intense divergence of rates of growth.

## 3. Convergence and orthodoxy

The great majority of theories that predict convergence of regional development patterns are related to orthodoxy. They are normally associated with neoclassical theory and assume the idea of a non-frictional environment. (Agents know the world without great information costs, therefore they form their expectations correctly, and there are no barriers to the flow of goods and factors and prices are flexible.) In this world the imbalance between development levels among regions tends to disappear.

What those theorists have in mind is the fact that capital has decreasing marginal returns.[3] Therefore, as capital accumulation proceeds, and as the stock of capital increases, there is a reduction in the marginal return to capital. As capital has two alternatives – the first gives it a smaller marginal return (richer regions) and the second one a larger marginal return (poorer regions) – it will migrate to the region in which the marginal productivity is larger. Therefore, capital would flow from more developed regions, as they have a larger stock of capital, to regions where the capital accumulation is not so developed. This makes clear the tendency towards homogenization of patterns of growth. This process is made easy by liberalization and globalization since those two processes accelerate the action of market mechanisms, as they remove the frictions of exogenous elements that slow down the economic relations among nations.

Those theories discount the role of money in the process of growth. This is perfectly understandable since, in their macroeconomic theory, money has a neutral role and so does not interfere in the growth trends of the economy as a whole. There is, therefore, no reason for it to interfere in the growth trends of regional economies, unless there are short-run imperfections that make agents mal-form their expectations and, thus, there is room for short-run non-neutrality of money. However, as the economy passes from the short-run period to the long-run, the intervention of money in the growth pattern of the economy is eliminated and growth becomes only a function of real variables. And it is precisely those real variables which lead to the homogeneity of growth patterns.

## 4. Heterodoxy and divergence

Some schools of economic thought have undermined the idea that uneven patterns of regional economic development tended to be eliminated by market forces. They argued that, instead of a natural tendency towards regional economic harmony, there was a natural tendency towards divergence of initially unequal growth trends. Nevertheless, those analyses were based on real variables. Money was never taken seriously at the regional level.

Myrdal (1972) was one of the pioneers in verifying that, when there is a force that deviates the economy from its equilibrium position, there is no guarantee that this economy will be taken to the previous point again by any natural force. Conversely, the process may be in exactly the opposite direction: the initial disequilibrium can be accentuated. Therefore, the economic process may be subject to vicious circles. This idea is perfectly applicable to regional economic analysis.

Other theories were developed aiming to demonstrate that this tendency to amplify the initial inequality of development levels was valid. Among those theories was Dependency Theory.[4] This theory demonstrated that underdevelopment and development were two joint aspects of the process of capitalist development. Therefore, it was the underdevelopment of some countries/regions that made possible the development of others. International inequalities were reproduced within each country and so the regional inequalities tended to be functional to capitalist accumulation and could not be eliminated through market mechanisms. What made those inequalities so special for understanding the process of capitalist accumulation was the extraction of surplus from the peripheral economies by the central economies. This is not a homogenous school of thought and so there are different theoretical reasons presented for this extraction of surplus. But all the theories associated with the broad classification of Dependency Theory analysed the regional problem in real terms. Occasionally they did analyse the role of the financial system. However, this was done in the sense that the transference of surplus was mediated by the financial system. Therefore, this analysis did not allow money to play a real role; it was just a veil to a real process of surplus extraction.

Kaldor (1970) also analysed the dynamic of regional growth in terms of divergence. He identified some cumulative processes that were the consequence of differences in the level of productivity between regions. The main element that determined competitiveness (and thus external demand) was related to the rate of growth of each economy. Therefore, the more dynamic the economy, the more its productivity grows and, consequently, the higher the rate of growth of the economy. Growth was itself a positive function of growth. Thus, an original differential of rates of growth tended to be amplified instead of reduced.

All theories considered so far started from a monetary framework, if any at all, that considers money as an element with minimal importance. And so, logically, money could not have any important role to play in this whole story. Chick and Dow, on the contrary, develop the argument concerning the non-neutrality of money, with the banking system as supplier of private money. Consequently they incorporate money in the theory as a non-neutral element. In doing so, they filled a gap in regional theories, introducing the financial system as a relevant element in order to explain the vicious circle of growth generated at the regional level. They put together elements related to the real sphere of regional analysis and the financial behaviour of agents under rather different economic regional structures, and then elaborated a theory of vicious cycles in a monetary production economy (Dow 1982, 1987, 1990).

As post-Keynesian theory demonstrated, in order for investment to take place, it is necessary that the marginal efficiency of capital is equal, at the margin, to the interest rate. Therefore, the higher the interest rate, the lower the level of investment. The interest rate, contrary to the classical tradition, is a monetary phenomenon determined by the supply and demand of money. As investment takes place the demand for finance is increased, so there is the need for some agents to accept becoming less liquid in order for the rate of interest not to increase. Normally, the sector supposed to accept a less liquid position is the banking system. If they do so, they create extra finance; they increase the liquidity of the economy and re-establish their liquid position by the end of the process. Another form of increasing the liquidity of the economy is the consent of the Monetary Authority in expanding the money supply. Therefore, if there is a limit to the expansion of the money supply in one region, and this limit does not exist in the other region, there is a tendency in the second to grow more rapidly than the first. Thus, the analysis of the process of regional growth depends on the behaviour of agents in relation to liquidity in each system.

The lower the level of per capita income of an economy, the more agents will use cash instead of deposits. This causes a leak in the flow of loans/deposits on which the money multiplier is based. Therefore, each time banks extend credit towards a backward region, they receive less deposits as a consequence of this credit extension than if they were doing the same thing in a richer economy. This has a negative impact on the pattern of growth of the poorer economies, as the capacity of private money creation is more constrained in peripheral regions than in central ones. On the other hand, these peripheral economies tend to be more unstable than the central ones. Given the higher instability, agents present a higher liquidity preference in these economies (because of precautionary and speculation motives). And, so, in the periphery, banks are again penalized because of the drain of deposits from those regions to the central ones, as a result of the higher liquidity preference (Dow 1982, 1990; and Chick and Dow 1988).

Another important aspect of this analysis is the openness of regional economies. Peripheral economies present a higher marginal propensity to import than central ones. This causes a drain of the finance created in peripheral regions towards richer regions and this reduces the capacity of banks to create money through the money multiplier and thus to finance economic growth. This element has important impacts on both the money and income multipliers. Those effects tend to reduce the growth potential of peripheral systems and amplify growth in central systems (Dow 1982).

Finally, we should analyse one of the important peculiarities of regional economies in terms of the demand for liquidity. Since one assumes that there is no barrier to capital movements in regional economies, agents will prefer to speculate with assets that have higher liquidity, as a consequence of more solid institutional arrangements. Moreover, agents in the periphery will have a higher liquidity preference as a consequence of the higher instability of those regions, as pointed out previously. As central regions present more solid institutional arrangements, their assets are more liquid. So, peripheral agents tend to speculate with central assets. The higher liquidity preference in itself is a problem in terms of the creation of finance, but there is an extra problem that refers to the use of central assets to speculate. This causes an extra drain of finance from the peripheral regions towards central regions via the capital account (Dow 1982; Chick and Dow 1988).

Banks that have their head offices in the central regions could, however, create credit in the periphery, returning part of the finance that was drained from that system by market mechanisms. However, it is not so easy to assume that this will happen effectively. Centre's banks form their expectations in relation to the

197

periphery on a remote basis. This discriminates against the creation of credit in those regions, especially when we assume an uncertain world where conventions are the basis for expectations formation (Dow 1990; Amado 1997).

On the other hand, up to this point we have only considered the liquidity preference of firms and households. Banks also present a liquidity preference function and this would vary according to their expectations with respect to each economy, and with the uncertainty with which these expectations are held. As peripheral regions are more unstable all banks would keep larger reserves in those regions. And this again will constrain the availability of finance and reduce the growth potential of those economies (Dow 1990).

Those elements that lead to uneven patterns of regional development can only be counteracted by an exogenous element that is not related to the private logic of accumulation. This element can only be the State.

This position, however, is not consensual among the post-Keynesian stream. Davidson (1992), proposing a new arrangement for the international financial system, considers the case of regions to be a good example of what he calls Unionized Monetary Systems (UMS). He points out that part of the regional dynamic is associated with the reconstitution of the liquidity levels of the region, through the action of the State. This system has the advantage of reducing exchange risk, since they have an absolutely fixed exchange rate, as they have the same monetary unit. However, he seems to underestimate the negative impacts of the market mechanism on the monetary dynamic of the regions which has been discussed by Chick and Dow on several occasions. He overemphasizes the exogenous and voluntarist position of the State in the economic dynamic.

To summarize, an analysis that assumes a non-neutral money and a monetary production economy under uncertainty could only arrive at a view of money as having an effective role to play at the regional level. This non-neutrality is the consequence of market forces and tends to reinforce initial inequalities in the trend of growth of regional economies. Moreover, the regional analysis cannot separate the real from the monetary sphere in order to understand the dynamic of accumulation of regional economies. Those conclusions that were true for national economies were applied to the regional level through an adequate treatment of money and the behaviour of agents toward this peculiar asset.

## 5. Globalization, internationalization of the peripheral financial system and a new regional dynamic

As previously noted, the 1990s were characterized by an intense process of liberalization of the external relations of nations. Not only was external trade liberalized, but this process had a profound impact on the capital account of peripheral countries. This had many consequences, but one of the main consequences was the intensification of the vulnerability of these economies.[5] This can be easily perceived by the exchange crises which reached Latin America and Asia. In a certain sense we can say that this vulnerability even undermined some of the results of the mainstream model and led some theorists to consider new assumptions to be necessary for understanding this new reality (Silva and Andrade 1998).

In Mercosul this process was marked especially by the case of Argentina, that undertook a rapid and intense process of internationalization of its financial system. Brazil internationalized a significant part of its financial system; however this process did not reach the same scale as Argentina. (In Argentina, in 1998, the private foreign banks held 45.5 per cent of total deposits, 48 per cent of total loans and 51.2 per cent of total assets; in Brazil, also in 1998, they held 8.3 per cent of deposits, 12.2 per cent of loans and 14.2 per cent of assets; Amado and Silva (1999).)[6]

This tended to promote the financial integration of the bloc, led not by the sovereign decision of the countries, but by market mechanisms. This is so because the international banks that entered the Brazilian market were the same that were entering the Argentinian market. The strategies of the banks were mainly based on their operations in the region as a whole and not isolated by country. This can be discerned from some statements of the head officers of the main banks involved in the process (Amado 1997).

The Brazilian internationalization of the financial system was followed by two other processes. On the one hand, there was a strong process of financial concentration, and, on the other hand, there was the loss of the regional character of the banking system. In this period private banks that did not have their head offices in the centre (São Paulo and Rio de Janeiro) were incorporated with other nationwide and international banks. This twofold process tended to create two kinds of problems. The concentration of the banking system in the central region tended to enhance regional disparities, as discussed in the first part of the chapter. On the other hand, since this process was associated with the internationalization of these banks, the decision-making process became more fragile and this created extra problems for the extension of credit to the national peripheries.

As was previously observed, one of the reasons that led to divergence of growth patterns with respect to regional economies is the behaviour of the centre banks when extending credit to the periphery. Since the information that those banks have on the economies of the periphery are less reliable than information on the economy of the centre, the banks are more restrictive in the extension of credit to peripheral regions and this creates liquidity constraints for those regions. When dealing with international banks in national peripheral economies, this process is intensified, since the country as a whole does not present a very solid information base for the decision-making process[7] and the internal peripheral regional economies present an even less reliable base of information. And so, the actions of those banks tend to be even more restrictive in those regions than the national banks.

The definition of the strategy of those international banks in terms of their actions in Mercosul tends, as well, to stress the spatial concentration of the financial system. As the theoretical model and the operations of those banks in Mercosul demonstrates, the tendency is to integrate the centre of the two main countries (Argentina and Brazil), that is the region on the South of São Paulo and Buenos Aires, and to reduce the participation of those banks in the periphery of those countries. That is, the Brazilian economic centre integrates with the Argentinian economic centre and the national peripheries disintegrate in relation to the other national periphery and to the bloc periphery as a whole. In Brazil this can be observed by the increase in the number of municipalities that do not have any kind of financial provision following the intensification of the process of internationalization and concentration of the banking system. In Brazil in 1994, 23 per cent of the towns/cities did not have financial institutions; in 1998, 31 per cent of towns had no financial services (Amado and Silva 1999).

In the case of Mercosul there is another element that puts strong limits on the idea of monetary union within the bloc. The stabilization plans of Brazil and Argentina in the 1990s were based on the idea of exchange anchors. The exchange regime of Brazil had a certain flexibility, however in the Argentinian case flexibility was nil, which made the country lose its monetary policy tools. After the external crises of 1998, Brazil left this regime and entered a flexible exchange rate regime. Therefore, it is difficult to consider the possibility of homogenizing those two kinds of exchange regime in order to promote monetary union. Another issue is how far this homogenization is desirable, considering that the main proposal on this issue is to integrate Brazil with the Argentinian regime, which constitutes the transformation of those two countries into appendages of the USA.

## 6. Epilogue

It is important to consider whether it is possible for these two countries to deal with the degree of monetary rigidity that this kind of solution asks for. Moreover, it is fundamental to consider the consequences of the loss of the monetary tool for dealing with the process of development of these countries.

In this sense, the analysis of the institutional development of these countries is fundamental. The State provided the main pillars of the industrialization process of these countries and played an especially important role in the provision of finance and funding of the growth process. The liberalization process and the rigidity that the monetary regimes of Argentina and Brazil adopted in the 1990s eliminated the possibility of State action in financing development. This goes exactly in the opposite direction of what should be the case according to a model that assumes the non-neutrality of money, in which one of the roles of the State should be to create adequate institutional mechanisms and support those mechanisms in order to remove financial bottlenecks in the process of development.

Therefore, a process of monetary/financial integration conducted along the lines that have been proposed by the policy makers in Mercosul tends to create further financial constraints in the region and emphasizes the divergence of growth rates among the economic regions inside the bloc.

# Notes

1  The author gratefully acknowledges the financial support of CNPq.
2  Mercosul is the Common Market of the South and is formed by Argentina, Brazil, Uruguai and Paraguai.
3  There are recent attempts to derive models which present a tendency toward convergence at the same time as assuming increasing marginal returns (Sala-I-Martim 1996).
4  See Furtado (1964, 1971, 1982), Paz and Sunkel (1975), Prebisch (1970), Rodriguez (1981), Baran (1957), dos Santos (1970), Frank (1967) and Cardoso (1972, 1979).
5  This can be observed by the impacts of the emerging markets' external crisis that began with the Mexican crisis in 1995. All this crises had deep consequences for the external and internal positions of Mercosul countries, especially Brazil and Argentina, demonstrating the increased vulnerability of these countries. For further details see Silva (1999) and Andrade et al. (2000).
6  There is a significant difference of dimension with respect to the internationalization of the two financial systems. The internationalization of Argentina is much more intense than for Brazil. However, until the middle of the decade, Brazil had only a marginal participation of international banks in its financial system and by the end of the decade these figures were expressive.
7  This was the basis for the models that deal with herd behaviour.

# References

Amado, A. (1997) *Disparate Regional Development in Brazil: A Monetary Production Approach.* Aldershot: Ashgate.
Amado, A. M. (1998) 'Impactos Regionais do Recente Processo de Concentração Bancária no Brasil', In *Proceedings of the III Encontro de Economia Política.*
Amado, A. M. and Silva, L. A. S. (1999) 'Integração Monetário-Financeira do Mercosul', In *Proceedings of the XXVI Encontro de Economia*, ANPEC.
Andrade, J. P., Silva, M. L. F. and Carneiro, F. G. (2000) 'Contrasting Monetary Policies Within the Mercosul Experiment', *Economia Aplicada* 4(2): 223–232
Baran, P. A. (1957) *The Political Economy of Growth.* London: John Calder.
Cardoso, F. H. (1972) 'Dependency and Development in Latin America', *New Left Review* July-August.
Cardoso, F. H. and Faletto, E. (1979) *Dependence and Development in Latin America.* Berkeley: University of California Press.
Chick, V. and Dow, S. (1988) 'A Post-Keynesiana Perspective on the Relation Between Banking and Regional Development', in P. Arestis (ed.), *Post-Keynesian Monetary Economics.* Aldershot: Edward Elgar.
Chick, V. and Dow, S. (1997) 'Competition and The Future of the European Banking and Financial System', in A. Cohen, H. Hagemann and J. Smithin (eds), *Money, Financial Institutions and Macroeconomics.* Kluwer, pp. 253–70.
dos Santos, T. (1970) 'The Structure of Dependence', *American Economic Review* 60(2).
Dow, S. C. (1982) 'The Regional Composition of the Money Multiplier Process', *Scottish Journal of Political Economy* 29(1).
Dow, S. C. (1987) 'The Treatment of Money in Regional Economics', *Journal of Regional Science* 27(1).
Dow, S. C. (1990) *Financial Markets and regional Economic Development: The Canadian Experience.* Aldershot, Avebury.

Frank, A. G. (1967) *Capitalism and Underdevelopment in Latin America*. New York: Monthly Review Press.

Furtado, C. (1964) *Development and Underdevelopment*. Berkely: University of California Press.

Furtado, C. (1971) *Teoria e Política do Desenvolvimento Econômico*. São Paulo: Editora Nacional.

Furtado, C. (1982) *A Nova Dependência*. Rio de Janeiro: Paz e Terra.

Frank, A.G. (1967) *Capitalism and Underdevelopment in Latin America*. New York: Monthly Review Press.

Furtado, C. (1971) *Teoria e Política do Desenvolvimento Econômico*. São Paulo: Editora Nacional.

Furtado, C. (1964) *Development and Underdevelopment*. Berkeley: University of California Press.

Furtado, C. (1982) *A Nova Dependência*. Rio de Janeiro: Paz e Terra.

Kaldor, N. (1970) 'The Case for Regional Policies', *Scottish Journal of Political Economy* 17.

Keynes, J. M. (1936) *The General Theory of Employment, Interest and Money*. London: Macmillan.

Lipietz, A. (1988) *O Capital e seu Espaço*. São Paulo: Nobel.

Myrdal, G. (1972) *Economic Theory and Underdeveloped Regions*. London: Gerald Duckworth.

Paz, P. and Sunkel, O. (1975) *El Subdesarrollo Latino Americano y La Teoria del Desarrollo*. Mexico: Siglo Veintiuno.

Prebisch, R. (1970) *Transformacion e Desarrollo: La Gran Tarea de La América Latina*. México: Fondo de Cultura Económica.

Rodriguez, O. (1981) *Teoria do Subdesenvolvimento da CEPAL*. Rio de Janeiro: Editora Forense-Universitária.

Silva, M. L. (1999) *Modern Exchange-Rate Regimes, Stabilisation Programmes and Co-Ordination of Macroeconomic Policies*. Aldershot: Ashgate.

Silva, M. L. F. and Andrade, J. P. (1998) 'Contrasting or Convergent Views on Currency Crisis: Mainstream versus Keynesian Approaches', in *Proceedings of the XXVI Encontro Nacional de Economia*, ANPEC.

# 20

# ASSESSING CREDITWORTHINESS AND SMALL-FIRM BANK LENDING

*Jochen Runde*[1]

Credit relations are a central theme in post-Keynesian thought to which Victoria Chick has contributed in numerous writings.[2] And as she has worked on the financing of small businesses in particular, it seemed appropriate to use the present occasion to say something about an important determinant of credit relations in the small-firm sector, namely the procedures that banks use to assess small-firm loan applications. Whereas such assessments were once the preserve of largely autonomous local or regional branch managers, the last decade or so has seen a strong movement towards the centralisation and automation of lending decisions. The transition is now so advanced that the relationship managers who serve as banks' points of contact with small-firm clients, often have little or no discretion over whether an application is granted. What follows considers some implications of this shift for small-firm borrowing, drawing on a series of interviews conducted with the major UK clearing banks in 1995.

Section 1 outlines the epistemological basis of the lending decision before and after the shift described above. Section 2 gives reasons for this shift and Section 3 explores possible implications for the availability of bank finance for small firms. Section 4 concludes.

## 1. Case- vs class-based judgements

Lending decisions are based on lenders' beliefs about the creditworthiness of potential borrowers. Questions about how such beliefs are arrived at, and the nature of information employed, are therefore central to the study of credit relations.

Despite its emphasis on uncertainty and asymmetric information, however, the mainstream theoretical literature on credit relationships has little to say about these questions. The reason for this is that most of this literature employs the expected utility model and thereby assumes that economic actors are able to assign a unique probability to each of the possible outcomes they are uncertain about (the returns on a business venture, for example). The drawback of this approach is not only that this assumption is heroic in the extreme, but also that it forestalls

203

questions about how agents actually arrive at their probabilities. They are simply assumed to 'have' well-defined probability functions, usually taken to correspond to objective frequencies, and the analysis proceeds from there.

Rather than proceeding in this way, then, it is useful to distinguish between *case*- and *class-based* judgements of probability. Case-based judgements of probability are best understood as a weighing of the balance of the arguments (on the basis of the information available) for and against a particular conclusion. Judgements of this kind are typically qualitative and take the following form: '*x* on evidence *e* is more probable than not-*x* on evidence *e*', or '*x* on evidence *e* is more probable than *y* on evidence *e*'. That such judgements are in fact probability judgements may sound strange to those accustomed to thinking about probabilities as numerical ratios. But the idea should be familiar enough from everyday life. In a court of law, for example, the guilt of a defendant is not decided on the basis of the number of times similar persons have been found guilty of a similar crime in similar situations, but on the basis of the arguments for and against the defendant's guilt on the basis of whatever is known about the specifics of the case. The same is true of the traditional 'judgemental' lending decision, based predominantly on a weighing up of information specific to the applicant firm and its proposed venture.

Class-based judgements of probability are beliefs about possible outcomes based on the frequency such outcomes have occurred in similar instances in the past. Thus a cunning gambler's judgement of the probability that the next toss of the weighted die will land six up may be based on a knowledge of the relative frequency with which six has come up in a long sequence of past throws. Similarly, a banker's judgement of the probability that an applicant will default on loan may be based on his or her knowledge about the default rate in a class of similar business ventures.

The essential difference between these two approaches is that whereas case-based judgements of probability are made in respect of individual cases as individual cases, class-based judgements of probability focus on individual cases only insofar as they are members of a *class* of similar cases. In the context of the lending decision, this difference translates into whether the lender asks:

1   'is *this* applicant *x* creditworthy, given what I know about his or her particular situation?'; or
2   'is this *type* of applicant creditworthy, given what I know about the average quality of borrowers of this type?'

The transition from 'judgemental' decision making to statistically based (credit-scoring) techniques in small-firm lending entails a shift from 1 to 2.[3]

## 2. Why class-based assessment?

The benefits of moving from case- to class-based assessments fall into four categories. First are various savings in the processing of individual applications: reductions in time and personnel required for face-to-face interaction with clients; reductions in skill levels needed to screen applications; reductions in time spent actually making decisions; learning by doing efficiencies accruing from standardised procedures; increased speed of processing reducing customer dissatisfaction; and the fact that class-based assessment systems generally require less information than their case-based counterparts.

Second are various benefits stemming from the consistency that class-based assessment procedures impose on lending across the branch networks of individual banks. Foremost here is that it becomes possible to control centrally the volume and quality of lending. Consistency also facilitates internal audits and the identification of systematic problems with particular classes of borrowers or particular branches, as well as the generation of data about individual account and aggregate portfolio performance. Finally, clients may value the fact that they would receive similar treatment wherever their branch is located.

Third is the improved performance of loans that class-based procedures might bring. Class-based procedures also facilitate the tracking and analysis of data and, to some extent, the validation of the systems employed. In particular, scoring formulations can be tested for consistency against a variety of samples and, given a sufficiently stable economic environment, in terms of predictive success.

Finally, there are a number of sector-specific reasons why small firms may be suited to class-based assessment: (i) unlike larger firms, small firms typically do not have a ready market valuation, are subject to relatively lower accounting and information reporting requirements, and tend to lack the financial expertise and experience necessary to provide the information that banks might want to see; (ii) class-based assessments are based on the assumed 'sameness' of the members of classes of similar firms, an assumption that is most likely to be met in the small-firm sector (and which is also most suited to providing large samples of similar loans to work on); and (iii) class-based assessment procedures benefit from scale economies where, as is typically the case in the small-firm sector, the size of individual loans is small and the costs of individual assessment and processing high, relative to the size of the loan.

## 3. Implications for small-firm bank lending

### Faceless banking

The movement from case- to class-based assessment procedures tends to reduce face-to-face interaction between bank managers and their clients. Indeed, some advocates of credit scoring believe that it removes altogether the need to interview applicants for small-firm loans. How then may this increase in the 'distance' between bank managers and their small-firm clients affect small-firm lending?

First, class-based assessment procedures allow banks to maintain an arm's length relationship with their small-firm clients. This makes it easier for banks to extend and roll over short-term finance in good times and withdraw it in bad (Hughes 1994: 219); prevents any improvement in their generally low level of knowledge of firm- and industry-specific knowledge (Binks *et al.* 1988, 1990); and, accordingly, reinforces their inability and unwillingness to have a voice in, and assist their small-firm clients on, anything other than basic financial matters. Second is the possibility that, far from reducing what are already seen as excessive collateral requirements, the shift towards class-based assessment procedures may provide mutually reinforcing arguments for increasing them. On the one hand, the resulting increase in 'distance' between banks and their small-firm clients is likely to undermine the role of trust and reputation in their relationships. If this should translate into increased fears about moral hazard on the part of borrowers, banks may be led to raise collateral requirements. On the other hand, maintaining or increasing collateral requirements may justify banks in neglecting the acquisition of firm- or industry-specific knowledge about their small-firm clients. If this reasoning is correct, moreover, banks' incentive to price risk will be reduced. Finally, class-based assessment procedures may prejudice unusual or exotic applications.

These negative implications are mitigated by the following factors. All of the banks interviewed reported an increase in medium-term lending to small firms over the preceding five years (enhancing the prospects of longer-term relationships between banks and their small-firm customers) and a number argued that the efficiencies achieved through class-based procedures would allow relationship managers to spend more time with their clients. Also, having gone through a credit-scoring exercise was felt to increase the productivity of interviews by helping the client to focus on key issues and by taking the emotion out of the lending decision. A number of the banks conduct regular site visits, moreover, and some of them provide seminars, information packs and so on to their small-firm customers. Finally, a number of the banks interviewed indicated that small firms were 'control averse', actually preferring to maintain anonymous relations with their bankers, and that (relatively rare) exotic applications are dealt with on their own merits in case-based terms.

Nevertheless, the dominant tendency was towards an increasingly anonymous 'hands-off' relationship between banks and their small-firm clients. The accompanying emphasis on the (average) quality of classes of loan applicants (as opposed to the quality of individual cases) inevitably brings a 'playing the numbers' aspect to small-firm lending. This leads to two important analogies with the insurance industry: banks' incentive to assess the intrinsic riskiness of individual clients as accurately as possible and the possibility of adverse selection and moral hazard problems.

### *Improvements in the accuracy of individual assessments of creditworthiness*

An oft-repeated argument in favour of class-based assessment procedures is that they provide more accurate predictions than their case-based counterparts. This argument is seldom questioned, no doubt due to the aura of scientificity that surrounds the methods employed. In fact, however, it is an open question whether the desired improvements will actually be achieved for any given case. There are two main reasons for this. First, the class-based approach is narrowly inductive, aiming to predict the quality of potential borrowers strictly on the basis of past experience with borrowers of a similar type. As such, it faces all the standard problems of inductive inference when applied in an open and dynamic world. Second, and even given a suitably stable economic environment and the absence of adverse selection and moral hazard problems (see below), the class-based approach is restricted to measuring the creditworthiness of applicants on the basis of their membership of a class of similar applicants grouped together on the basis of some shared, general characteristics (more specific or particular differences between members of that class are assumed to be randomly distributed and therefore irrelevant). The trouble is that this may lead to the neglect of specific information that may be both readily available and relevant to the loan application. The traditional approach is better suited to picking up differences of this kind.

The move towards class-based assessments of loan applications does not guarantee improvements in the quality of small-firm lending. It follows that there may be no benefits to small firms from this source.

### Asymmetric information and the problems of adverse selection and moral hazard

The economic literature on credit rationing is dominated by the information theoretic approach precipitated by Stiglitz and Weiss (1981, henceforth S&W). This approach focuses on problems of adverse selection (AS) and moral hazard (MH) that may arise when banks have imperfect information about individual borrowers or their investment projects. AS occurs in the following way. Suppose banks charge a pooling rate of interest on loans to some class of borrowers (being unable to distinguish between the riskiness of their individual projects), whereas borrowers within that class are aware of the riskiness of their projects and are prepared to pay interest rates that reflect this risk. If the interest rate then rises, the proportion of loans taken up by high-risk borrowers will rise as low-risk borrowers drop out. MH problems arise when risk-taking behaviour changes in response to changes in the interest rate and other terms of the contract. S&W focus on the possibility that borrowers may pursue riskier projects in response to interest rate rises.

In both cases, increases in the rate of interest may increase the average riskiness of the loans issued by banks. It is then possible that there may be a point at which the positive effect on banks' expected revenues of increases in the interest rate are outweighed by decreases in revenue that follow from AS and MH effects. Banks may accordingly be led to set a ceiling on the interest rate at this point and, given that they are constrained by liquidity and balance sheet considerations of their own, to ration credit. S&W show that similar arguments apply with respect to collateral requirements, that increased collateral requirements (beyond some point) may decrease the returns to the bank by either decreasing the average degree of risk aversion of its pool of borrowers or, in an intertemporal context, by inducing individual borrowers to undertake riskier projects.

How is this reasoning affected by the transition from case- to class-based assessment procedures? The traditional case-based approach differs somewhat from the scenario presupposed by S&W. In particular, where a locally based lending officer has personal-, firm- or industry-specific knowledge about loan applicants and their proposed projects, there is scope for the matching lending to the particular circumstances of individual applicants (rather than posting a pooling offer for some class of borrowers). Moreover, since loans are typically issued by different lending officers in different regions, the scope for systematic biases are that much less than under class-based systems. From this perspective, the introduction of class-based assessment procedures may leave banks relatively more open to AS problems, and, for similar kinds of reasons, to MH problems.

Against this conclusion is the possibility that asymmetric information problems may be reduced to the extent that class-based assessment procedures facilitate finer partitionings of borrowers that could then be priced separately. The banks interviewed differed in the extent to which they were attempting to price risk. But all of them indicated that it was desirable to do so, at least within limits, and that the pricing of risk would increase as class-based assessment procedures are refined and developed. There is reason to be sceptical about the extent to which class-based methods will lead to dramatic improvements over their case-based counterparts in the classification of borrowers into different risk groups (see below). But even granting some improvement in this respect, this is unlikely to do much to enhance the quality of banks' lending to small firms through the reduction of AS or MH problems *per se*. The reason is that problems of the type analysed by S&W may not be as significant in the small-firm sector as is sometimes thought. This can be seen by considering some of the assumptions on which their model of AS and MH is based.[4]

With respect to *Adverse Selection*, two key assumptions are:

(i) *The level of interest that firms are prepared to pay on loans is directly related to the riskiness of their proposed projects.* Individual (borrower) firms' investment projects earn a gross return $R_i$ with probability $p_i$ or fail completely and earn zero (in which case the bank loses the principal and any accrued interest on the loan). The expected gross returns $E[R_i] = R$ are assumed to be equal for each firm (the $p_i$'s and $R_i$'s will in general be different, reflecting the different risk/return combinations offered by the different firms). This last condition is crucial because it implies assumption (i). To see this, suppose that all of the (risk neutral) firms want to invest a fixed amount $K$ and have $W$ of their own to invest in the project (the size of the loan will then be equal to $K - W = L$). Let $r$ denote the interest rate on loans charged by the banks and $b$ the maximum expected return that borrowers would earn from investing $W$ in some alternative project. The expected profit for the period of the $i$th firm will then be

$$E(\pi_i) = p_i[R_i - (1+r)(K-W)]. \tag{1}$$

It is evident from (1) that as $r$ rises, low return firms will begin to drop out. For it is a necessary condition for a firm to take a loan that $R_i - (1 + r)(K - W) > 0$ (although it will of course only do so as long as $E(\pi) > (1 + b)W$. Because higher $R_i$'s are necessarily accompanied by higher levels of risk (lower $p_i$'s, because $E[R_i] = R$), it follows that the level of interest that firms are prepared to pay on loans is directly related to their riskiness.

(ii) *Individual borrowers know their $p_i$'s and $R_i$'s; banks only know that the expected gross return of all borrowers is R.* Assumption (i) is open to various objections. First, it places extreme demands on firms' capacity to assess the risk of their projects and to match this to particular interest rates. I shall return to this point in the discussion of (ii) below. Second, the posited direct relationship between the interest rate and the riskiness of borrowers may be reversed in a situation that is just as plausible as the one assumed by S&W. Suppose that all firms have a common gross return $R^g$ if successful but different probabilities of succeeding (de Meza and Webb 1987). The expected profit for the period of the ith firm is then

$$E(\pi_i) = p_i[R^g - (1 + r)(K - W)]. \tag{2}$$

As before, the firm will only borrow so long as $E(\pi_i) > (1+b)W$. But in this case, over some ranges of the variables, higher-risk borrowers will *withdraw* from the market as the interest rate rises, and the proportion of low-risk borrowers demanding loans will rise.

This theoretical indeterminacy about the relationship between the level of interest that small firms are prepared to pay on loans on the one hand, and their riskiness (profitability) on the other, was mirrored in the interviews conducted with the banks. But an interesting point that emerged here was that although most of the banks claimed that they were (or would be) attempting to price risk, some of them indicated that low-risk borrowers are sometimes actually charged *higher* interest rates on loans than are high-risk borrowers. If so, this would indicate that such borrowers are irrational or, more likely, that they are unaware of the riskiness of their projects and/or that they should be able to obtain credit on better terms than they are currently receiving. Either way, however, assumption (i) is violated in this case.

With respect (ii), borrowers *do* typically have private information not accessible to their bankers. The question is whether such information would be relevant to the bank's decision to refuse or grant a loan. Borrowers typically know more than do their bank about such things as the technology employed, local demand conditions, supply relationships and so on. Banks are likely to know relatively more about the typical pitfalls small businesses face, the macroeconomic climate, financial management and, importantly, the hit rate of ventures of similar kinds. An interesting possibility that emerged from the interviews was, contrary to the assumptions of S&W, that the banks often achieve a more realistic assessments of the prospects of the individual borrowers' ventures than do the borrowers themselves. The reasons for this are partly that small firms often lack financial expertise and have less information than does the bank about the success rates of ventures of similar kinds. Further, and as their historically high failure rates suggest (Daly 1990), they tend to be unduly optimistic about their prospects of success (de Meza and Southey 1996). If so, a significant proportion of small firms may be over-keen to borrow at prevailing rates and banks may be justified in turning them away. Again any unsatisfied demand for credit at these rates will not be due to AS along the lines of S&W.

On the *moral hazard* side of the argument, two key assumptions are:

(iii) *The level of interest that firms are prepared to pay on their loans is directly related to the riskiness of the proposed projects.* This assumption is identical to (i) above, but in this case the firms are assumed to be identical and to choose from a range of investment projects with varying levels of riskiness.

(iv) *The bank is unable to observe the actions of the borrower, namely the riskiness of the project he or she undertakes.* The first of these assumptions was already considered above. Even if it is granted, however, the image of small firms having a portfolio of possible investment projects, each of them offering a different risk/return combination and all of them being implementable at will in response to variations in the interest rate, seems implausible. The problem is not only that the necessary financial and forecasting skills are typically not available to small firms. More importantly, it flies in the face of the normal order of things, namely that ideas for business ventures almost invariably precede questions about their financing and that the bulk of small-firm lending is made to firms that are already established and where instant variations in the nature of investment projects pursued are not feasible. Also, with high and increasing sanctions that apply to loan failures (loss of credit ratings), it is by no means clear that small-firm borrowers would deliberately choose riskier projects when faced with higher rates of interest.

Assumption (iv), in contrast, *is* plausible: small firms typically do know more than do their banks about how they use the money loaned to them. Moreover, private information of this kind does provide scope for MH, even if perhaps not of the kind considered by S&W. The responses of the banks on this issue suggested that it is useful to distinguish between *ex ante* MH (where potential borrowers deliberately misrepresent their position prior to securing a loan), a strong form of *ex post* MH (where borrowers' post-contract behaviour violates the formal terms of the loan contract) and a weaker form of *ex post* MH (where existing borrowers take actions which, while not necessarily at variance with the formal terms of the loan contract, are not in the banks' best interests). The general view was that the first two forms of MH are rare. This was attributed to the 'basic honesty' of the majority of borrowers, reinforced, in the case of *ex ante* MH, by the fact that some of the information provided by the applicant is verifiable, and in the case of *ex post* MH, by legal sanctions and the threat of the loss of credit ratings. Moreover, as the majority of small-firm borrowers are pre-existing clients of the bank, some screening is possible. Overall, the banks were sceptical about the idea that more extreme forms of MH may be directly related to the interest rate.

Weaker forms of *ex post* MH were regarded as more common, however, particularly as manifested in small-firm borrowers attempting to cope with financial difficulties without notifying and/or requesting assistance from the bank. It has been argued that *ex post* informational asymmetries of a related kind may lead to credit rationing. Williamson (1986), for example, suggests that banks may respond to the possibility of borrowers falsely declaring returns that are insufficient to repay their loans, by committing themselves to costly monitoring in the event of bankruptcy. Given that higher loan rates are likely to lead to increases in genuine bankruptcies, they are also likely to lead to higher monitoring costs. If so, the bank may attempt to avoid raising monitoring costs by choosing a non-market clearing loan rate. The kind of MH that Williamson has in mind here is of the stronger, fraudulent variety that, according to the banks interviewed, is only rarely encountered in practice. It is nevertheless possible that weaker forms of *ex post* MH could conceivably have similar effects. But again, the possibility that banks may set loan rates specifically with a view to avoiding self-imposed high monitoring costs seems far-fetched.

For all of these reasons, then, AS and MH problems *à la* S&W seem unlikely to be dominant causes of credit rationing in the small-firm sector. Certainly all of the banks interviewed denied setting interest rate ceilings in order to avoid AS and expressed scepticism about any significant link between the interest rate and the incidence of MH. These responses were all the more noteworthy in view of the fact that many of them admitted to adhering to implicit interest rate ceilings for other reasons: to avoid placing further pressure on small firms whose survival prospects may already be marginal, to avoid losing market share, and to avoid the possible political pressure that might accompany significant interest rate increases in what is an important and relatively fragile sector of the economy. All in all, then, if there is an unsatisfied demand for small-firm credit at these ceiling rates, its dominant causes appear likely to be other than AS or MH problems. If so, and even if the shift towards class-based procedures does lead to overall improvements in the assessment of the creditworthiness of individual firms, it is unlikely to have much impact on the climate for small-firm lending through the reduction of these problems *per se*.

### Efficiency gains and competition

It was suggested above that banks have adopted class-based methods to reduce the assessment and processing costs involved in small-firm lending. Whether the savings achieved will actually improve the conditions for small-firm lending from banks, however, is an open question. This is something that will depend on a variety of other factors, not least the profitability of the banks' other operations and the level of competition between banks. That said, the good news is that class-based assessment procedures have and promise to continue to enhance competition in small-firm lending. Application procedures have been streamlined in recent years and the turnaround time of loan applications dramatically reduced. The costs to small firms of shopping around to find the best available terms, now enhanced by the internet, are accordingly lower than they have ever been and look set to fall still further.

## 4. Summary

Small-firm lending has become an increasingly impersonal affair with the banks adopting an 'arm's-length'/'playing the numbers' approach to lending. Although this development has some positive implications for small firms, two of the more important ones are likely to be negative: banks are likely to remain relatively poorly informed about their small-firm customer businesses activities and to have an incentive to increase their emphasis on collateral as a result.

Given a suitably stable economic environment, it is possible that the use of class-based assessment methods may lead to improvements in the average quality of loans to small firms. The downside is that an exclusive reliance on these methods makes it difficult to employ specific information about applicants (information that is more readily available to lending officers employing the traditional case-based approach). It is not clear that class-based loan assessment procedures will lead to general improvements in the accuracy of individual assessments of small-firm creditworthiness.

Adverse selection and moral hazard problems may be less significant than is suggested by the theoretical literature on credit rationing. If so, the transition from case- to class-based assessment procedures will be unlikely to have much of an impact on the climate for small-firm lending, even if informational asymmetries are reduced by more effective screening procedures.

A major driver of the move towards class-based assessment procedures is the reduction of the costs of assessing and processing loan applications. It is possible that the adoption of such procedures may benefit banks even without dramatic improvements in the quality of loans to small firms. The positive implication for small firms is that transactions costs involved in applying for bank loans have been dramatically reduced and the possibility that the market will accordingly become more competitive one.

The oft-repeated argument that the reduction of private information would make it easier for small firms to secure loan finance stands testimony to influence of the asymmetric information theory of credit rationing. Cowling and Sugden (1993: 18–19), for example, support 'a process of decentralisation of decision making by the larger banks and the provision of more localised funding, taking into account the merits and prospects of individual firms. This would help reduce the distance maintained in the relationship and may provide the basis for the provision of cheaper, longer-term funding. On the part of small firms this would require greater co-operation with banks and reductions in the level of private information.' It is clearly possible that if the banks could re-establish closer relations with their small-firm clients and thereby make greater use of more specific information about them, this might result in an improved quality of lending. The trouble with the proposal, however, is that it fails to recognise the substantial economies in the assessment and processing of loan applications afforded by class-based assessment procedures. These economies form a significant barrier to a return to case-based assessment in the small-firm sector.

## Notes

1 This is an abridged version of a paper written for an ESRC Centre for Business Research project on *Information, monitoring and the financing of small and medium sized businesses*. I am grateful to Alan Hughes and Jörg Bibow for comments on the longer version.
2 For example, Chick (1997, 2000) and Chick and Dow (1996).
3 Credit-scoring systems assess applications in terms of financial and non-financial characteristics determined on the basis of the bank's experience with similar applicants in the past. Credit scoring is usually conducted using a table that allocates points in respect of each characteristic depending on the applicant's responses. The sum total of points achieved are then compared to a predetermined cutoff point. If the applicant's score falls below this threshold, the application is rejected.
4 A simplified version of their model is used here (see Blanchard and Fisher 1989: 480–4; Hillier and Ibrahimo 1993).

## References

Binks, M. R., Ennew, C. T. and Reed, G. V. (1988) *The Survey by the Forum of Private Business on Banks and Small Firms*. London: Forum of Private Business.

Binks, M. R., Ennew, C. T. and Reed, G. V. (1990) *Small Businesses and their Banks*. London: Forum of Private Business.

Blanchard, O. J. and Fisher, S. (1989) *Lectures on Macroeconomics*. Cambridge, MA: MIT Press.

Chick, V. (1997) 'Some Reflections on Financial Fragility in Banking and Finance', *Journal of Economic Issues* 31: 535–41.

Chick, V. (2000) 'The Regions and Small Business in Bankers' Europe', in Toporowski (ed.), *Political Economy and the New Capitalism: Essays in Memory of Sam Aaronovitch*. London: Routledge.

Chick, V. and Dow, S. C. (1996) 'Regulation and Differences in Financial Institutions', *Journal of Economic Issues* 30: 517–23.

Cowling, M. and Sugden, R. (1993) 'Small Firm Lending Contracts: Do Banks Differentiate Between Firms?', *Occasional Paper in Industrial Strategy*, Vol. 15. Research Centre for Industrial Strategy, Birmingham University.

Daly, M. (1990) 'The 1980s – A Decade of Growth in Enterprise – Data on VAT Registrations and Deregistrations', *The Employment Gazette*, November.

de Meza, D. and Southey, C. (1996) 'The Borrower's Curse: Optimism, Finance and Entrepreneurship'. *The Economic Journal* 106: 375–86.

de Meza, D. and Webb, D. C. (1987) 'Too Much Investment: A Problem of Asymmetric Information', *Quarterly Journal of Economics* 102: 281–92.

Dow, S. C. (1996) 'Horizontalism: A Critique', *Cambridge Journal of Economics* 20: 497–508.

Hillier, B. and Ibrahimo, M. V. (1993) 'Asymmetric Information and Models of Credit Rationing', *Bulletin of Economic Research* 45: 271–304.

Hughes, A. (1994) 'The "Problems" of Finance for Smaller Businesses', in N. Dimsdale, and M. Prevezer (eds), *Capital Markets and Corporate Governance*. Oxford: Clarendon Press, pp. 209–34.

Stiglitz, J. E. and Weiss, A. (1981) 'Credit Rationing in Markets with Imperfect Information', *American Economic Review* 71: 393–410.

Williamson, S. (1986) 'Costly Monitoring, Financial Intermediation, and Equilibrium Credit Rationing', *Journal of Monetary Economics* 18: 157–79.

# 21

# WOMEN'S WORK OR WORK FOR WOMEN?

*Peter A. Riach and Judith Rich*

## 1. Introduction

In the decade between the death of Joan Robinson and the appointment of Victoria Chick in 1993, there were no female professors of economics in the UK. Her interest in the position of women in academia was influenced not only by her own career progression, but also by her own experience, as well as that of other female students (Chick 1992: 81). We analyse the position of women in academia with this in mind.

Women and men continue to be concentrated in different occupational categories (horizontal segregation) and women as compared to men tend to be in lower status, lower-paid job categories within occupations (vertical segregation). This persistent segregation is seen as one of the main reasons why gender earnings differentials continue to exist (Bergmann 1986: 86; Gunderson 1989: 67). While descriptive statistics can tell us whether female shares have changed by comparing two years of workforce data, they can tell us little about any of the processes that may be contributing to changes in segregation or even the magnitude of segregation in any given year. Numerous studies of occupational segregation have used indexes to measure the level of segregation of a workforce. Usually these studies seek to explain '... to what degree is segregation a barrier to gender equality, and how effective are employment equity policies in dismantling this barrier?' (Blackburn *et al.* 1993: 335). However, researchers using different indexes to measure the level of segregation over similar time periods, in the same country, find conflicting results for the magnitude of segregation and whether, over time, segregation has increased or decreased (Charles and Grusky 1995: 946; Karmel and Maclachlan 1988; OECD 1985). These and other studies concerned about rigorous measurement have raised the serious issue of the structure of these indexes and what constitutes an appropriate measure of segregation.

A further important consideration of this debate is to avoid inappropriate policy analysis and recommendations from incorrect measurement of occupational gender segregation. Society's concern with equality of opportunity has led to equal employment opportunity and affirmative action legislation in many countries. Equal employment opportunity and affirmative action programmes are designed to redress differential treatment of targeted groups in the selection, hiring, recruitment and promotion process. These policies, if successful, will increase the representation of females in male dominated areas and increase the representation of males in female dominated areas. In the case of female/male differences, this ultimately leads to a change in the gender ratio of individual job categories, particularly an increase in female representation at the higher levels of the organisation. Affirmative action is especially relevant to redressing vertical segregation.

A necessarily limited summary of the (sometimes intense) debate on the issue of measurement of segregation is presented in the following discussion which identifies a fruitful approach to analysing segregation. This is the Karmel–Maclachlan index or *IP*. This index measure is then used to analyse vertical gender segregation of academic staff in the university sectors of the UK and Australia to demonstrate how *IP* and its decomposition can be applied. We then use these findings to comment on equal employment opportunity policy in the UK.

## 2. The measurement of segregation

What can index measurement indicate about the segregated nature of a workforce? Three different effects need to be isolated. Segregation can increase because individual job categories become more gender segregated (female or male); or because there has been employment growth in female or male dominated jobs; or because there has been an increase in the number of females participating in the workforce who choose, or are crowded into, female-dominated jobs. Of course, changes in individual choice may also have an impact here, particularly if women (and men) choose to invest more in human capital and in gaining training in skills generally regarded as non-traditional for their sex.

One can identify two broad areas of agreement regarding various index measures that have been proposed (see Blackburn *et al.* 1990, 1993, 1995; Boisso *et al.* 1994; Charles and Grusky 1995, 1998; Cortese, Falk and Cohen 1976; James and Taeuber 1985; Karmel and Maclachlan 1988; Taeuber and Taeuber 1976; Watts 1992, 1995, 1998). First, there is broad consensus that a measure of segregation should meet six criteria to ensure that researchers can identify a change in the level of segregation due purely to changes in the sex ratio of occupational classifications. These six criteria are: organisational equivalence, size invariance, gender symmetry, the 'principle of transfers', occupations invariance and composition invariance. Critically, a measure of occupational segregation needs to be free of any effects from changes in the gender shares of total employment and changes in the occupational distribution of total employment (satisfying the two criteria of occupations invariance and composition invariance). Researchers sometimes specify this as the measure being 'margin free'. An index should identify changes in occupational sex segregation that are due to changes in the sex ratio of occupational groups, individual occupational categories or individual job categories. Very few indexes that have been proposed meet these criteria. The Karmel and Maclachlan index, *IP*, with its decomposition procedure can identify the contribution of a change in the gender shares of individual occupational classifications to the overall change in the level of segregation (the composition effect).

Second, the *IP* index is to be preferred to the index of dissimilarity, *ID* (and its standardised form), which is the preferred measure of many researchers. Contributions in the 1990s support earlier assessments of *ID*s' failings with many researchers regarding *ID* as an unsatisfactory measure of segregation (Blackburn *et al.* 1993; Boisso *et al.* 1994; Charles and Grusky 1995; White 1985: 217; Watts 1992). Neither standardisation of the index nor decomposition of *ID* provide satisfactory methods of overcoming *ID*'s lack of occupations invariance (Charles and Grusky 1995: 935; Watts 1992: 482–3).

Karmel and Maclachlan (1988) define an index, *ID*, such that

$$IP = \frac{1}{T} \sum |M_i - a(M_i + F_i)|$$

$$\frac{1}{T} \sum |(1 - a)(M_i - aF_i)|,$$

where $T$, $a$, $M_i$, $F_i$ are respectively total employment, the male share of total employment and the numbers of males and females in occupation $i$.

This index denotes the proportion of employed people who would have to change jobs to achieve a sex ratio for each occupation equal to the male/female ratio for total employment. The occupational structure of employment of the workforce and the overall gender shares of employment are kept constant. *IP* meets the criteria of organisational equivalence, size invariance, gender symmetry and the weak principle of transfers (Watts 1998).

The total percentage change in the index over time can be decomposed into Composition and Mix effects, where the latter can be broken up into Occupation, Gender and Interaction effects (for details of this decomposition procedure see Karmel and Maclachlan 1988: 190–1). The Composition effect isolates the contribution of the change in the gender composition of occupations to the total change in segregation. The Composition effect is both composition invariant and occupations invariant, that is, it is margin free. A reduction of female/male differences in the selection, hiring, recruitment and promotion process ultimately leads to a change in the gender ratio of individual occupations. The Composition effect can assist in assessing whether various equal employment opportunity and affirmative action programmes that have been implemented within organisations have been effective, as it quantifies the effect of changes in the gender shares of individual occupations. The Occupation effect isolates the impact of the change in the occupational structure over time. The Gender effect isolates the contribution of the change in female workforce participation to the total change in segregation.

## 3. Measuring segregation in academic employment in the universities of the UK, the US and Australia

Using *IP* to measure vertical gender segregation within the university sector can identify whether the university sector has become more or less segregated, and the contribution of a change in the gender ratio of individual academic levels to the overall change in the level of segregation.

The level of segregation in universities may have increased for three reasons. First, the number of females entering academic employment could have increased and been unevenly distributed across the academic levels (which will be identified by the gender effect). Second, occupational categories that are less gender integrated may have increased in relative terms (which will be identified by the occupation effect). Third, individual academic appointment levels may have become more sex segregated (indicated by a positive composition effect).

Legislative differences between the UK, the US and Australia make a comparison of segregation in these three countries of some interest. It has been illegal to discriminate on the basis of gender (and race) in Australia, in all States and federally, for over fifteen years, in the UK for over twenty years, and in the US for over thirty years. While Australia and the US have affirmative action legislation, the UK does not. All have equal employment opportunity legislation. Ultimately, successful policies will redress inequality of treatment (e.g. in pay) and reduce the gender share imbalance in (higher level) individual job classifications (addressing vertical segregation). Changes in individual (female or male) choices may lead to more balanced gender representation in jobs and thus contribute to a lesser or greater extent to any decline in segregation in occupations. Nevertheless, the policies themselves would encourage and support these choices and improve the individual's chance of success in obtaining an appointment or promotion.

Since 1994 polytechnics in the UK have been incorporated into the university sector. Prior to this, data on academic staff in the university sector refer to the 'old' universities in Great Britain. So there is necessarily a break in the series of data for the UK. The two time periods for the UK are not comparable given that the polytechnics and the 'old' university sector may have had different proportional representation of women in academic employment categories and the data prior to 1994/5 only cover universities in Great Britain. Therefore, comparison of vertical segregation in academic employment in the universities of the UK and Australia is made for the more recent period from 1994 to 1998. Data availability on academic staff in the US university sector limits the comparison between the three countries to the period mid to late 1980s to 1994.

Table 21.1 shows that women are relatively underrepresented at the more senior academic levels in all three countries with however in the US female representation at the more senior levels is somewhat higher than in the UK and Australia.

The results for the measurement of segregation in full-time staff across appointment levels for the UK and Australia for the period 1994–1998 , using *IP*, are reported in Table 21.2. $IP_1$ refers to the first year and $IP_2$ to the last year for which

*Table 21.1* Female share by appointment level in the university sectors of the US (1995), the UK (1997/8) and Australia (1998), full-time staff (%)

| US | 1995 | UK | 1998 | Australia | 1998 |
|---|---|---|---|---|---|
| Professor | 17.8 | Professor | 9.3 | Professor | 11.7 |
| Associate/Prof | 31.8 | Reader/Snr | | Associate/Prof | 16.1 |
| Assistant/Prof | 43.6 | Lecturer | 20.5 | Snr Lecturer | 26.0 |
| Instructor | 50.4 | Lecturer | 34.6 | Lecturer | 40.2 |
| Lecturer | 54.3 | Researchers | 36.9 | Assistant Lecturer | 48.0 |
| Other | 44.4 | Others | 39.0 | | |
| Total | 34.6 | Total | 30.9 | Total | 32.3 |

*Sources*: US Department of Education, *Digest of Education Statistics*, 1998. University Statistical Record, *University Statistics*, Vol. 1, 1997/8. Department of Employment, Education and Training, *Higher Education Statistics*, unpublished data, 1998.

*Table 21.2 IP*, Composition, Gender and Occupation effects for the UK, the US and Australia, full-time academic staff

| Country | $IP_1$ | $IP_2$ | Composition effect (%) | Gender effect (%) | Occupation effect (%) | Total change (%) |
|---|---|---|---|---|---|---|
| *1994–8* | | | | | | |
| UK | 0.0701 | 0.0734 | −8.65 | 6.94 | 4.00 | 4.66 |
| Australia | 0.1140 | 0.1094 | −12.99 | 4.75 | 2.98 | −4.16 |
| *1988/9–1993/4* | | | | | | |
| Great Britain | 0.0719 | 0.0838 | −6.92 | 15.51 | 2.56 | 15.18 |
| *1985–93* | | | | | | |
| US | 0.1094 | 0.1100 | −13.30 | 12.50 | −0.43 | 0.54 |
| *1989–94* | | | | | | |
| Australia | 0.1245 | 0.1144 | −16.52 | 10.21 | −6.44 | −8.45 |

data were available. While not directly comparable, calculations for the three countries over the mid-1980s to mid-1990s are included in this table.

While the level of vertical segregation by gender decreased in Australia from 1994 to 1998, it increased in the UK. Australia recorded the largest improvement in segregation with a fall of 4.2 per cent over the period. The increase in the UK was due to the increase in the number of female staff entering the universities. In both countries however, negative composition effects were recorded indicating that academic appointment levels have become more integrated. While in both countries fewer staff would have had to change appointment levels in 1998 as compared to 1994 to achieve zero segregation, the change in Australia was one and a half times greater than the change in the UK (−12.99 as compared to −8.65). The earlier period analysed also indicates that in all countries individual academic categories became less segregated with Great Britain showing the smallest percentage change.

## 4. Comments on equal employment opportunity in the universities

The decrease in the level of vertical segregation in Australian universities, in particular the contribution of the integration of the sexes across the academic hierarchy to this decline (identified and measured by the Composition effect), suggests that changes are occurring. Some may argue that this progress is slow given the continuing low level of representation of women at the more senior levels of academia and they may question the success of equal employment opportunity and affirmative action programmes.

Some tentative conclusions can be made on equal employment opportunity and affirmative action programmes. Universities in Australia were covered in the first stage of the affirmative action legislation in 1986. The results suggest some measure of success has been achieved (see also Burton 1997; Glass and McInnes 1989: 40; Wieneke and Durham 1992). In the UK, those assessing equal employment opportunity programmes have found them to be limited in their approach and effectiveness, with little progress made beyond monitoring and assessment of recruitment and promotion (Heward and Taylor 1992; Webb 1988; Williams *et al.* 1989).

The opportunity for women to reach senior levels in the higher education sector may be limited by recruitment and promotion procedures which appear neutral (based on merit), but which actually maintain differential treatment of males and females. The issue of defining merit objectively in academia has been raised in Australia by Allen (1990) and Bacchi (1993) and in Great Britain by Kennedy (1995). It is suggested that the promotion process is structured in ways which reduce the success rate of females. Collinson (1987) has found similar practices, which reduced the success rate of females in recruitment and promotion procedures, in other large organisations (Collinson 1987, 1988).

Bergmann (1996) raises, in general, the issue of defining merit and the use of merit-based criteria in hiring and promotion in the labour market. This is a contentious issue because the strongest argument made against equal employment opportunity and affirmative action programmes is that less qualified individuals will get jobs. In other words it is argued that affirmative action violates the principle of merit in job hiring, without demonstrating that labour market hires are in fact always based on merit. Individuals could be hired because they are relatives, friends or informally recommended. The criteria used in hiring and promotion may not be the only possible ones capable of indicating the desired abilities required for the job. If there is not one outstanding candidate for the job, then choosing may be arbitrary (Bergmann 1996).

A major recent study of affirmative action in the US finds little support for this criticism of affirmative action. This study found that: 'When Affirmative Action is used in recruiting, it generally does not lead to lower credentials or performance of women and minorities hired'. (Holzer and Neumark 2000: 240). In fact, affirmative action may introduce a refreshing transparency and accountability into the hiring process, ensuring the more efficient use of an organisation's labour resource. Furthermore Holzer and Neumark stated: 'Overall, the more intensive search, evaluation, and training that accompany Affirmative Action appear to offset any tendencies of the policy to lead to hiring of less-qualified or less-productive women and minorities'. (Holzer and Neumark 2000: 240).

Empirical studies testing actual market participants and the hiring process (sending matched pairs of actors or matched pairs of letters to advertised job vacancies) indicate that screening for jobs, based on criteria other than merit, occurs on a depressingly persistent basis in many countries (Riach and Rich 1987, 1991, 1995; Fix and Struyk 1993; Neumark 1996; Jowell and Prescott-Clarke 1970). Studies of promotion within organisations suggest that unequal treatment is part of the explanation for the persistence of vertical job segregation (see e.g. Halaby 1979; Hartmann 1987; Paulin and Mellor 1996). Friedman (1981) has argued that this is in fact the case for women academics in the US higher education sector.

The decline in segregation at each academic level in Australia was found to be greater than in the US or the UK. The slow change occurring in the UK may be due, in part, to the lack of effective equal employment opportunity programmes coupled with the fact that the UK has no affirmative action legislation. Both Australia and the US have affirmative action legislation but the legislation in the US is more stringent, with quotas required to be meet as part of compliance, which is not the case in Australia. The greater change occurring in Australia suggests that management in Australian universities may have a stronger commitment to improving the position of women (and minority groups). Certainly the goals of the universities and other organisations need to be integrated more closely with the goals of affirmative action.

## 5. A review of equal employment opportunity policy in the UK

In view of this relatively limited reduction in vertical segregation within the British higher education sector, it is pertinent to review policy. The Equal Opportunities Commission was established twenty-five years ago. There is evidence that it may be having some impact in opening up professional employment to women at the initial recruitment level (Riach and Rich, forthcoming). It clearly has been less successful in facilitating female representation in posts more senior in the job hierarchy. Consequently we turn now to consider policies which could be effective in ensuring greater female representation at more senior levels.

The current British approach to equality of employment opportunity is *anti-discriminatory*, *complaint-based*, with the enforcement body cast in a *passive* role. In other words discrimination on the basis of sex is illegal and a rejected applicant has the onus of activating the legislation and demonstrating that sex was the reason for the rejection. Frequently rejected applicants will not be aware, let alone able to demonstrate, that sex was the criterion for their rejection.

Experimental studies of recruitment have demonstrated the uninformative, and sometime dishonest, nature of rejection letters (McIntosh and Smith 1974; Riach and Rich 1987, 1991). The first policy option therefore would be to take action to enable this *anti-discriminatory, complaint-based, passive*, enforcement process to operate. The recommendation is that a brief curriculum vitae, listing qualifications and experience, be circulated to all unsuccessful applicants. This would either provide prima facie evidence of discrimination, or allay the suspicions of rejected applicants. We first suggested this policy in 1987 (Riach and Rich 1987). In 1998 one of us applied, unsuccessfully, for a job with New York University. We were most impressed when, several weeks later, just such a curriculum vitae of the successful candidate arrived in the mail. If such a procedure is acceptable to New York University, we fail to see why it could not become universal.

The second policy option would be to turn the Equal Opportunities Commission's role from a passive to an active one; that is to empower the Equal Opportunities Commission to conduct random audits of hiring and personnel practices. If employers were required to keep all records of job applications for a period of twelve months, and obliged to justify decisions on short-listing for interview and final choice of candidate, in the event of random audit, it would reinforce the pressure for scrupulousness in the hiring decision, which derives from the former proposal.

An appropriate analogy can be drawn here with the capital market. Public corporations have various duties with respect to reporting to shareholders, potential shareholders and the business community at large. They are also subject to independent financial audit, and they are usually required to satisfy an independent commission about various aspects of their financial activities. In effect, capitalist economies provide a range of regulations and checks to protect the owners of financial capital against unscrupulous practices and guard against the waste of this resource. Therefore it seems entirely appropriate that similar protection be afforded the owners of human capital, and that steps be taken to prevent it being wasted through employers using screening devices, such as sex, for purposes unrelated to job performance. Barbara Bergmann has also advocated such a policy (see Bergmann 1986: 158).

The third policy option is to switch from a complaint-based procedure, where the onus is on applicants as complainants, to a procedure where the onus would be on employers to justify their employment decisions. Just such a proposal was included in the policy of the British Labour Party in 1991 – 'Instead of women having to prove discrimination the employers will have to prove non-discrimination.' (Labour Party 1991). In May 2000 the European Parliament legislated to shift the burden of proof from complainants to respondents in recognition of the difficulty applicants have in obtaining evidence.

The fourth and final policy option is to switch from an anti-discriminatory approach to one of affirmative action. This inevitably invokes fierce controversy and opposition from the privileged group – often white, middle-class, 'prime-age', protestant men.

Perhaps a simple parable might concentrate awareness of this approach as a 'policy of last resort'. Envisage a labour market where employment is initially as a trainee with one member of a set of training firms. The general practice at the end of this training period is for each training firm to recruit from amongst its own set of trainees. One trainer, however, which is overwhelmingly male-staffed and whose best trainee is female, decides to recruit in the external labour market. A 'superior' male applicant is appointed. The rejected female then finds that the vast majority of other training firms select internally, so she is unable to compete for employment. We suspect that many readers would agree that this woman had been badly done by, but none of the previous three policies would be effective – given the superiority of the particular male applicant for the externally advertised post. If, however, a policy of affirmative action were in existence, the male-dominated firm would have had to think long and hard about rejecting a woman who was their best current trainee.

Women not infrequently oppose affirmative action because they want to be able to demonstrate unequivocally that they got the job 'on their merits'. This is understandable but we believe the interests of future generations are worth a concession from the current generation of women. It is only by getting a significant group of women into superior positions, where they can demonstrate their talents, that the prejudice will be broken down. Previous generations of women have paid a high price in enduring gross inequality of pay and employment opportunity. We believe that enduring some innuendo about their sexually privileged status would be a relatively minor price for the current generation to pay. Affirmative action legislation, nevertheless, does not guarantee compliance as many of the annual reports from the affirmative action agency in Australia confirm. Moreover, compliance does not guarantee effectiveness (Rosenbaum 1985; Bergmann 1996).

The extent of vertical segregation remaining in Britain, twenty-five years after the establishment of the Equal Opportunities Commission, indicates the need for a change in policy direction. A shift away from a complaint-based strategy to a procedure where the burden of proof is on employers seems inevitable, in the light of recent European Union legislation. We believe that it will also be necessary for the Equal Opportunities Commission to be empowered, and financed, to move to an active, investigative role, and that targets may ultimately be necessary to ensure the elimination, or at least minimisation, of vertical segregation.

## References

Allen, F. (1990) 'Indicators of Academic Excellence: Is There a Link between Merit and Reward?', *Australian Journal of Education* 34(1): 87–98.

Bacchi, C. (1993) 'The Brick Wall: Why So Few Become Senior Academics', *The Australian Universities Review* 36(1): 36–41.

Bergmann, B. (1986) *The Economic Emergence of Women*. New York: Basic Books.

Bergmann, B. (1996) *In Defence of Affirmative Action*. New York: Basic Books.

Blackburn, R., Siltanen, J. and Jarman, J. (1990) 'Measuring Occupational Gender Segregation', *Sociological Research Group, Social and Political Sciences, Working Paper No. 3*, University of Cambridge.

Blackburn, R., Jarman, J. and Siltanen, J. (1993) 'The Analysis of Occupational Gender Segregation Over Time and Place: Considerations of Measurement and Some New Evidence', *Work, Employment and Society* 7(3): 335–62.

Blackburn, R., Siltanen, J. and Jarman, J. (1995) 'The Measurement of Occupational Gender Segregation: Current Problems and a New Approach', *Journal of the Royal Statistical Society, Series A* 158(Part 2): 319–31.

Boisso, D., Hayes, K., Hirschberg, J. and Silber, J. (1994) 'Occupational Segregation in the Multidimensional Case: Decomposition and Tests of Significance', *Journal of Econometrics* 61: 161–71.

Burton, C. (1997) *Gender Equity in Australian University Staffing*, Department of Employment, Education, Training and Youth Affairs. Canberra: AGPS.

Charles, M. and Grusky, D. (1995) 'Models for Describing the Underlying Structure of Sex Segregation', *American Journal of Sociology* 100(4): 931–71.

Charles, M. and Grusky, D. (1998) 'The Past, Present and Future of Sex Segregation Methodology', *Demography* 35: 497–504.

Chick, V. (1992) 'Victoria Chick', in P. Arestis and M. Sawyer (eds), *A Biographical Dictionary of Dissenting Economists*. Aldershot: Edward Elgar (second edition forthcoming).

Collinson, D. (1987) 'A Question of Equal Opportunities – A Survey of Staff in a Large Insurance Company', *Personnel Review* 16(1): 1–16.

Collinson, D. (1988) *Barriers to Fair Selection: A Multi-sector Study of Recruitment Practices*, Equal Opportunities Commission Research Series, London: HMSO.

Cortese, C., Falk, R. F. and Cohen, J. (1976) 'Further Considerations on the Methodological Analysis of Segregation Indices', *American Sociological Review* 41: 630–7.

Department of Employment, Education and Training (1989, 1994, 1996, 1998) *Selected Higher Education Statistics*. Canberra: AGPS.

Fix, M. and Struyck, R. (1993) *Clear and Convincing Evidence: Measurement of Discrimination in America*. Washington: The Urban Institute Press.

Friedman, J. (1981) 'Congress, the Courts, and Sex-Based Employment Discrimination in Higher Education: A Tale of Two Titles', *Vanderbilt Law Review* 34: 37–69.

Glass, C. and McInnes, B. (1989) 'Equal Employment Opportunity Structures and Unions: Conflict or Cooperation?', *The Australian Universities' Review* 32(2): 40.

Gunderson, M. (1989) 'Male–Female Wage Differentials and Policy Responses', *Journal of Economic Literature* 27: 46–72.

Halaby, C. (1979) 'Job-Specific Sex Differences in Organisational Reward Attainment: Wage Discrimination vs Rank Segregation', *Social Forces* 58(1): 108–27.

Hartmann, H. (1987) 'Internal Labour Markets and Gender: A Case Study of Promotion', in C. Brown and J. Pechman (eds), *Gender in the Workplace*. Washington, DC: The Brookings Institution.

Heward, C. and Taylor, P. (1992) 'Women at the Top in Higher Education: Equal Opportunities Policies in Action?', *Policy and Politics* 20(2): 112–21.

Holzer, H. and Neumark, D. (2000) 'What Does Affirmative Action Do?', *Industrial and Labor Relations Review* 53(2): 240–71.

James, D. and Taeuber, K. (1985) 'Measures of Segregation', in N. B. Tuma (ed.), *Sociological Methodology*. San Francisco: Jossey-Bass.

Jones, J. and Castle, J. (1989) 'Women in Higher Education – Changes in the "80s?"', *The Australian Universities' Review* 32(2): 6–8.

Jowell, R. and Prescott-Clarke, P. (1970) 'Racial Discrimination and White-Collar Workers in Britain', *Race* 11: 397–417.

Karmel, T. and Maclachlan, M. (1988) 'Occupational Sex Segregation – Increasing or Decreasing', *Economic Record* 64(186): 187–95.

Kennedy, H. (1995) 'Prisoners of Gender', *The Times Higher Education Supplement 3*, November: 15–16.

Labour Party (1991) *A New Ministry for Women*. London: Labour Party.

McIntosh, N. and Smith, D. (1974) *The Extent of Racial Discrimination*, Political and Economic Planning Broadsheet No. 547, London: Political and Economic Planning Institute.

Neumark, D. (1996) 'Sex Discrimination in Restaurant Hiring: An Audit Study', *Quarterly Journal of Economics* 111: 915–42.

OECD (1985) *The Integration of Women into the Economy*. Paris.

Paulin, E. and Mellor, J. (1996) 'Gender, Race, and Promotions within a Private-Sector Firm', *Industrial Relations* 35(2): 276–95.

Riach, P. and Rich, J. (1987) 'Testing for Sexual Discrimination in the Labour Market', *Australian Economic Papers* 26: 165–78.

Riach, P. and Rich, J. (1991) 'Testing for Racial Discrimination in the Labour Market', *Cambridge Journal of Economics* 15: 239–56.

Riach, P. and Rich, J. (1995) 'An Investigation of Gender Discrimination in Labor Hiring', *Eastern Economic Journal* 21: 343–56.

Rosenbaum, J. (1985) 'Jobs, Job Status, and Women's Gains From Affirmative Action: Implications for Comparable Worth', in H. Hartmann (ed.), *Comparable Worth: New Directions for Research*. Washington DC: National Academy Press.

Taeuber, K. and Taeuber, A. (1976) 'A Practitioner's Perspective on the Index of Dissimiliarity', *American Sociological Review* 41: 884–9.

US Department of Education (1992, 1996, 1998) *Digest of Education Statistics*. National Center for Education Statistics.

University Statistical Record (1988/9, 1993/4, 1994/5, 1997/8) *University Statistics*, Vols 1 and 2. London: HMSO.

Watts, M. (1992) 'How Should Occupational Sex Segregation Be Measured?', *Work, Employment and Society* 6(3): 475–87.

Watts, M. (1995) 'The Use and Abuse of Measures of Occupational Gender Segregation: A Critical Review', *Occasional Paper No. 210*, Department of Economics, University of Newcastle.

Watts, M. (1998) 'Occupational Gender Segregation: Index Measurement and Econometric Modelling', *Demography* 35(4): 489–96.

Webb, J. (1988) 'The Ivory Tower: Positive Action for Women in Higher Education', in A. Coyle and J. Skinner (eds), *Women and Work: Positive Action for Change*. London: Macmillan Education.

White, M. (1985) 'Segregation and Diversity Measures in Population Distribution', *Population Index* 52(2): 198–221.

Wieneke, C. and Durham, M. (1992) 'Regulating the Equality Agenda: EEO in Higher Education', *The Australian Universities Review* 35(2): 30–5.

Williams, J., Cocking, J. and Davies, L. (1989) *Words or Deeds? A Review of Equal Opportunity Policies in Higher Education*. London: Commission for Racial Equality.

# VICTORIA CHICK'S PUBLICATIONS

## 1. Books

(1995) (ed., with P. Arestis). *Finance, Development and Structural Change*. Edward Elgar, pp. xxiii, 305.

(1992). P. Arestis and S. C. Dow (eds), *On Money, Method and Keynes: Selected Essays by Victoria Chick*. Macmillan/St Martin's Press, pp. xvi, 227. Articles reprinted in this volume are marked below with *.

(1992) (ed., with P. Arestis). *Recent Developments in Post-Keynesian Economics*. Edward Elgar, pp. xxii, 193.

(1983). *Macroeconomics after Keynes: A Reconsideration of the General Theory*. Dedington, Oxford: Philip Allan, pp. ix, 373. Published in USA by MIT Press. *Translations:*

    (1984). *La macroeconomia dopo Keynes*, Bologna: Il Mulino, pp. 581.

    (1990). *La macroeconomia según Keynes: Una revision de la teoria general*. Madrid: Alianza Editorial, pp. 412.

    (1991). *Keinzu to Keinzian no Makaro Keizaigaku* (Macroeconomics of Keynes and the Keynesians). Tokyo: Nihon Keizai Hyoron Sha, pp. ix, 533.

    (1993). *Macroeconomia após Keynes: Um Reexame da 'Teoria Geral'*. Editora Forense Universitária, pp. xiii, 416.

(1976). *Transnational Corporations and the Evolution of the International Monetary System*, Transnational Corporations Research Project (Sydney University) Research Monograph.

    (1979). An updated version appears in G. J. Crough (ed.), *Transnational Banking and the World Economy*. Sydney University, pp. 129–177.

(1973). *The Theory of Monetary Policy*, Gray-Mills.

    (1977). Revised edition, Basil Blackwell, pp. v, 161.

    (1982). Translation: *La Teoria della Politica Monetaria*, with an additional essay, Milan, Feltrinelli, pp. x, 247.

## 2. Chapters in books

(2001). 'Cassandra as Optimist', in R. Bellofiore and D. Papadimitriou (eds), *Financial Keynesianism and Market Instability: The Legacy of Hyman Minsky*. Edward Elgar, Vol. 1, pp. 35–46.

(2000). 'The Regions and Small Businesses in Bankers' Europe', in J. Toporowski (ed.), *Political Economy and the New Capitalism: Essays in Memory of Sam Aaronovitch*. Routledge, pp. 167–78.

(2000). 'Money and Effective Demand', in J. Smithin (ed.), *What is Money?* Routledge, pp. 124–38.

(2000) (with M. dos Anjos). 'Liquidity and Potential Surprise', in P. Earl and S. F. Frowen (eds), *Economics as an Art of Thought: Essays in Memory of G. L. S. Shackle.* Routledge, pp. 242–68.

(1999). 'Deflation and Redistribution: Austerity Policies in Britain in the 1920s', in J. T. J. M. van der Linden and A. J. C. Manders (eds), *The Economics of Income Distribution: Heterodox Approaches.* Kluwer, pp. 77–126.

(1998). 'Finance and Investment in the Context of Development', in J. Halevi and J.-M. Fontaine (eds), *Restoring Demand in the World Economy: Trade, Finance and Technology.* Edward Elgar, pp. 95–106.

(1998). 'Dissent and Continuity: John Maynard Keynes', in R. P. F. Holt and S. Pressman (eds), *Economics and its Discontents: Twentieth Century Dissenting Economists.* Edward Elgar, pp. 135–54.

(1998). 'A Struggle to Escape: Equilibrium in *The General Theory*', in S. Sharma (ed.), *John Maynard Keynes: Keynesianism into the Twenty-First Century.* Edward Elgar, pp. 40–50.

(1997). 'Comment on G.R. Steele's Paper', in S. F. Frowen (ed.), *Hayek: Economist and Social Philosopher – A Critical Retrospect.* Macmillan, pp. 256–7.

(1997) (with S. C. Dow). 'Competition and the Future of the European Banking and Financial System', in J. Smithin, H. Hagemann and A. Cohen (eds), *Money, Financial Institutions and Macroeconomics.* Boston: Kluwer, pp. 253–70.

(1997). 'Comment on Silke Tober's Paper', in S. F. Frowen and J. Hölscher (eds), *The German Currency Union of 1990: A Critical Assessment.* London: Macmillan.

(1997) (with M. Caserta). 'Provisional Equilibrium and Macroeconomic Theory', in P. Arestis, G. Palma and M. C. Sawyer (eds), *Markets, Employment and Economic Policy: Essays in Honour of G. C. Harcourt*, Vol. 2. Routledge, pp. 223–37.

(1997). 'The Multiplier and Finance', chapter 11 in G. C. Harcourt and P. A. Riach (eds), *A 'Second Edition' of the General Theory.* Routledge, pp. 154–72.

(1995). 'Order out of Chaos in Economics? Some Lessons from the Philosophy of Science', in S. C. Dow and J. Hillard (eds), *Keynes, Knowledge and Uncertainty.* Edward Elgar, pp. 25–42.

(1995) (with S. C. Dow). 'Wettbewerb und die Zukunft des europäischen Banken- und Finanzsystems (Competition and the Future of the European Banking and Financial System)', in C. Thomasberger (ed.), *Europäische Geldpolitik zwischen Marktzwängen und neuen institutionellen Regelungen (New Institutions for European Monetary Integration).* Marburg: Metropolis-Verlag, pp. 293–321.

(1993). 'Sources of Finance, Recent Changes in Bank Behaviour and the Theory of Investment and Interest' (revised), in P. Arestis (ed.), *Money and Banking: Issues for the 21st Century.* Macmillan, pp. 55–74.

(1993). 'The Evolution of the Banking System and the Theory of Monetary Policy', in S. F. Frowen (ed.), *Monetary Theory and Monetary Policy: New Tracks for the 1990s.* Macmillan, pp. 79–92.

(1993). 'Some Scenarios for Money and Banking in the EC and their Regional Implications', in I. H. Rima (ed.), *The Political Economy of Global Restructuring, Volume II: Trade and Finance.* Edward Elgar, pp. 190–200.

(1992). 'The Small Firm under Uncertainty: A Puzzle of *The General Theory*', in B. Gerrard and J. Hillard (eds), *The Philosophy and Economics of J. M. Keynes.* Edward Elgar, pp. 149–64.

(1991). 'Keynes's Monetary Theory: A Partial Survey', in J. Jespersen, (ed.), *Nye Keynestolkninger: Metode, Politik og Etik*, Proceedings of the conference 'New

Developments in the Interpretation of the Work of John Maynard Keynes' (5–6 October 1990), Institut for Samfundsøkonomi og Planlægning, Roskilde University, 89–101.

(1993). Reprinted (in English) in *Revista de Economia Politica* (São Paolo), 13(4), 125–34.

*(1990). 'Some Methodological Considerations in the Theory of Speculation', in D. E. Moggridge (ed.), *Perspectives on the History of Economic Thought, Volume IV: Keynes, Macroeconomics and Method*. Aldershot: Edward Elgar, pp. 113–124.

(1990). 'Comment on Professor Hartog's Paper', in K. Groenveld, J. A. H. Maks and J. Muysken (eds), *Economic Policy and the Market Process*. Amsterdam: North Holland, pp. 195–8.

(1989). 'Discussion (of Tim Congdon's Paper)', in R. Hill (ed.), *Keynes, Money and Monetarism*, Proceedings of the Eighth Keynes Seminar, Keynes College, University of Kent at Canterbury. Macmillan, pp. 73–81.

(1989). 'Comment on the Minford-Davis and Peterson Papers', in J. Muyskens and C. de Neubourg (eds), *Unemployment in Europe*. Macmillan for the European Production Study Group, pp. 357–60.

(1989). 'A *Teoria Geral* de Keynes 50 Anos Depois: O Que Resta' ('Keynes's *General Theory* after 50 Years: What Remains?'), In E. J. Amadeo Swaelen (ed.), *John M. Keynes: Cinqüenta Anos da Teoria Geral*. Instituto de Planejamento Econômico e Social, Serie PNPE, Rio de Janeiro, pp. 33–43.

(1988). 'Sources of Finance, Recent Changes in Bank Behaviour and the Theory of Investment and Interest', in P. Arestis (ed.), *Contemporary Issues in Money and Banking*. Macmillan, pp. 30–48.

(1985). 'Time and the Wage-Unit in Keynes's Method', in T. Lawson and H. Pesaran (eds), *Keynes' Economics: Methodological Issues*. Croom Helm, pp. 195–208.

*(1984). 'Monetary Increases and their Consequences: Streams, Backwaters and Floods', in A. Ingham and A. M. Ulph (eds), *Demand, Equilibrium and Trade: Essays in Honour of Ivor F. Pearce*. Macmillan, pp. 237–50.

*(1981). 'On the Structure of the Theory of Monetary Policy', in D. Currie, R. Nobay and D. Peel (eds), *Macroeconomic Analysis: Essays in Macroeconomics and Econometrics*. London: Croom Helm, pp. 178–208.

(1979). 'Monetarist Views of Inflation' in D. Heathfield. (ed.), *Perspectives on Inflation: Models and Policy*. Longmans, pp. 37–69. Translation in Japanese published by Nihon Keizai Hysron Sha.

(1982). Included in Italian translation of *The Theory of Monetary Policy* as an Appendix.

# 3. Journal articles

(2001) 'Über Geld und Geldtheorien', *Zeitschrift für kritische Sozialwissenschaft*, 123(2), 227–44.

(2000) (with S. C. Dow). 'Financial Integration in Europe: A Post Keynesian Perspective', *Archives of Economic History*, 11(1–2), 21–40.

(1998). 'On Knowing One's Place: The Role of Formalism in Economics', *Economic Journal*, 108, 1859–69.

(1997). 'Some Reflections on Financial Fragility in Banking and Finance', *Journal of Economic Issues*, 31(2), 535–41.

(1996). 'Equilibrium and Determination in Open Systems', *History of Economics Review*, No. 25, 172–83.

(1996). 'A Struggle to Escape: Equilibrium in *The General Theory*', *Ekonomska Misao i Praksa* (Dubrovnic), 5, 345–62; (1998).

(1998). Reprinted in S. Sharma, *John Maynard Keynes: Keynesianism into the Twenty-first Century*. Edward Elgar, pp. 40–50.

(1996) (with S. C. Dow). 'Regulation and Differences in Financial Institutions', *Journal of Economic Issues*, 30(2), 517–23.

(1995). 'Comment on "Government Debt and Sustainable Fiscal Policy"', *Economic Notes* (Banca Monte dei Paschi di Siena), 24(3), 581–4.

(1995). 'Is there a Case for Post Keynesian Economics?', *Scottish Journal of Political Economy*, 42(1), 20–36.

(1991). 'Hicks and Keynes on Liquidity Preference: A Methodological Approach', *Review of Political Economy*, 3(3), 309–19.

(1990). 'On the Place of *Value and Capital* in Monetary Theory', *Greek Economic Review*, Vol. 12, Supplement: *The Monetary Economics of Sir John Hicks*, Autumn, pp. 53–71; (1992). In Portuguese ('Sobre o lugar de *Valor e capital* na teoria monetaria') in *Revista Brasiliera de Economia*, 46(1), 97–116.

(1988) (with S.C. Dow). 'A Post Keynesian Perspective on the Relation between Banking and Regional Development', *Thames Papers in Political Economy*, 1–22.

(1988). Reprinted in P. Arestis (ed.), *Post Keynesian Monetary Economics: New Approaches to Financial Modelling*. Edward Elgar, pp. 219–50.

(1987). 'Are the *General Theory's* Central Contributions still Valid?', *Journal of Economic Studies*, special issue, J. Pheby (ed.): The *General Theory and After: Essays in Post Keynesianism*, 14(4), pp. 5–12.

(1991). Reprinted in M. Blaug (ed.), *John Maynard Keynes*, Vol. II, pp. 353–60. Pioneers in Economics series, Edward Elgar.

(1987). 'Speculation, the Rate of Interest and the Rate of Profit', *Journal of Post Keynesian Economics*, Fall, 124–32.

*(1986). 'The Evolution of the Banking System and the Theory of Saving, Investment and Interest', *Économies et sociétés*, Cahiers de l'ISMEA, Serie 'Monnaie et Production', No. 3, pp. 111–26.

(1994). Published in Portuguese as 'A Evolução do Sistema Bancario e a teoria da Poupança, do Investimento e dos Juros", *Ensaios FEE* (Fundação de Economia e Estatistica, Porto Allegre, Brazil), 15(1), 9–23.

(1996). Reprinted in M. Musella and C. Panico (eds), *The Money Supply in the Economic Process: A Post Keynesian Perspective*, in the series The International Library of Critical Writings in Economics, Series Editor M. Blaug. Edward Elgar.

*(1983). 'A Question of Relevance: *The General Theory* in Keynes's Time and Ours', *South African Journal of Economics*, 5, 388–406. (Invited article for a Keynes Centenary issue, revised and extended from the French version.)

(1983). 'La "Teoria generale" ai tempi di Keynes e oggi', *Politica ed Economia*, 14 maggio, 55–64.

*(1982). 'Comment on "*ISLM* – An Explanation"' (by Sir John Hicks), *Journal of Post Keynesian Economics*, 4, 439–44.

(1989). Reprinted in J. C. Wood and R. N. Woods (eds), *Sir John Hicks: Critical Assessments*. Routledge. Vol. III, pp. 302–6.

(1982). 'Une question de pertinence: La *Theorie Generale* du temps de Keynes et aujourd'hui', *L'Actualité économique*, 58, 61–8.

(1981). 'Reply to Professor Harrison' (on 'The Nature of the Keynesian Revolution') *Australian Economic Papers*, 20, 405–8.

*(1978). 'The Nature of the Keynesian Revolution: A Reassessment', *Australian Economic Papers*, 17, 1–20.

(1983). Reprinted in J. C. Wood (ed.), *John Maynard Keynes: Critical Assessments*. Croom Helm.

*(1978). 'Keynes' Theory, Keynesian Policy and the Post-War Inflation', *British Review of Economic Issues*, 1, 1–24.

*(1978). 'Unresolved Questions in Monetary Theory: A Critical Review', *De Economist*, 36–60.

*(1978). 'Keynesians, Monetarists, and Keynes: The End of the Debate – or the Beginning?', *Thames Papers in Political Economy*, Spring, 1–15.

(1985). Revised and reprinted in P. Arestis and A. Skouras (eds), *Post-Keynesian Economic Theory: A Challenge to Neo-Classical Economics*, Wheatsheaf Books (UK) and M.E. Sharpe (USA).

*(1973). 'Financial Counterparts of Saving and Investment and Inconsistency in Some Macro Models', *Weltwirtschaftliches Archiv*, Band 109, Heft 4, 621–43.

# 4. Other published work

## (i) Encyclopaedia entries

(1996). J. M. Keynes, in *International Encyclopaedia of Business and Management*. International Thompson Business Press.

(1998). Reprinted in *The IBEM Handbook of Management Thinking*. International Thompson Business Press, pp. 345–54.

(1995). 'Quantity Theory of Money', in A. Kuper and J. Kuper (eds), *The Social Science Encyclopaedia*, 2nd edn. Routledge and Kegan Paul, pp. 553–4.

(1994). 'Speculation', in P. Arestis and M. C. Sawyer (eds), *The Elgar Companion to Radical Political Economy*. Edward Elgar, pp. 380–84.

(1992). J. M. Keynes, in P. Arestis and M. C. Sawyer (eds), *Biographical Dictionary of Dissenting Economists*. Edward Elgar, pp. 310–18.

(2000). Second edition, pp. 360–68. To appear in Bulgarian in *Economic Thought*, published by the Bulgarian Academy of Sciences.

(1992). Victoria Chick, in P. Arestis and M. C. Sawyer (eds), *Biographical Dictionary of Dissenting Economists*. Edward Elgar, pp. 81–6.

(2000). Second edition, pp. 101–7.

*(1988). 'Money', in P. Deane and J. Kuper (eds), *A Lexicon of Economics*. Routledge and Kegan Paul, pp. 267–9.

(1987). 'Alan Coddington', in J. Eatwell, M. Milgate and P. Newman (eds), *The New Palgrave: A Dictionary of Economic Theory and Doctrine*. Macmillan, Vol. I, p. 463.

'Finance and Saving', *The New Palgrave* (*ibid.*), Vol. II, pp. 336–7.

'Silvio Gesell', *The New Palgrave* (*ibid.*), Vol. II, p. 520.

'Hugh Townshend', *The New Palgrave* (*ibid.*), Vol. IV, p. 662.

(1985). 'Monetary Policy; Monetarism; Quantity Theory of Money', in A. Kuper and J. Kuper (eds), *The Social Science Encyclopaedia*. Routledge and Kegan Paul.

(1988). Reprinted in P. Deane and J. Kuper (eds), *A Lexicon of Economics*. Routledge and Kegan Paul, pp. 261–72.

## (ii) Interviews

(1999). in C. Usabiaga Ibáñez, *The Current State of Macroeconomics: Leading Thinkers in Conversation*. Macmillan, pp. 52–74.

(1995). in J. E. King, *Conversations with Post Keynesians*. Macmillan, pp. 93–112.

(1995). in B. Snowdon, H. Vane and P. Wynarczyk, *A Modern Guide to Macroeconomics*. Edward Elgar, pp. 398–407.

(1997). French translation: *La pensée économique moderne*. Ediscience International, pp. 431–41.

***(iii) Introductions to books***

(1995) (with P. Arestis). Introduction, to V. Chick and P. Arestis (eds), *Finance, Development and Structural Change: Post Keynesian Perspectives*. Edward Elgar, pp. xv–xxiii.

(1992) (with P. Arestis). 'Introduction', to V. Chick and P. Arestis (eds), *Recent Developments in Post-Keynesian Economics*, Edward Elgar, pp. xi–xxii.

(1989). Foreword, to E. J. Amadeo, *Keynes's Principle of Effective Demand*. Edward Elgar, pp. ix–xii.

(1995). Foreword, to R. Studart, *Investment Finance in Economic Development*. Routledge, pp. viii–x.

***(iv) Newspaper article***

(1987). 'Money Matters' (feature article on *The General Theory*), *The Times Higher Education Supplement* 2 January, p. 8.

## 5.  Forthcoming publications

(2002). 'Keynes's Theory of Investment and Necessary Compromise', in S. C. Dow and J. Hillard (eds), *Keynes, Uncertainty and the Global Economy; Beyond Keynes*, Vol. II. Edward Elgar.

(2001)(with Sheila Dow) 'Formalism, Logic and Reality: A Keynesian Analysis', *Cambridge Journal of Economics* 25(6).

'An Equilibrium of Action'. *Cambridge Journal of Economics*.

'Caravale's Contributions to the Theory of Equilibrium and their Relevance to Understanding Keynes', in S. Nisticò and D. Tosato (eds), *Competing Economic Theories*. Routledge.

## 6.  Work in progress

***(i) Books***

(ed.), *Keynes and the Post-Keynesians*. Macmillan.

(ed.), *The Challenge of Endogenous Money*: Proceedings of a Conference held in Berlin, March 2001.

(ed.), *Monetary Macroeconomies: Essays in Theory and Method*, Edward Elgar.

*Macroeconomics After Keynes*, Second edition. Edward Elgar.

***(ii) Articles and Contributions to books***

'Keynes and the Post-Keynesians: A Survey and Evaluation', for the Kent Keynes Conference. To be published in *Keynes and the Post-Keynesians*, Macmillan.

'Money in Keynes, the Bastard Keynesians and the Post Keynesians'.

'Liquidity Preference and the Monetary Circuit: Methodological Issues'.

'How Best to Study Money'.

'Why Does the Euro Split both Labour and Conservatives?'.

'Theory, Method and Mode of Thought in the *General Theory*'.

'The Methodology of Karl Niebyl'.

# INDEX